"Paper or Plastic?"

Energy, Environment,
and Consumerism
in Sweden and America

Rita J. Erickson

PRAEGER

Westport, Connecticut
London

Library of Congress Cataloging-in-Publication Data

Erickson, Rita J.
    "Paper or plastic?" : energy, environment, and consumerism in
Sweden and America / Rita J. Erickson.
      p. cm.
    Includes bibliographical references and index.
    ISBN 0–275–95766–7 (alk. paper)
    1. Dwellings—Energy conservation—Sweden. 2. Dwellings—Energy
conservation—United States. 3. Environmental protection—Sweden.
4. Environmental protection—United States. I. Title.
TJ163.5.D86E75   1997
306.3—dc21   96–54489

British Library Cataloguing in Publication Data is available.

Library of Congress Catalog Card Number: 96–54489
ISBN: 0–275–95766–7

First published in 1997

Praeger Publishers, 88 Post Road West, Westport, CT 06881
An imprint of Greenwood Publishing Group, Inc.

Printed in the United States of America

The paper used in this book complies with the
Permanent Paper Standard issued by the National
Information Standards Organization (Z39.48–1984).

10 9 8 7 6 5 4 3 2 1

I would like to dedicate this book to

Shelia Wann Reaves (1939–1992)

and to Bahá'ís everywhere.

Contents

Acknowledgments

Let's start with infrastructure: I wish to thank the National Science Foundation for a generous two-year research and writing grant (NSF DBS–9207519) from its Anthropology and Human Dimensions of Global Change Programs. Anthropology program officer Stuart Plattner was especially encouraging of my work. Sincere thanks also to other substantial financial contributors to the Foley–Munka Ljungby research over time: The Swedish Building Research Council, American-Scandinavian Foundation, and Swedish Institute. The University of Minnesota, Fulbright Foundation, Minnesota Department of Energy and Economic Development, and Center for Urban and Regional Affairs also underwrote the project in various ways.

My study of Foley and Munka Ljungby was aided and enriched by many people in the United States and in Sweden. The first round of research formed the basis for my dissertation in cultural anthropology at the University of Minnesota, and in that context I would like to thank my indefatigable advisor and continuing friend, Luther P. Gerlach. Anthropologist Frank C. Miller is a long-time source of heartwarming support. Wanda Olson, University Extension Housing Technology Specialist, generously shares time and knowledge—as does economist Michael Alexander of the Minnesota Department of Public Service. Special thanks go to Lee Schipper, Senior Staff Scientist at the Lawrence Berkeley Laboratory, who supported this project from the start with data and his unique personal energy.

A sincere and warm thank you to all residents of Foley and Munka Ljungby—especially to those who completed that 10-page questionnaire! I am very grateful to the core households for faithfully meeting the demands of research participation and for so warmly opening their homes to me (an asterisk denotes household participation in both the 1980s and the 1990s research):

MUNKA LJUNGBY
CORE HOUSEHOLDS

Arne and Gunilla Andersson
Emmy Andersson
John-Erik and Gärd Andersson and children
*Leif and Ann-Christin Andersson and
  children
Walter and Stina Andersson
*Janse and Lisbet Bengtsson and daughters
Rune and Brita Bergkvist and sons
Arvid and Anna Lisa Borgqvist
Kenneth and Eva-Karin Broberg and
  children
Jürgen and Eva Börner and sons
*Björn and Gun Dahlberg and children
Lars and Lena Ejehag and children
Maj-Britt Ekberg and children
Istvan and Etelka Horvath and children
Gerth and Kerstin Johansson
Nisse and Inga-Brit Knutsson and children
*Filip and Christine Larsson and daughters
Magnus Månsson and Katarina Levau-
  Månsson
*Tommy Nilsson and Kerstin Larsson and
  children
Mats and Marie Nilsson
Lennart and Margaret Nordstrand and
  children
Bo and Gerd Ousbeck and children
Göran and Gun Persson and daughters
Kenth and Lena Persson and daughters
Per-Arne and Karin Persson and children
*Erik and Anna Viola Röijer and children
Wolfgang and Birgitta Schieler and children
*Birger and Kerstin Segerström and
  daughters
*Lars-Erik and Solveig Söderberg and
  daughters
Jan and Karin Sörensson and daughters
Bengt and Ann-Britt Städe and children
Christer and Lena Städe and children
Christer Svensson
Ivar and Gurli Svensson
Leif and Kristina Tennare and children
Rune and Kerstin Viebke and children

FOLEY
CORE HOUSEHOLDS

Jack and Pat Abfalter and children
Al and Penny Jo Albrecht
Dick and Sandy Anderson
Pete and Pat Atwood and daughters
Gary and Dawna Beack and children
*Paul and Frances Bronder and children
Harry and Esther Dahler
Tom and Lou Demarais and sons
Jason and Barb Dziuk and children
Charles and Markey Duensing and sons
*Terry and Jane Ernst and children
Lyle and Lynn Freudenberg and children
Bill and Julie Garceau and children
George and Cordy Heroux and children
*Karl and Betty Johnson and children
Delroy and Lana Kampa and sons
Fritz and Viola Larson
Tim and Sally Lloyd and children
Doug and Sharon Meyer and children
Dave and Sandy Mollner
Dave and Dianne Mosford and daughter
Pat and Bonnie Ogg and daughters
Wayne and Kay Olson
Raymond and Deanna Ostby and
  children
*Mike and Pam Premo and sons
Tim and Kim Rhonemus
*Bill and Rita Samsa and children
LeeRoy and Dixie Shore and children
Mark and Sheryll Storry and children
Jayson Stricker and Melissa Tolmie
John and Sophie Svihel and son
Bruce and Sandy Thompson and sons
Syl & Mary Margaret Tomporowski
*Brian and Judy Weis and children
Dale and Pat Wojciehowski and
  daughters
*Ron and Mary Ann Youso and children

Minnesota Extension Service educators in Foley were generous with their time and information, as were the St. Cloud personnel of the Northern States Power Company. In Foley in the 1980s, Brian and Jan Thompson shared their home and their friendship with me. In the 1990s Bill Bronder kindly lent me a room, and his mother and neighbor, Fran, welcomed me often for a cup of tea. Research assistants Sheryll Storry (1980s) and Judy Weis (1990s) were both efficient and a pleasure to work with. Foley mayor Karl Berlin introduced the project to the community and supported it over time.

In Sweden, the Department of Social and Economic Geography at the University of Lund hosted me as guest researcher, both in the 1980s and the 1990s. I want to thank Department Chair Olof Wärneryd for his gracious help, and also geographers Reinhold Castensson and P. O. Hallin for breaking the ground with an earlier research project in Munka Ljungby and for their pre-fieldwork encouragement. Hallin, who joined me in Munka and Foley in the 1990s to investigate environmentalism, is a delightful, insightful colleague and friend. Lund ethnologist Orvar Löfgren and social anthropologist Alf Hornborg were most welcoming to me, and discussions with them were stimulating and affirming. Geographer Ann-Cathrine Åquist bolstered me in Lund during initial research preparation. Philip Moding of SSK, Malmö, has remained an expansive source of encouragement and help.

During Munka Ljungby fieldwork in the 1980s I lived with Torkil and Gunilla Nilson, and we established a close and lasting American–Swedish connection of our own. In the 1990s it was my very good fortune to share the home of Stina Pålsson. Karin Nilsson's enthusiasm for the project made her an ideal research assistant during both fieldwork periods. Thanks go to the personnel of Ängelholm's kommun, especially Secretary Åke Nilsson, and also to Jan Grönberg, marketing head at Ängelholms Energiverk.

Colleagues Bruce Hackett, P. O. Hallin, Sharon Kemp, Loren Lutzenhiser, Michael Noble, Lee Schipper, and Harold Wilhite read and commented on the manuscript for this book. I thank them heartily for their thoughtful critiques, time, and encouragement. And for nearly five decades of love and support, I thank my parents, Leonard and Edna Erickson.

Introduction

"PAPER OR PLASTIC?"

The best answer to the question of paper or plastic, posed at checkout lines in American grocery stores, is "Neither, I brought my own bags." "Paper or plastic?" is a microcosm of the complex consumption choices of daily life—for economic, social, aesthetic, environmental, and infrastructural factors may all be involved in this apparently simple decision. Well-intended consumers in both Sweden and America want to choose that which is least harmful to the environment. They deliberate over paper-versus-plastic and similar issues but torture themselves with minutiae because they lack more-general guidelines for their decisions. And they rarely break free from the framework of conventional options to initiate alternatives or to question consumption more fundamentally.

I originally began fieldwork to investigate the relative roles technology and behavior played in determining Sweden's lesser per capita residential energy consumption (between 70 and 80 percent of the U.S. figure in 1980). However, the scope of my research soon expanded to include environmental awareness and consumerism, for it was clear that household energy use does not occur in a vacuum and that these important related dimensions should also be addressed. To what extent are consumers aware of the cultural precedents and environmental consequences of their energy consumption? Consumerism is at heart of energy and environment problems, and it underlies much social injustice as well.

This book addresses issues of energy, environment, and consumerism as they engage ordinary citizens in everyday life. Although the Swedish social welfare state and America's competitive capitalism represent quite different contexts for energy and environment decisions, both are essentially variations of industrial consumer society. Both have continuous economic growth as predicate and goal, and both socialize their members to believe that they can somehow have it all: cheap energy and food, a clean environment, boundless physical mobility, upward social mobility, and a very comfortable lifestyle. And both share a materialist worldview (by which I do not mean consumerist but rather empirical or positivist, the antithesis of spiritual). One contention of this book is that an ecological perspective and spiritual change are necessary for lasting resolution of problems of energy, environment, and social justice. An essential step in this process is outgrowing consumerist mentality.

Economist Paul Ekins (1991) defines consumerism as a cultural orientation maintaining that the "possession and use of an increasing number and variety of goods and services is the principal cultural aspiration and the surest perceived route to personal happiness, social status and national success." Consumerism thrives in Sweden as well as in America. When asked why shopping and consumption of goods are so important in contemporary life, informants in both locales said that they believe that buying things was an attempt to fill a gap in life. Americans identified this missing dimension to be spiritual; Swedes said it was lack of contact with nature or lack of inner life.

As will be seen, consumers in both Sweden and America dislocate the patterns and choices of daily life from larger problems and trends. Although they may lament environmental pollution or the disproportionate energy consumed by industrial societies, they do not associate these issues with their own energy use choices. Nor do they acknowledge the energy and resources demanded for the manufacture of an ever-expanding array of consumer goods or link environmental damage to the products they buy. Such dislocation is reflected in contradictory statements consumers make. For example, they say that consumption (in the abstract) should be decreased, but also that they do not want to change their personal style of living or threaten jobs. Also, even though Americans declare that they are prepared to pay more to protect the environment, they want energy-saving or pro-environmental activities to pay *them*, either through very short payback time or (preferably) through immediate monetary reward.

When asked to conserve energy or the environment, people are being asked to contradict what they have been taught constitutes successful functioning in industrial consumer society. Enervated by the many demands of a fast-paced, money-market system, they choose to save money and time over energy and the environment. Additionally, they accede to social norms and goals that foster consumption and not conservation. The view of consumers presented here is not that they are hypnotized, but that they are indeed enmeshed, trapped. Lacking the psychic energy and the discipline to overcome habit and conserve, consumers say that they need, even wish for, some external authority to force them to do so. Both Americans (grudgingly) and Swedes (more sympathetically) identify government as the appropriate enforcing agent, but both groups doubt that the necessary political will currently exists in politicians or in government institutions.

Some findings from my fieldwork translate readily into policy recommendations. However, this book does not have as its main purpose the offering of cross-cultural insights in order to fine-tune energy use and decrease demand.

Rather, it is the consideration of the broader and more critical questions about industrial consumerism which emerged from the thicket of investigating energy use and environmental awareness in daily life. These are very tough, politically sensitive connections. Foleyans and Munka Ljungbyans are not the only ones making contradictory statements. One also finds doublespeak at the institutional level—for example, one tenet of the Organization for Economic Cooperation and Development statement on sustainability reads "adopting simpler lifestyles while maintaining current standards of living" (OECD 1995).

In the conclusion, various ways out of the impasse are addressed. Many citizens are now ahead of their governments, expressing support for progressive energy and environmental changes. Yet, the conundrum is that progressive legislation dies in legislatures, victim of what representatives think their constituents want and victim of lobbyists for vested interests. The impulse for lasting change in energy use and environmental relationship must originate instead from a sense of stewardship, and humility, and desire for justice. Spiritual will, not merely political will, is needed in order to achieve this radical evolution.

ENERGY AND DAILY LIFE IN SWEDEN AND AMERICA

Certain questions tantalized American energy analysts after the oil traumas of the 1970s. They wondered enviously how Swedes could use so much less energy than Americans did while maintaining their notoriously comfortable way of life. (Per capita, Swedes used 60 percent of the overall energy, and from 70 to 80 percent of the residential energy, that Americans did [Schipper and Lichtenberg 1976, Hambraeus and Stillesjö 1977].) Did Swedes use less residential energy because their daily lives differed markedly from those of Americans? Or were Sweden's tighter-constructed houses and smaller, more efficient appliances primarily responsible for its lower consumption? In the absence of ground-level detail about daily life, stereotypes were invoked to explain the consumption difference. These stereotypes portrayed Swedes as conscientious energy conservers, who lived simply and did tasks by hand. In contrast, Americans were thoughtless energy gluttons, living on a lavish scale and addicted to machines.

As a cultural anthropologist, I wanted to answer these questions and test the stereotypes firsthand. To do so, I conducted fieldwork in the early 1980s, and again a dozen years later, in the small towns of Munka Ljungby (Skåne) and Foley (Minnesota). Each time, I distributed questionnaires community wide to obtain information about housing infrastructure, household appliances, vehicles and travel, and opinions on energy and environment issues. Actual fuel consumption was measured as well, using both utility billing records and self-report. Core groups of households kept checklists of their daily energy-using activities over several weeks and were interviewed about the factors shaping their patterns and choices. Interviews also allowed household members to elaborate on qualitative issues—such as connections they perceived between energy and environment, time, and economy; obstacles to conservation; relationship to nature; consumerism; and quality of life.

Surprisingly, I found that Foleyans used *less* heating fuel, on the average, than did Munka Ljungbyans. And though Munka Ljungbyans used less fuel for all household operations other than space heating (here called *household fuel*), this difference was not as great as expected, given national-level statistics. Because daily household routines were strikingly similar in the two communities, I concluded that technology was more influential than behavior in determining Sweden's lower energy consumption. However, some differences in behavior were marked. The stereotypes of Swedish conservers and American wasters were confirmed by some aspects of daily life but were punctured (fascinatingly) by others. Striking differences in worldview and self-image appeared as well.

On returning to Munka Ljungby (or "Munka," as its residents say) and Foley in the early 1990s, I found residents of both towns to be profoundly bored by the topic of energy. Relatively stable energy supplies (and *declining* fuel prices in Foley) had dispelled feelings of urgency over energy issues. Able to accommodate slowly rising fuel prices and saturated with energy information from an earlier state conservation campaign, Munka Ljungbyans also had lost interest in energy.

Disproportionate consumption of energy by America and by industrialized countries in general continues. The average resident of an industrial country consumes 10 times the energy of one in a developing country (Durning 1992). Further, America uses 35 times as much energy per capita as India (Stern, Young, and Druckman 1992). With roughly 5 percent of the world's population, America demanded 25 percent of world energy consumed in 1995. In contrast, all European OECD members consumed 18 percent of the global total (Energy Information Administration 1996).

Residential energy demand in both Sweden and the United States decreased after the oil crises of the 1970s, and fluctuated from 1979 through 1983. Demand has been rising gradually since the mid-1980s, when oil and other fuel prices stabilized, but has not returned to its pre-crisis levels (U.S. Department of Energy 1995; Swedish Central Bureau of Statistics 1994). Since the late 1970s Sweden's per capita total energy consumption has stayed at around 60 percent, and its per capita residential energy consumption at about 80 percent, that of the United States (U.S. Department of Commerce 1996).

In the 1990s I found that the earlier consumption relationships persisted between Foley and Munka Ljungby: Foleyans continued to use less fuel for heating their homes, and Munka Ljungbyans continued to use less household fuel. However, these gaps had widened since the 1980s. Foley's heating fuel demand decreased over time, but Munka's increased. Household fuel demand decreased in both communities, but Foley's (higher) average household demand decreased only negligibly, while Munka's (lower) demand decreased substantially.

Many energy-saving improvements in housing construction and household technology have been introduced over the past decade, but such improvements have leveled off since 1994 (Schipper 1996a). Further, efficiency gained through technological improvements can be offset by what is called the take-back effect. In Foley, for example, greater efficiency of refrigerators and water heaters resulted in lower operating costs and led to the purchase of larger-capacity models, because these could be operated nearly as cheaply as smaller models. Some conserving habits begun in times of energy crisis persist, such as selecting lower indoor temperatures or running only full loads in dishwashers and clotheswashers, as I found in both Munka Ljungby and Foley. However, other behaviors rebound when prices fall or when initial price shocks diminish, and in the absence of conservation reminders from the media. Although I found little evidence of rebound behavior inside households, it was blatant with regard to mobility. Both Swedes and Americans are driving faster than they did in the 1980s, and authorities in both countries complain about speeding. (Both time scarcity and affordable energy prices encourage going fast.) Munka Ljungbyans and Foleyans drive more on local errands than they did in the 1980s as well. Additionally, in Munka Ljungby the frequency of baths, more energy intensive than showers, rose.

CONSUMPTION AND THE ENVIRONMENT

Direct energy demand is just one manifestation of the broader consumption ethos of industrial societies, whose disproportionate resource demand and environmental damage are widely recognized. The United States still "leads" the world in resource consumption, but Europe's demand is rising rapidly. During the last decade, automobiles exceeded households in number, consumption of processed frozen foods doubled, and soft drink consumption increased by one third there. And the newly industrializing nations represent a fast-multiplying demand for consumer goods. Based on constant dollars, the world's people have consumed as many goods and services since 1950 as all previous generations combined (Durning 1992).

What are the environmental consequences of this inexorably rising consumption? Industrial living depends on the very commodities that are the most energy intensive and environmentally damaging, such as fuels, metals, chemicals, and paper. Industrial countries, representing one fourth of the world's population, consume 75 percent of its fuels, 80 percent of its iron and steel, 81 percent of its paper, and 86 percent of its aluminum and chemicals (Durning 1992).

Environmental concerns have now entered popular awareness. In *Environmental Values in American Culture*, Willett Kempton, James Boster, and Jennifer Hartley (1995) document substantial concern for the environment in diverse groups across the nation. They cite findings from a 1990 Gallup poll in which 73 percent of respondents said they consider themselves to be environmentalists. In their own survey, 87 percent of the general public sample agreed that an intrinsic obligation to protect the environment exists.

Foleyans and Munka Ljungbyans now focus their attention on the environment—if not as fervently as they focused on energy in the late 1970s, when they felt personal economic threats or heard government appeals for conservation. Government messages to Swedish citizens currently center on recycling and the problem of mounting garbage. Recycling is what Foleyans and Munka Ljungbyans want to talk about, bringing it up almost reflexively after any mention of environment or energy. Recycling is the pro-environmental activity they participate in most widely as well.

I investigated environmental awareness in Foley and Munka Ljungby: How do residents respond to warnings of compounding environmental damage? What energy-environment links do they perceive? Do they recognize any environmental consequences of their ways of life, and does this awareness influence their own daily choices? To what extent do they engage in pro-environmental activities?

As will be seen, some residents of both Foley and Munka Ljungby are skeptical about reports of ozone depletion or global warming projections. Others, though accepting the authenticity of such reports, are overwhelmed by the complexity of these and other environmental problems. Neither of these views inspires change. Whereas Foleyans regard "the environment" as a distant and abstract entity, Munka Ljungbyans express a more immediate and personal connection to it. However, members of neither community link their personal daily activities to environmental problems. They speak instead of the rain forest or the whales, remote and exotic concerns to which they can donate money without changing their own daily routines or comfort levels. Likewise, most householders disapprove of industrial spoilage of the environment, but they do not acknowledge, or perhaps not even fully recognize, that industry exists largely to provide consumers with the things they want (or will learn to want!).

Nature is closely integrated into Swedish life. More Swedes feel a personal need for contact with the natural world, and appreciation of nature is more widespread in Sweden than in America. However, experiences in nature can be regarded as products to be consumed in Sweden as well—as scenic, photogenic, or recreational antidotes to industrial worklife.

AFFLUENCE, DISCONTENT, AND RESISTANCE TO CHANGE

Both Sweden and America have greatly increased their energy efficiency, but reduction of direct energy (fuel) demand means little if consumption of energy and resources to produce material goods continues unabated. Mirroring national trends, marked increases in saturation of appliances and entertainment equipment, as well as increases in ownership of duplicates, occurred in both Foley and Munka Ljungby over time.

Numerous surveys reveal what we all recite: increased affluence does not bring greater happiness. Periodic polls taken by Chicago's National Opinion

Research Center, for example, indicate that no more Americans report being "very happy" now than did in 1957. This very happy faction has remained at about one third of the population, despite a near doubling in personal consumption expenditures (cited in Durning 1992). Further, people say they want fewer things and more time than they have now. A survey reported in a 1989 *Fortune* magazine showed that 75 percent of working Americans between the ages of 25 and 49 would like "to see our country return to a simpler lifestyle, with less emphasis on material success." In a recent survey conducted by *Time* magazine and CNN television, 69 percent of respondents said that they would like to "slow down and live a more relaxed life," and 61 percent agreed that "earning a living today requires so much effort that it's difficult to find time to enjoy life" (surveys cited in Elgin 1993).

Scandinavian surveys yield similar findings. For example, 76 percent of Norwegians polled in 1975 indicated that they found their standard of living already too high. When later asked which they would choose, a raise in pay or more free time, 58 percent said they would choose time over money (cited in Nørgård and Christensen 1992–93). Surveys in Denmark report a steady increase in stated preference for time over money: 44 percent in 1964, 57 percent in 1975, and 70 percent in 1987 (cited in Nørgård 1995). In a 1978 U.S. Department of Labor study, 84 percent said they would like to trade some or all of future income for additional free time (cited in Schor 1992). Majorities of questionnaire respondents in both Foley and Munka Ljungby also said they would choose time over a pay raise: 61 and 70 percent, respectively.

If material prosperity does not increase happiness, and surveys reveal desires both for environmental protection and for a simpler way of life, why is there not more substantive change? Although they express certain frustrations with consumerist society, Foleyans and Munka Ljungbyans largely accept its values and comply with economic and social mandates to consume and conform. As is documented here, many feel no dissonance between the larger environmental and social ideals they claim and their own consumption levels and patterns of daily life. Conspicuous consumption is much in evidence in both towns. Although overall time spent in shopping has declined in both communities since the 1980s, Foleyans continue to shop for longer periods than Munka Ljungbyans, and "shopaholics" are more readily identified there.

Of course, membership in industrial society ascribes some degree of participation in consumption and environmental damage. Interviews revealed the limitations, even distortions, of the industrial worldview, and the social and cultural traps in which consumers are caught. But how and where to consensually limit consumption when it is believed that individuality as well as social identity is expressed through material means? Consumption has been called "sacrosanct" in America, where no one questions the rights of individuals to consume in any manner they please (Sobel 1981). Swedes, highly conformist, have been restrained from similar expressions of affluence by *lagom*, their cultural principle of moderation. Now, however, *lagom* faces redefinition in a new era of shopping malls, two-car households, and greatly expanded television broadcasting, most of which comes from America.

Sweden and America differ profoundly in some respects, and these differences are highlighted in the next chapter. Sweden's politics have been more humane, and its energy and environmental policies more farsighted, than those of the United States. Its welfare state embodies the principles of the worth of every individual and of solidarity and extends these canons internationally. However, both Sweden and America are essentially variations of industrial consumer society. Sweden's economy is becoming more privatized, the role of the market and monetary considerations growing in importance. Sweden increasingly resembles America materially, and this material diffusion has social and psychological impact.

ORGANIZATION OF DISCUSSION

In the chapters that follow, the issues and questions raised here are considered in the light of fieldwork findings. In Chapter 1 the Swedish welfare state is contrasted with American capitalism in order to give a sense of the different contexts in which Foleyans and Munka Ljungbyans live. Energy and environmental policies are compared, and Sweden's economic, political, and identity problems of the 1990s are set forth. The communities of Foley and Munka Ljungby are described. Chapter 2 focuses on house contents, fuels, and fuel consumption. The images residents of each town hold about the other are reported, and the degree to which these stereotypes are fulfilled is traced through an examination of house contents. Fuels used in residences and fuel prices are compared, along with actual fuel consumption in sample households. Factors contributing to Munka Ljungby's lower household fuel demand, and those contributing to Foley's lower heating fuel demand, are presented.

Patterns of energy-using household activities are reported in Chapter 3, and notable differences are detailed. As with house contents, many aspects of daily routine counter stereotypes. In Chapter 4 perceptions and awareness of energy, and self-images, are contrasted for Foleyans and Munka Ljungbyans. Their knowledge of energy-saving strategies and the obstacles to conservation they identify are presented. In Chapter 5 individual rationales for consumption and the trade-offs among time, energy, money, and environment which underlie consumption decisions are related to larger cultural mandates; in Chapter 6 motives for conservation are similarly addressed.

The environmental focus which has displaced interest in energy is described in Chapter 7, and engagement in pro-environmental activities is contrasted for Foley and Munka Ljungby. Perceived connections between energy and environment and competing environmental and economic factors in decision making are described. Chapter 8 addresses various aspects of consumerism, including embodied energy, conspicuous consumption, status symbols, shopping, origins of the urge to buy, and voluntary simplicity. The relation of consumerism to fear is traced. In Chapter 9 some dimensions of worldview are compared for Foley and Munka: the "image of unlimited good" (Hornborg 1992); quality of life; and views of the future, potential fuel shortages, and collective versus individual solutions to energy and environmental problems. Discrepancies between ideal and real behavior are also explored. Culture traps and trade-offs are reviewed in the Conclusion. The self-limits of industrialism and various potential routes to change and sustainability are considered. Certain research procedures are detailed in the Appendixes.

Chapter 1

The Communities and Their Contexts

THE SWEDISH WELFARE STATE AND AMERICAN CAPITALISM

America feels ambivalent about Sweden, a "socialist" welfare state that had the nerve to succeed. The Swedish state provides its citizens with all of their basic needs—such as health care, education, unemployment insurance and retraining programs, and old age care—with no sacrifice of affluence or range of private consumption options. Swedish life expectancy is higher, and infant mortality rates lower, than in America. Per capita, Sweden spent just 40 percent of the U.S. total for health care expenditure (public and private) in 1994 (U.S. Department of Commerce 1996). That Sweden competes economically with the United States piques us further. Despite Sweden's relatively late industrialization, it quickly gained ascendancy in world markets. Sweden became known for its engineering virtuosity, and Swedish products such as steel, automobiles, paper, and chemicals are prized worldwide for their quality and durability. Modern Scandinavian aesthetics set the standard for interior design.

Politically, Sweden has long held a position of neutrality. It has engaged in no wars since the end of the Napoleonic conflicts in 1814. Sweden's political and economic aloofness is reflected in its refusals to join either NATO or the Common Market and in its contested and delayed entry into the European Community in late 1994. Yet Sweden is globally-oriented, in the 1990s contributing over five times as much per capita in official development assistance as the United States does (U.S. Department of Commerce 1996). Sweden is also politically active and outspoken, its activism perhaps best represented by the role Sweden serves in U.N. negotiations and peacekeeping and by the world leader it provided in Dag Hammarskjöld. Swedes freely pass judgment on American politics, both internal and external. They have long decried the racist treatment of blacks and other minorities in America (Myrdal 1944). Sweden was the first country to formally protest U.S. involvement in Vietnam and offered permanent refuge to draft resistors and defectors. In the late 1970s,

Americans learned that those self-satisfied Swedes possessed a higher standard of living than theirs, as measured by GNP, life expectancy, and per capita consumption of telephones, newspapers, and medical services. Reports that they managed to use less energy to sustain this standard (for example, Schipper and Lichtenberg 1976) further aroused envy and curiosity.

Sweden is often mislabeled a socialist country because of misperception of its economy as state-owned and its politics as centralized and unilateral. Actually, 80 percent of Sweden's industry and commerce is privately owned; the Swedish system has been called "state-administered capitalism" (Jamison, Eyerman, and Cramer 1990). And Sweden's representative parliamentary democracy encompasses nearly a dozen parties. In recent years, Social Democrat hegemony has been challenged by more-conservative coalitions.

In a welfare state, the provision of certain standards of income, health, and education is considered the political *right* of every citizen—in sharp contrast with the American view of such benefits as charity offered only to the deficient. Truly democratic, the Swedish welfare state actualizes the principle of the worth and dignity of every human being, and this conviction fosters compassionate solidarity which extends beyond Sweden to the rest of the globe as well. Contemporary Swedish citizens' rights and benefits stem from a history of decentralized politics and popular movements. A brief description of the development of the welfare state makes clearer the contrasts of the economic and political contexts in which Foleyans and Munka Ljungbyans live.

DEVELOPMENT OF THE SWEDISH WELFARE STATE

The Swedish system is characterized by consistent emphasis on the universality of rights and by solicitation of perspectives from all factions of society in shaping social policy. What were the origins of these organizing principles of egalitarianism and inclusiveness? In 1982 I asked a member of the *Riksdag*, the Swedish Parliament, why Sweden is more farsighted and compassionate than the United States. He answered, "It's because our legislators are mostly farmers and teachers, while yours are lawyers and businessmen." Such Swedish groundedness began early in Sweden's political history. Sweden's peasantry was never subjugated by a feudal order and was recognized as an independent estate in the strong national administrative system that was the legacy of the Great Power Era, the seventeenth-century period of Swedish control of the Baltic. Farmers had political strength both in Parliament and in local government.

Throughout the nineteenth century, Sweden was one of the poorest countries in Europe, overwhelmingly agrarian. However, it was comparatively advanced in literacy in that public education was introduced in 1842. Industrialization came relatively late to Sweden, in the 1870s. In 1884 the Swedish Parliament adopted the first comprehensive social insurance bill. Social welfare programs in other countries, such as Germany, were largely directed toward industrial workers, but Sweden's bill covered all citizens.

The Swedish welfare state was the product of an alliance between workers and farmers, with contributions from liberal intellectuals and university radicals of the 1880s. Both Christian morality and secular humanist values shaped the political platform, and consumer cooperatives were also influential. An early pattern of satisfying diverse interests continues today in government's widespread consulting with all political parties, scientists and researchers, and interest and citizens' groups as laws and policies are forged. Such inclusivity assures Swedish citizens that conclusions reached by their government are just.

The Swedish Social Democrat party was founded in 1889, and Social Democrats controlled the *Riksdag* for 44 years, from 1932 to 1976. In the 1930s reforms were introduced that established Sweden as a model for social welfare, providing genuine security for citizens in the event of illness or unemployment and in old age. Strong economic growth and expanded welfare coverage characterized the postwar period. Added benefits included preventive medical and dental care and various allowances, such as those for children until age 16, adult education, and job training.

In 1990 Sweden's public welfare sector was the largest in Europe: 35 percent of its GDP. Swedish taxes, of course, finance public sector benefits. Combined state and local income taxes levied on individuals average 30 percent up to the first 180,000 SEK (about $26,000 in 1997), and 50 percent after that. This may strike American readers as high, but such taxation provides all medical and dental care, unemployment insurance and retraining, accident and disability insurance, a minimum five weeks' paid vacation, and a variety of miscellaneous allowances for which the individual may be eligible (such as study or child allowances). In addition, Swedes can feel assured that no one in their country need suffer dire poverty or homelessness, and that tax moneys also support international aid and development assistance. In the 1990s a number of economic setbacks and social welfare problems emerged to challenge Sweden, and these are discussed in the last sections of this chapter.

SWEDISH ENERGY POLICY

Sweden's Fuel Dependence and Oil Reduction Campaign

Sweden has no domestic oil or natural gas resources. It has some coal and uranium deposits, but these are of such low grade that their mining is not feasible economically. Sweden's dependence on imported fuels has been marked since the turn of the century, when indigenous wood was displaced by imported coal and coke as central fuels for the industrializing nation. By the late 1930s, Sweden imported 70 percent of its fuel supply. During the second world war, however, such imports were restricted and accounted for only 30 percent of total fuel used (Wennerström 1976). Greater self-sufficiency was achieved in this crisis through a return to the use of firewood and government rationing of fuels. When constraints lifted at the war's end, national fuel consumption (and fuel imports) tripled rapidly.

By the 1970s oil constituted 70 percent of Sweden's total energy use, and coal and uranium, 10 percent. In the 1990s Sweden continues to import nearly 70 percent of its energy (oil forms nearly half of total energy consumed, up from its 1980s share). Sweden's chief indigenous energy sources are hydro-power, biomass, and wind.

In contrast to Sweden, the United States enjoys a bonanza of indigenous energy resources, both renewable and fossil. It need not import any of its natural gas but elects to purchase some gas and electricity from Canada. Likewise, the United States chooses to import oil: 46 percent in the mid-1970s, 30 percent in the mid-1980s, and 50 percent in 1994 (American Petroleum Institute 1995; U.S. Department of Commerce 1996).

Following the oil embargo of 1973, the Swedish state issued an energy policy statement with the dual objectives of reducing Sweden's oil dependence and developing indigenous and renewable energy sources. In support of the policy, the Social Democrats authored Sweden's comprehensive Energy Bill of 1975, which emphasized ensuring Sweden's energy supply in the long term through fuel conservation and use of domestic renewables. This bill launched an extensive research-and-development program to these ends. It stipulated guidelines for electricity provisioning: limited expansion of hydropower, continued nuclear development, and increased cogeneration (use of by-product heat from electricity generation for space heating).

An Energy Research and Development Commission was formed to coordi-nate Sweden's energy programs. In typical Swedish fashion, this commission consisted of representatives from across society. A new state Committee for Energy Savings began a massive campaign for reduction of oil dependence through conservation. The message sent out was that every citizen could, and *should*, help in this effort; and media bombarded citizens with reminders and tips on saving energy. State-salaried advisors on energy conservation (*energisparrådgivare*), positioned in most *kommuner* (municipalities), provided information and conducted free home energy audits. State aid was established for homeowners making energy-saving structural changes, including no- and low-interest loans and various types of subsidies.

In 1976 the Liberals replaced the Social Democrats as the party controlling the *Riksdag*, but they maintained the 1975 energy policies and programs. The oil-saving campaign was so successful that a new comprehensive energy policy was created in 1981. Its goals were to maintain zero energy growth and to reduce oil products from 70 to 40 percent of total energy consumption by 1990. By 1983 Sweden already had achieved most of the oil-reduction objective. State subsidies of homeowners' energy-saving changes were reduced in 1981 and gone by 1986. A sizable reduction in the number of energy advisors occurred as well.

Swedish reports reveal impressive reductions in energy demand. Sweden used about the same amount of energy for residential heating in 1990 as it did in 1970, despite a 28 percent increase in the number of houses (Holm and Thun-berg 1993). And since 1970, industry's energy consumption has decreased 14 percent, even though production has increased 17 percent (NUTEK, the Swedish National Board for Industrial and Technical Development). Other statistics temper this good news, however. NUTEK also reports that energy for transportation has *increased* by 40 percent since 1970: greater automotive efficiency was offset by an increase in the number of automobiles. Also, half of all goods are now transported by truck in Sweden, as opposed to more-efficient freight trains (Holm and Thunberg 1993). Energy analyst Are Kjeang (1989) relates that energy use declined from 1980 to 1984 but increased in 1985 due to stabilizing and then decreasing oil prices. Kjeang adds that the decline in residential energy demand during the late 1980s can be attributed in large part to milder winters in recent years and to the greater efficiency on paper that results from the changeover from oil to electricity. (Electricity consumption is calculated only from point of use, excluding losses incurred in its production or distribution. Additionally, there are no conversion losses in electrical heating systems or appliances.) Currently, Swedish energy demand is on its way up again (Schipper and Meyers et al. 1992), and NUTEK projects that by 2005, energy demand will exceed supply by from 3 to 9 TWh.

Sweden has half a million homes with direct electric heat, 70 percent of which were built after 1960. This construction trend peaked in the 1970s, and though electricity is still the preferred residential heating fuel, waterborne systems are now more commonly installed than baseboard electric systems. Combination furnaces, able to use electricity or wood, are also becoming more widespread.

SHIFTING U.S. ENERGY POLICY

The comprehensive and consistent policies formed swiftly by the Swedes in response to the oil crisis contrast sharply with America's reaction. The atmosphere surrounding energy issues in the United States was discordant, filled with conflicting reports and uncertainties, strident factionalism, and discontinuities. In 1975 the U.S. Energy Policy Conservation Act was passed, and in 1977 the Department of Energy and many state energy agencies were founded. Government-sponsored programs were established to explore for fossil fuels, investigate renewables, and develop synthetic fuels. Residential energy programs introduced included fuel bill assistance and weatherization schemes, restrictions on the shutting off of fuels by utility companies during the winter, mandated provision of low-cost energy audits by utility companies, and energy-demand labeling of major appliances. In addition, tax deductions for energy-conserving structural changes or the acquisition of energy-efficient appliances were introduced. During the late 1970s both government and utility companies urged energy conservation.

After 1980, however, President Carter's "moral equivalent of war" was abrogated by President Reagan's denial of the existence of energy problems. Emphasis switched from conservation and alternative fuels to exploration for fossil fuel deposits and nuclear power research and development. Earlier legislative proposals regulating the windfall profits of petroleum companies were not enacted. Reagan threatened to dismantle the Department of Energy (DOE). Although this drastic measure was not effected, the budgets for the solar fuel and fossil fuels conservation divisions and the Energy Information Administration were reduced sharply, while nuclear energy and weapon allotments were increased. Many state energy agencies experienced large cuts in federal funding as well. By the late 1980s there were no longer any tax deductions or subsidies for improving housing energy efficiency. In 1990 the U.S. federal government spent less than half as much on energy research, development, and demonstration projects as it did ten years earlier (Holdren 1992). The United States tried to reduce imports of oil through conservation and increased domestic production, and succeeded fairly well with these strategies. In 1994, however, the United States imported half its total petroleum demand, that year marking a 40-year low in domestic oil production (American Petroleum Institute 1995).

NUCLEAR POWER IN SWEDEN

The results of a popular referendum on nuclear power held in 1980 led the *Riksdag* to declare shortly thereafter that all Swedish reactors would be phased out by the year 2010. (Reactors under construction at the time of the referendum were to be completed.) In 1994, however, the *Riksdag* voted against making the referendum decision law. What happened? Sweden's 1975 research-and-development program for renewable energy technologies and energy efficiency continued into the early 1980s. With the continuous addition of reactors, peaking at 12 in 1985, nuclear power production nearly tripled. In order to sell this additional power, producers reduced electricity prices considerably in 1983. These reductions and falling world market oil prices made alternative technologies less attractive economically, and the renewables program faltered.

After the 1986 Chernobyl accident, discussion ensued about decommissioning some nuclear reactors. However, the proposal was stalled by the power industry, various electricity-intensive industries, and trade unions. The government said that it would decommission reactors only if economically feasible ways of generating electricity were found—and of course, the reactors' low operating cost is difficult to match.

In 1992 the Swedish State Power Board (*Vattenfall*) became a state-owned company, leaving its traditional status as a government-directed entity. Reflecting the national trend toward increased privatization, this act transformed the Swedish electricity market, formerly consisting of local monopolies, to a competitive arena in which customers can select any producer. Sweden now plans to export electricity to the continent, where prices are higher. In 1993 Sweden was the eighth-largest nuclear power generator in the world (U.S. Department of Commerce 1996). Nuclear power generated fully 43 percent of Sweden's electricity in 1994 (United Nations 1994). Deregulation, internationalization, and economic considerations, along with Sweden's current high dependence on electricity, make dubious the decommissioning of all nuclear reactors by 2010.

Munka Ljungby and the Nuclear Power Issue

Munka Ljungby opinion is divided with regard to nuclear power, and individuals expressed internal ambivalence about this issue as well. Those who support nuclear power emphasize its environmental advantages: no emissions and no further development of wild rivers for hydropower. They also view positively the contribution of nuclear power to Sweden's economic development. One Munka area resident using only solar and wood energy in her home was nonetheless emphatic about the value of nuclear power for industry. Those Munka Ljungbyans who oppose nuclear power emphasize its dangers and the problem of storing radioactive spent fuel.

Some consumers say they conserve electricity in order to decrease dependence on nuclear power. One such informant expressed strong feelings about nuclear dangers:

The big question is nuclear waste storage and the potential for leaks. It's not right to leave a life-threatening situation to the coming generations. In fact, it's reprehensible. We [Swedes] can't leave our reactors up just because others will leave theirs up, as some argue.

Nuclear discussions usually contained references to the situations in other countries by both proponents and opponents:

I'm not so much against it, because I really have little influence. Besides, other lands nearby have nuclear plants: Russia, Germany, France. . . . At least they are not burning coal like Poland: a pure catastrophe!

The Swedish state gave Russia and Poland money to build up their reactors and make them safer. They are really close and really *dangerous*!

Renewable Alternatives to Nuclear Power

Founded in 1991, the Swedish National Board for Industrial and Technological Development (NUTEK) has as one of its missions the safeguarding of environmental goals from encroachment by energy development strategies. NUTEK also stimulates research in renewables, especially wind power. Its publications focus on energy efficiency and alternative, pro-environmental energy sources.

Wind Power. Wind-generation subsidies were rescinded in the mid-1980s, but supports up to 35 percent of wind generator construction costs for individual citizens, cooperatives, and power companies were reinstated in 1991. Additionally, NUTEK established wind power advisors to provide information on wind power and the construction of wind generators. In response to these stimuli, one hundred new generators were built by 1994. Local groups throughout Skåne, a region noted for its winds, have formed small power cooperatives to build generators and sell power to the grid.

Swedes agree that windmills have the advantage of being nonpolluting. Controversy exists, however, over how they look and how noisy they are. Several Munka Ljungbyans emphasized how unattractive windmills were to them personally. Additionally, the city of Ängelholm fears that generators would mar the scenery along the coast and reduce tourist revenues. "What would be perfect would be a windmill on every lot, but that would never, ever be acceptable to the neighbors," said one Munka Ljungbyan. "It would be 'disruptive' and would not be neat and tidy with the lawn." Another bristled: "Destroy the landscape? No one says they think the electric power line support towers are ugly or complains much about the drone of highway traffic."

Solar Energy. Sweden takes pride in its leadership position in solar cell research, and NUTEK emphasizes solar energy as a valuable complement to electricity after the year 2000. The high cost of solar energy has prevented the development of large systems, but its price is now declining as efficiencies improve. Swedish state subsidies to cover roughly one fourth of total solar system cost have been reinstituted for residential solar collectors. Munka Ljungbyans did not bring up the subject of solar power, but one study circle in the area had built a solar collector.

Biomass. In the early 1980s plantations of fast-growing trees were planted in central Sweden, and in the south, peat was the focus of energy speculation. Biomass is currently favored once again, in that its use results in no net addition of carbon dioxide to the atmosphere. NUTEK is supporting biomass research, and Sweden is regarded as the world's leader in techniques for the gasification of biomass. The *Riksdag* recently allocated 1 billion *kronor* ($143 million) to support power plant conversion to biomass.

ENVIRONMENTAL POLICIES IN SWEDEN

Sweden leads the world in environmentalism. Sweden was the first country to establish an environmental protection agency, the first to pass environmental protection legislation, and one of the most vigorous supporters of research in environmental science and technology. Sweden initiated the first major U.N. Conference on the Environment, held in Stockholm in 1972. Jamison, Eyerman, and Cramer (1990) trace the evolution of Sweden's environmental sensibility in *The Making of the New Environmental Consciousness.* They write that awareness grew out of a long-standing concern with preservation of natural resources—specifically, the minerals and timber upon which Sweden's seventeenth-century Great Power Era and its rapid industrialization in the late nineteenth century depended. Forestry and natural history early acquired scientific status in Sweden, the "land of Linnaeus." In 1909 the Swedish Society for the Conservation of Nature was established, along with various state conservation agencies. Swedish royal investigative commissions on nature protection and water pollution were active before World War II. That these commissions followed the tradition of widespread consulting across society increased state responsiveness to warnings from scientists expressing environmental concern.

Several events in the 1960s heightened Sweden's environmental concern, among them the publication of Carson's *Silent Spring* and a national debate on mercury pollution. Expansion of hydropower through development of rivers became highly controversial during the 1960s. And in 1969 microbiologist Björn Gillberg, "Sweden's Ralph Nader"(Jamison, Eyerman, and Cramer 1990), published a book on genetic damage caused by food additives and industrial chemicals. In 1967 the National Environmental Protection Agency was created, the first of similar agencies to be established in other countries. Two years later Sweden's Environmental Protection Act was passed, characterized as "the strongest and most rigorous legislation that could be found anywhere" (Ibid.).

Swedish environmentalism expanded its focus beyond protection of threatened species and pristine environments to address human survival and limits to growth. Sweden's Green Party formed in 1980 and usually wins seats in the *Riksdag*. In 1989 the Stockholm Environmental Institute (SEI) was established by the *Riksdag* as an independent foundation to carry out global environmental research building on the 1972 U.N. Conference on the Environment and the work of the World Commission for Environment and Development (the Brundtland Commission). The SEI translated Agenda 21 from the 1992 U.N. Conference on Environment and Development (the "Rio Conference") into an action plan for Sweden, in which *kommuner* play an integral role. (Agenda 21 states that every country is obliged to ensure that its activities do not cause environmental damage in other countries.)

Current Swedish environmental guidelines preclude further development of rivers for hydroelectricity. Sweden's goals for cleaner air are ambitious as well: By 2000, Sweden hopes to reduce sulfur emissions by 80 percent, and nitrous oxide by 30 percent, from their 1980 levels. Carbon dioxide emissions will stay at their 1990 level until 2000, and then will be decreased (Swedish Institute 1992). Sweden is well aware of the success of America's stricter emissions controls. Leaded gas was outlawed in Sweden in 1994. NUTEK continues to promote catalytic converters, more-efficient (and electric) cars, and ethanol.

Sweden taxes carbon dioxide and other pollutants from fossil fuels universally. It also taxes both gasoline and diesel fuel heavily, although this was originally done to increase general revenues rather than to protect the environment. Sweden's example contrasts with America's attempts at a comprehensive Btu tax, attacked by lobbyists from the petroleum and hydroelectric industries; agriculture; and national associations of manufacturers, truckers, and ethanol and methanol producers. The tax shrank to 4.3 cents per gallon of gasoline, and any message to consumers became absorbed by reductions in crude oil prices.

Sweden's strong commitment to environmental protection contrasts sharply with the situation in the United States, where pro-environment goals are hard won and then still vulnerable to reversals when power turns over. At this writing, Republicans seek to dismantle such basic legislation as the Clean Air and Clean Water Acts. An environmental laggard, America was the last major developed nation to ratify (in 1994) the International Convention on Biological Diversity from the Rio Conference. Sweden is caught in goals whose fulfillment is mutually-conflicting, however—for example, how to decommission nuclear reactors, reduce fossil fuel consumption, and avoid further development of wild rivers for hydroelectricity and at the same time continue to succeed in the world market in order to maintain domestic prosperity and expansive welfare rights? (Conflicting desires were expressed by consumers as well—such as wanting cleaner air but also increased mobility. These will be described for both Munka Ljungby and Foley in later chapters.)

SWEDEN'S CRISES: ECONOMIC, POLITICAL, AND IDENTITY

In the early 1990s Sweden faced multiple crises of unprecedented magnitude, and speculations about the demise of the welfare state appeared in U.S. media.

Economic Crisis

In the early 1990s Sweden, with a growing trade deficit and high inflation rates, experienced its worst economic conditions since the 1930s depression. The unemployment rate was 10 percent in 1994, distressing in a society where the usual range is from 3 to 5 percent, and where the traditional goal is full employment. One quarter of youth aged 18 to 24 were then unemployed (*DN*, 2/10/94). A growing national debt made maintaining social welfare benefits a pressing problem: slowed economic growth in the 1970s and 1980s, and negative growth in the early 1990s, had undercut tax supports. Since 1994 Sweden's overall economic situation has improved somewhat, with lower unemployment and positive GDP.

In part this improvement is the result of substantial cuts in a variety of social welfare benefits. Sweden also revamped its retirement system to achieve savings for the state, urging citizens to establish individual retirement plans and to increase personal savings. The general retirement age was increased from 65 to 66 years as well. A major quandary for Sweden is the degree to which it can maintain its generous immigration policy and extension of benefits to immigrants and refugees in the face of shrinking resources. In 1992 nearly 6 percent of the Swedish population consisted of immigrants (U.S. Department of Commerce 1996). In 1993 nearly 60,000 non-Nordic citizens obtained residence permits in Sweden, which entitled them to the exact same rights and benefits as native Swedes. Of these, nearly half were Bosnians. The Swedish state devoted nearly $1.75 billion—2 percent of its total national budget—to its immigrant population in 1994 (Swedish Department of Culture 1994). In March 1995 Sweden began deporting Cubans and investigating ways to expel Bosnians, due to budget concerns and to fears of nationalist backlash. These events signal momentous changes in a country known as a liberal and generous haven.

As well as challenging social welfare policy, economic concerns increasingly rival or take precedence over environmental considerations. For example, the provision of jobs and the bolstering of regional economy were central arguments for constructing the Öresund bridge between Malmö and Copenhagen, a project protested by some environmentalists. Also, the postal service reported that direct mail advertising, seen as a nuisance and a waste of resources by many Swedes, provided one fourth of its income. It warned that citizens putting up "No advertising, thanks" (*Ingen reklam, tack*) stickers on their mailboxes would directly threaten their own postal carrier's job (*NST* [*Nordvästra Skånes Tidningar*, a regional newspaper] 3/20/94)!

Political Crisis

Domestically and internationally, Sweden faces an era of new and complex questions, accompanied by political disillusionment. Swedes are expressing unprecedented cynicism about their political process. In response to an interview question about what had changed in Sweden since the 1980s, one Munka Ljungbyan said simply, "People have given up. Government leaders will do as they want." A seasoned local official in his 70s agreed, reflecting:

There have been big changes over the last 10 to 20 years. . . . Before, we considered our politicians to be honorable: we had confidence in them. Now, they are just *spittoons*. Politics has become a personality cult . . . and all parties are saying the *same thing*.

In late 1994 Sweden voted to join the European Community. However, a sizable (47%) minority voted against membership, feeling it would compromise Sweden's distinctiveness and independence. Fears expressed in the media debate over membership included losing the traditional right of common access to land (*allemansrätt*) and being forced to adopt the Community's environmental and health standards, considered lower than Sweden's.

Growing immigration has resulted in an increasingly heterogeneous population in Sweden. In the 1990s new political parties formed out of nationalist and racist backlash. Hostilities have occurred that shock and sadden most Swedes, ranging from physical attacks to the burning of a mosque. Other social problems seem to be worsening in Sweden as well. *NST* reports increasing incidence of vandalism and violence, including muggings, rape, and knife fights. Newspaper stories often focus on "troubled youth," whose problems are said to be due to alcohol (a long-standing concern in Sweden) and being left alone too much.

Identity Crisis

Sweden increasingly resembles America, materially. Highway culture was evident in the early 1980s, with uniform cloverleafs and gas station-quick shop combinations. Such homogenization has since expanded in the form of shopping centers and warehouse-style grocery and discount stores. Now, charge cards are much more numerous, and gasoline and supermarket chains offer discounts and special buys to their card holders. Direct mail ads with American-style glossy layouts have proliferated. Television programming has expanded mightily, much of it imported from or modeled on U.S. TV. Much of what is happening in Sweden supports McKibben's (1992) reflection that the world is not becoming a global village, but rather a global convenience store.

Although Swedes have not taken the step the French did in outlawing English loan words, and only a few Munka Ljungbyans expressed frustration with the trend, American terms and phrases have permeated the Swedish language. Certain sports terms were borrowed long ago, such as sudden death and time-out. The greatest infusion of English is evident in names of products or their features, like the Supervoice answering machine or Electrolux's No Frost line of refrigerators. Disney characters have long appeared on Swedish clothing, and Levi's have been around for decades. But now clothing labels are often in English, frequently incorporating the words "natural" or "cotton." Such labels in 1994 included L.O.G.G. (Label of Graded Goods), Friend of Nature, World Class Woman, and (my favorite) Nature Calling. Other English intrusions are Nordic Light, a Swedish face cream, and Urban Center, the name of a private medical practice in Ängelholm. Travel and leisure vocabularies are also rife with English. You *parkera* your car and *checka in* at a hotel, or go *camping* in your *campare*. Want to camp but don't have a *campare*, just a *pickup*? Buy a *Toppola*, the brand name for what converts a *pickup* to a *campare*. Or you can stay at home and *skippa* the whole thing.

Urban life continues to take on American dimensions. Date books and cellular telephones (called "yuppies' teddy bears" by the Swedes) are now common. One radio program I heard solicited callers' frustrations with modern life. In addition to general resentments over increased stress, crowding, and people being too hurried to chat, two memorable complaints were customers paying for just a liter of milk with grocery charge cards and people using their cellular phones in movie theaters! Talk radio came to Sweden in the 1990s. Most of the talk is benign pleasantry, rather than shock radio, however.

FOLEY AND MUNKA LJUNGBY: SUBURBANIZING SMALL TOWNS

Though no claim is made that Foley and Munka Ljungby typify America and Sweden, or even their respective regions, they were matched along several dimensions relevant to comparing energy use, consumerism, and daily life. They exemplify a type of community found with increasing frequency in both countries: the suburbanizing small town. Foley and Munka Ljungby lie in farm country and were formerly agricultural service centers. Foley is located in the heart of the state of Minnesota, 70 miles northwest of the Twin Cities of Minneapolis and St. Paul. Munka Ljungby is located very near the west coast of Skåne, Sweden's southernmost province, and is 60 miles north of the city of Malmö. Foley's population in 1982 was 1,600; by 1993 it had grown to 1,900.

Munka Ljungby, somewhat bigger, had 2,300 residents in 1982 and 2,600 in 1994.

The larger center into whose sphere Foley has been drawn is St. Cloud, a city of 49,000 in 1992, located 14 miles to its west. Munka's nearest city is Ängelholm, just 3 miles to the west, which had a population of 20,000 in 1994. Ängelholm's *kommun*, a unit of government frequently translated as municipality but which is more similar to a small U.S. county, had a 1994 population of 36,000. Both St. Cloud and Ängelholm are industrial and government centers. Roughly half of the working population (slightly more in Munka, slightly less in Foley) commuted to another town or city to work in the 1980s. A decade later, however, two thirds of Munka workers commuted, largely to Ängelholm.

Foley has a concentrated commercial zone of about four square blocks in area; Munka's shops are less numerous and more diffuse. In addition to a small center consisting of a grocery store, post office, bank, and four retail shops, other Munka stores are scattered throughout the central residential sector, often located in remodeled houses. Although similar shops and services (restaurant, bakery, hardware, clothing, gift, grocery, gasoline, and florist) are available in Foley and Munka, residents shop frequently in St. Cloud or Ängelholm. Both towns have light industry in their budding industrial parks. There are two churches in Munka Ljungby (one state Lutheran church and one Protestant free church) and four in Foley (two Lutheran, one Catholic, and one Presbyterian). Each town has grade schools and a middle school. Foley has a high school, but for their roughly equivalent *gymnasium*, Munka youth must go to Ängelholm. *Nordvästra Skånes Folkhögskola*, a combination liberal arts and technical institute similar to a community college, is located in the center of Munka. Each community has its own library, nursing home, and medical and dental services. Munka has a day-care center as well. Foley is the Seat of Benton County and publishes a newspaper, the *Benton County News*.

One can travel by bus between Munka Ljungby and Ängelholm, but there is no public transportation between Foley and St. Cloud, apart from a van which runs once weekly. The railroad goes through Foley, but there is no passenger service. The railroad tracks outside Munka were torn up in the early 1960s, and a highway now covers their former route. From Ängelholm, one can make train connections to the rest of Sweden. In St. Cloud, cross-Minnesota bus service is available.

Evidence of past and current links with agriculture is apparent in both towns in the forms of farmers' cooperatives, seed and feed stores, and meat packing plants. Where streets and backyards end, fields begin. Landscapes are also similar, consisting of relatively flat plains broken by thick stands of trees.

Although a range of occupations is held by the residents of each town, most Foleyans and Munka Ljungbyans can be characterized as working class, employed in factories, construction, and retail shops, or as lower-level civil servants. Young families with school-age children dominate the populations, closely followed by retired people. Munka Ljungby is ethnically homogeneous, consisting almost entirely of native Swedes. The ethnic background of most Foleyans is either Polish, German, or Swedish.

The oldest housing stock in each town is found in the central sector, where commercial buildings are also located. Subdivisions of housing from the 1960s, 1970s, 1980s, and early 1990s surround this older nucleus. There are apartment complexes in each community, but residence is typified by the detached single-family dwelling, which is the focus of this research. Most of Munka Ljungby's newer houses are brick or stucco, but many of its pre-1960s houses are wood frame. Frame with wood or metal siding dominates in Foley.

The towns differ greatly with regard to weather. Foley lies at the 45th parallel, and Munka Ljungby is at the 56th (which cuts across the south of Hudson Bay). However, Munka's milder maritime climate, influenced by the Gulf Stream, produces a less extreme temperature range and less snow than Foley's landlocked Siberian climate. Thirty-year January temperature averages are 31° F for Munka and 8° F for Foley; July averages are 62° F and 70° F, respectively. Only a Swedish town north of the Arctic Circle would experience winters as cold as Foley's, but then its summers would be much cooler. Use of degree-day statistics can adjust for temperature dissimilarities in order to compare winter heating fuel consumption meaningfully, however.

Housing, retail offerings, and industrial parks expanded in both Munka Ljungby and Foley since the early 1980s. Munka now has video shops, a tanning salon, an acupuncturist, a massage therapist, two physical therapists, and a second bank. A public pool was built. A multistory apartment complex for retired persons was constructed, including public rooms for meetings and a public restaurant. The nursing home for the aged was expanded. A long-term health care center is under construction. The Munka grocery added a greenhouse wing. Just east of town on a new paved road is a new golf course, and on the outskirts of Ängelholm can now be found a warehouse-style grocery store and a McDonald's.

Foley lost one each of two earlier pharmacies, grocery stores, and auto dealerships, as well as its only movie theater. However, it gained a new library and city hall complex, high school, and fire station. A nature trail for walking was created on the edge of town. Whereas Ängelholm's retail offerings have grown only moderately since the early 1980s, St. Cloud's have boomed, incorporating many representatives of national chains.

Local Power Companies

Ängelholms Energiverk is trusted and has a positive reputation among Munka Ljungbyans. The *Energiverk* supplies more than half of local electricity demand and contributes to district heating in Ängelholm with waste heat from its electricity generation as well. It was among the first power companies in the country to use biomass (wood chips and peat) and also among the first to adopt natural gas. In 1991 a combination furnace (*kombipanna*) capable of using either biomass or natural gas was installed. Also, *Ängelholms Energiverk* is experimenting with a wind turbine for electricity generation.

Trends toward deregulation and privatization in Sweden are reflected in changes in language used by and about power companies. The *Energiverk* was formerly a "power authority," operating for profit but under state regulation. Now it is a power company, whose former "subscribers" are now customers. Earlier, billing records were public information, but now written permission from customers is required for access to them.

Energiverk customers pay for their electricity in advance, based on estimated use. Bills are sent out four times per year, but only one is actual; the other three are estimates. Additionally, there is a fixed charge, based on the size of fuses and how much individual households take from the grid. A typical charge of this type would be $150 annually. Reduced electricity rates are offered during the night (10 p.m. to 6 a.m.) and over the entire summer, when cheap hydroelectricity is plentiful. About 6 percent of customers take advantage of this discounted night rate, according to *Energiverk* marketing head Jan Grönberg. *Ängelholms Energiverk* does not conduct energy audits but can arrange them with a subcontractor for its customers, who then pay the fee.

Northern States Power (NSP) is the utility company supplying Foley with natural gas and electricity. In the early 1980s many Foleyans regarded NSP with suspicion, wondering why a power company would reverse itself and begin to urge conservation. Additionally, private companies were suspected of collusion to create, or at least to profit from, the energy shortages of the 1970s. (Such consumer attitudes are detailed in Chapter 4). In the 1990s the problem of storing NSP's nuclear waste continues to antagonize some Foleyans. NSP generates electricity through coal- and nuclear-fired plants and is currently experimenting with biomass (alfalfa) and wind energy.

In contrast to *Energiverk* procedures, NSP sends Foleyans electricity and natural gas bills each month, based on actual use. Foleyans do not pay for consumption in advance, although the "budget helper" option distributes estimated annual usage across 12 months to level out high winter bills. NSP offers various beneficial programs to its customers. These include home energy audits (free since 1990, and $10 earlier); rebates for buying energy-efficient appliances; appliance recycling (a $50 savings bond gift, along with free appliance pickup and disposal); summer energy discounts for those who agree to cycle air-conditioning; and sales of energy-efficient home lighting products. The company also maintains "Ask NSP," recorded messages on a variety of energy-related topics which the public may phone in to hear.

A reduction in the number of energy audits performed by NSP reflects declining concern over energy conservation. An average of six to eight annual audits in the town of Foley in the early 1980s has shrunk to one or two in the 1990s. In contrast, NSP reports that its appliance recycling program, initiated in 1992, has exceeded projections. Purchase of energy-efficient lightbulbs has been only "lukewarm," which NSP personnel feel is due to high initial cost of the bulbs and low electricity prices. Earlier, NSP offered "rate breaks": lower price per unit of electricity and natural gas for high-volume users. This practice has since been discontinued. Electricity and natural gas prices are currently fairly stable.

Chapter 2

House Contents and Fuel Consumption

IMAGES OF THE OTHER

In the 1980s I asked the residents of Foley and Munka Ljungby how they envisioned life in the other community. Answers from Foley portray the Swedes as modest consumers in a difficult environment, living on a smaller scale and using less energy, with sophisticated political views and greater levels of physical activity. The following quotations are typical of Foleyans' conceptions of Sweden:

I would imagine that the houses are much smaller in area and smaller overall. They are probably built on smaller lots. Fewer families would have cars, and the cars that exist are smaller on average. Attitudes tend to be more cosmopolitan.

I would guess it wouldn't be a lot different, but they surely use a lot less energy than we do, because it costs a lot more. They use smaller cars, bicycles and walk more than we do. I'm sure they would wash dishes by hand, mow grass by push mower, and so on.

Their climate has made them hardy and aware of energy. I'm sure they conserve energy more than we do and probably always have. They get out for more walks and do outdoor sports much more than here. They do seem healthier than us. They must be peace-loving as they don't join wars any more.

They are more-conservative energy users. We probably have more convenience items and gadgets. Our energy is probably more plentiful and cheaper.

Swedish ambivalence toward America was summarized by one Munka Ljungbyan as "America: the land of everything good and everything bad." Several Munka families saw America as the land of material excess, the land of two cars per family and the electric toothbrush. Munka Ljungbyans described Americans as shortsighted, selfish, and wasteful consumers; living on a huge scale; politically naïve; physically inert; and surrounded by luxury:

People there use more than we, per inhabitant. They have big cars, and at *least* two. Everything is big. There are more household appliances; they even have electric toothbrushes! The U.S. is the land of overflowing abundance.

There's more waste in America, much more. Americans can't walk *two meters*. America is the land of opportunity, but they take an egoistic, selfish approach to material goods. Every American looks out for himself. Profits guide too much, and that goes for energy, also.

Swedes are more developed, both regarding lifestyle and energy savings. I don't believe that the Americans save the way we do—either money or energy. They live for the moment.

Americans are more wasteful. The U.S. uses much more electricity and gasoline than Sweden. There is flimsy construction in the U.S., and everything is air-conditioned. Americans don't bicycle so much. They don't bicycle when it rains.

Americans have more stuff of all sorts. There's a big gap between rich and poor, and certain rich groups use and waste a lot of energy. Americans all have their own bathrooms. America is the land of everything good and everything bad. [What's good and what's bad?] Technology and cultural and art life is good. "Coca-Cola culture" and the formation of powerful multinational companies and the oppression of workers' unions is bad.

American families have two big cars, electric toothbrushes and can openers, TVs in every room, thousands of lights. The U.S. is advanced in some areas but far behind in others. Americans think they are alone on the globe.

To what extent do Munka Ljungbyans and Foleyans fulfill these images? In this chapter, stereotypes are tested against fieldwork findings regarding house contents and actual fuel consumption. In the next chapter, household activities and daily routines will be similarly examined.

HOUSE CONTENTS

How different are homes in Foley and Munka Ljungby? To what extent do they conform to the stereotypes of small-scale Swedish living and "TVs in every room" in America? In order to answer these questions, community wide questionnaires solicited information about ownership of major and minor appliances and electronic equipment. Data from the 1980s questionnaires confirmed that more Foleyans owned certain items: black-and-white TVs, clothesdryers, and microwave ovens. Contrary to stereotype, however, more Munka households had dishwashers, automatic clotheswashers, color TVs, and videocassette recorders (VCRs). Shared trends since the initial research include increased saturation of all major appliances, increased ownership of duplicate or multiple items, more appliances with automatic functions, and proliferation of minor appliances.

Increased Saturation of All Major Appliances

Table 2.1 summarizes trends in saturation of selected appliances in Foley and Munka Ljungby. Percentages are based on questionnaire samples, which in the 1980s numbered 243 households in Foley and 110 in Munka. Respective sample sizes for the 1990s are 140 and 148 households.

Table 2.1
Appliance Saturation, Foley and Munka Ljungby
(Percent of Questionnaire Sample Households Containing)

Appliance	1980s		1990s	
	Foley	*Munka*	*Foley*	*Munka*
Dishwasher	33	57	41	72
Clotheswasher	80	94	90	97
Clothesdryer:				
Tumble-dryer	86	8	91	39
*Torkskåp**	n.a.	34	n.a.	28
Microwave Oven	33	2	92	75
VCR	5	11	79	75
Color TV	80	88	97	95
Black-and-White TV	55	27	24	9
Central air-conditioning	8	n.a.	29	n.a.

*A Swedish "drying cupboard," described in text

In the 1990s Munka continue to have more dishwashers and automatic clotheswashers than Foley, but Foley surpassed Munka slightly in number of VCRs and color TVs. VCR ownership grew from 5 to 79 percent in Foley by the 1990s, just above Munka's saturation level of 75 percent. Microwave ownership in Munka jumped from a negligible 2 percent in the 1980s, when microwaves were just being introduced in Sweden, to 75 percent a dozen years later. Foley's microwave ownership increased from 33 to 92 percent, a saturation second only to that for color television (97%). Color televisions spread in both communities, and black-and-white TVs decreased. Though still far below that in Foley, Munka Ljungby tumble-dryer saturation increased markedly, from 8 to 39 percent.

Homes having central air-conditioning nearly quadrupled in Foley, rising from 8 to 29 percent of the questionnaire samples. Additionally, the percentage of households owning more than one window unit more than doubled. No residential air-conditioning exists in Munka Ljungby; Swedes do not feel it is necessary, given their moderate climate.

Table 2.2 puts each community's 1990s saturations into national context.

Table 2.2
1990s Appliance Saturation for Foley and the US, Munka Ljungby and Sweden (Percent of Households Containing)*

Appliance	Foley	US	Munka	Sweden
Dishwasher	41	55	72	31
Clotheswasher	90	95	97	72
Clothesdryer:				
Tumble-dryer	91	89	39	18
Torkskåp**	n.a.	n.a.	28	***
Microwave Oven	92	84	75	37
VCR	79	***	75	88
Color TV	97	98	95	97
Central air-conditioning	29	44	n.a.	n.a.

*U.S. data are for single-family, owned houses in 1990 (EIA 1992b), with the exception of microwave oven saturation, which is for *all* dwellings in 1991 (EIA 1995). Swedish data are for all dwellings in 1991 (U.S. Department of Commerce 1996); saturation in single-family dwellings would be higher.
** A Swedish "drying cupboard," described in text
***Data not available

Increased Ownership of Duplicates or Multiples

Ownership of duplicate and multiple items, which formerly distinguished Foley, now characterizes Munka as well. The prime example of this trend is color television ownership. In the 1980s no one in either questionnaire sample owned more than two color sets, but by the 1990s one fourth of color TV owners in Foley and 18 percent in Munka had more than two sets. (Further, average screen size is larger in Munka: 28 inches, compared to 19 inches in Foley.) Also contrary to stereotype, more Munka Ljungbyans than Foleyans own stereos, CD players, and computers.

Trend toward Appliances with Automatic Features

A trend toward appliances with automatic features is quite apparent with regard to frost-free refrigerators, clothesdryers, and automatics clotheswashers, for example.

Frost-Free Refrigerators. Saturation of frost-free over manual-defrost refrigerators was similar for Foley and Munka over time and increased significantly in both communities. Fifty-four percent of the 1980s Foley sample owned a frost-free refrigerator, while this number rose to 86 percent in the 1990s. Saturation in Munka was 57 percent in the 1980s and 85 percent in the 1990s.

Clothesdryers. Ownership of tumble-dryers in Munka increased from 8 to 39 percent. (In Foley, an 86% saturation grew to 91%.) Earlier, another kind of dryer, the *torkskåp*, predominated in Munka Ljungby. The *torkskåp* (or "drying cupboard") is a metal cabinet in which wet clothes are draped over horizontal rods. The door is then closed, and a fan dries the clothes with heated air. Earlier, four times as many Munka Ljungbyans owned a *torkskåp* as owned a tumble-dryer. Now, slightly more Munka Ljungbyans own a tumble-dryer than a *torkskåp* (39 versus 28%). Owners said they prefer tumble-dryers because they produce softer clothes and towels. They added that it is easier to stuff clothes in tumble-dryers than to drape them in the *torkskåp*, in which clothes need two hours to dry. (No Munka Ljungbyan pointed this out, but a tumble-dryer uses half the energy of a *torkskåp*.)

Automatic Clotheswashers. In Foley, saturation of automatic clotheswashers increased from 85 to 96 percent, as these replaced wringer washers.

Proliferation of Minor Appliances and Gadgets

Small appliances are much less influential than major appliances in determining household fuel consumption. Annual energy consumption for lighting and for all small appliance needs for a four-person household has been estimated to be just 8 percent of total heating and household energy demand in the US—and 6 percent in Sweden (MEA 1978 and Harrysson 1981). Householders often wrongly identify smaller appliances as the culprits causing high energy demand. However, the collective demand of these "miscellaneous" appliances is significant (see Meier, Rainer, and Greenberg 1992)—and is of course multiplied by millions of households. Also, the energy and resources required for the manufacture and distribution of gadgets is not insignificant.

In the 1980s several small appliances fairly common in Foley were not found in Munka Ljungby. These include electric knives, blankets, can openers, garage door openers, and toothbrushes. Although the energy demanded by the above items would not increase Foley's household fuel demand significantly, Swedish awareness of such amenities as electric garage door openers perpetuates the stereotype of the American as sedentary and machine-addicted. A few appliances were found only in Munka Ljungby in the 1980s as well, however: the electric knife sharpener, juicer, and slicer for bread or meat. By the 1990s Munka had acquired some of the items that were formerly unique to Foley: the electric can opener, garage door opener, food processor, and toothbrush. The last item is of particular interest in that the electric toothbrush was cited by more than one Munka Ljungbyan at the time of initial research to illustrate that America was the land where "anything is possible." One reason for the appearance of electric toothbrushes in Munka is their endorsement by dentists, because scientific and health rationales carry much weight in Sweden. Several Munka households possess an item not found in Foley: a *kontaktgrill*, a small portable grill that could be used at the table. I also saw an electric wine opener in one Munka household, and more than one electric grass aerator, neither of which was in evidence in Foley.

One Munka woman recounted her surprise at the extent of her household inventory:

You get embarrassed when you count up what you have: food processor, electric mixer, microwave oven, vacuum cleaner, and so forth. Many that I have, I don't use very much . . . like the juicer or the electric drill.

Both Foleyans and Munka Ljungbyans have many appliances but use only a very few on a regular basis, as revealed by this last quotation and by core households' daily records of small apparatus use. Fieldwork findings corroborate those of sociologists Bruce Hackett and Loren Lutzenhiser (1990) that small appliance utility is a secondary phenomenon to the social significance of these possessions.

Sauna and *Stuga*

Electrically-heated saunas are common in Munka Ljungby, owned by 23 percent of the 1980s questionnaire sample households and rising to 35 percent later on. Even though they connote luxury to Americans, saunas use much less energy than one would expect: 4–5 kWh per half-hour session. It should be noted that one fourth of Swedish families own a *stuga*, or summer cottage, with implications for increased energy consumption, both direct (including travel fuels) and embodied in the form of furnishings. Few Munka Ljungbyans (just 6% of the 1990s questionnaire sample) own cottages, probably because Munka lies so near the sea.

Energy-Saving Improvements in Household Appliances

Significant gains have been made in the energy efficiency of both American and Swedish appliances during the past decade. American refrigerators, for example, now have smaller and more-efficient compressors which decrease energy demand. Both refrigerators and freezers are better insulated, and with freon-free foam replacing the fiberglass used earlier. The U.S. Department of Energy demand standard for refrigerators is the 75-watt bulb, and one Swedish ad claims that the Electrolux freezer uses no more energy than a 40-watt bulb. Water heaters likewise have better foam insulation, precluding the blankets used in America in the 1980s. Clotheswashers in Sweden and the United States offer choice of water level and temperature; dishwashers have both water- and energy-saving features. Further, though both American and Swedish dishwashers run off hot tap water, Swedish clotheswashers heat their own water internally.

Reflecting the new environmental emphasis, Swedish ads for refrigerators and freezers emphasize that they are freon-free and recyclable. Energy efficiency is mentioned, but only secondarily. Likewise, ads for tumble-dryers promote them as time-saving and producing soft clothes, and additionally as demanding less energy than the *torkskåp*. However, ads recommend buying a *torkskåp* as well, or keeping the old one, for drying outerwear and boots. (Just 6 percent of the 1990s Munka questionnaire sample had both tumbler and *torkskåp*.)

RESIDENTIAL FUELS IN FOLEY AND MUNKA LJUNGBY

In 1982 two thirds of Munka questionnaire sample houses were heated by oil and one third were heated by electricity, as shown in Table 2.3. Twelve years later, Munka Ljungby reflected the Swedish national shift away from oil: roughly half the houses were oil-heated and half were heated by electricity. Munka Ljungbyans use heating technologies nonexistent in Foley: heat pumps and ceramic stoves. A rarity in 1982, heat pumps operated in 15 percent of Munka houses in 1994. These devices operate on the principles of refrigeration, but instead of expelling heat, they extract it from outside air, water, or ground and raise it to a higher potential so that it can be used for winter heating. Owners enthusiastically report fuel-bill savings of one quarter to one half their previous totals. Other advantages cited were clean indoor air and not having to clean out oil or wood ash. Roughly 7 percent of the 1994 Munka sample used wood-burning ceramic stoves, or *kakelugnar*. These stoves were introduced into Sweden from the Netherlands in the 1600s. In the 1980s new wood stoves were constructed on the *kakelugn* principle, in which heated air circulates through convoluted pipe to yield maximum heat before being released up a chimney.

Table 2.3
Main Heating Fuel, Questionnaire Households

Main Heating Fuel	Foley 1980s	Foley 1990s
Oil	22%	10%
Natural Gas	70%	85%
Electricity	5%	4%
Wood	3%	1%

Main Heating Fuel	Munka 1980s	Munka 1990s
Oil	66%	49%
Natural Gas	n.a.	3%
Electricity	33%	48%
Wood	*	*

*Wood used in *kakelugnar* was largely supplementary to oil or electricity.

Questionnaire sample Ns:
   1980s: Foley, 243; Munka Ljungby, 110
   1990s: Foley, 140; Munka Ljungby, 148

Natural gas, purchased from Denmark, was introduced into Munka in 1991. Just 3 percent of the Munka sample reported heating with this fuel. In contrast, natural gas is the dominant heating fuel in Foley. In 1981 gas was used in 70 percent of homes there, increasing to 85 percent in 1993 as it replaced oil, wood, and electricity as the heating fuel of choice. In 1981 electricity heated only 5 percent of Foley homes, decreasing slightly to 4 percent in 1993. Wood as primary heating fuel decreased also, from 3 to 1 percent. The surge of wood use in Sweden and the United States in the late 1970s and early 1980s in response to hikes in oil prices has since declined.

It should be noted that many of Munka's furnaces are combination furnaces (*kombipannor*), capable of being fueled by some combination of oil, electricity, and wood. These were categorized according to which fuel residents reported using most.

Electricity is the only fuel used in Munka for household operations such as cooking and washing and drying clothes. Water is heated by electricity in electrically-heated homes and by oil in oil-heated homes. In Foley both natural gas and electricity are used for household purposes and remain fairly evenly divided as cooking fuel. Changes occurred for clothesdryers and water heaters, however. Over time, more households chose electric over natural gas clothes-dryers, and natural gas water heaters became more popular than electric. Electric appliances use less energy than natural gas appliances because they have no conversion losses in operation inside the household. Given current fuel prices, however, they are more expensive to operate.

FUEL PRICES

Household fuel costs represent only a tiny fraction of income for both Minnesotans and Swedes. On average, the percentage of household income spent for fuels (excluding gasoline) in Minnesota decreased over time, from 3 percent in 1981 to 2 percent in 1993. Respective Swedish percentages stayed essentially level at 3.7 and 3.6 percent (Minnesota Department of Public Service and Official Statistics of Sweden).

Table 2.4 shows fuel prices in Foley and Munka Ljungby in 1982 and 1994. Represented in 1982 constant dollars (nominal dollars adjusted for inflation), the prices of all fuels except electricity decreased markedly in both locations over time. Contrary to expectations, electricity cost more in Foley in the 1980s: 5 cents per kWh, compared with 3.5 cents in Munka Ljungby. By 1994 real electricity prices were similar in both locales. Fifteen percent of the 1994 kWh price in Munka is a state-imposed energy tax. Additionally, in 1990 all fuels became subject to MOMS, the Swedish value-added tax (25% in 1994, with fuels taxed at a slightly lower rate). Despite these taxes, electricity price infla-tion in the Munka area has been about the same as the Swedish consumer price index. Swedish electricity is the second cheapest in Europe, after Norway's. German prices are twice Sweden's, and Italian electricity costs over three times as much. Sweden's electricity prices are expected to increase as a consequence of domestic deregulation and electricity sales to other European Community member states.

Table 2.4
Fuel Prices in Foley and Munka Ljungby, 1982 and 1994
(Reported in 1982 constant dollars*)

Fuel	Foley Price	Munka Price	Foley Price as % of Munka Price
1 kWh electricity			
1982	$ .05	$ .035	143%
1994	$ .041	$ .038	108%
1 gallon gasoline			
1982	$1.26	$2.37	53%
1994	$ .78	$1.18	66%
1 gallon fuel oil			
1982	$1.00	$1.39	72%
1994	$ .64	$ .88	73%
1 ccf natural gas			
1982	$ .42	n.a.	n.a.
1994	$ .28	$ .55	51%
1 cord wood			
1982	$75.00	$90.00	83%
1994	$45.00	$52.00	87%

*The U.S. consumer price index was 74% that of Sweden for 1982–1994. Some of the downward shift apparent in Swedish prices is also due to currency exchange rates: the Swedish crown was 30% weaker against the dollar in 1994 than in 1982 (5.95 versus 7.72 crowns to the dollar).

The difference in gasoline prices in Foley and Munka decreased somewhat by 1994. What nobody in 1980s Foley would have predicted to happen did: oil products went *down* in price, even in nominal dollars! In Sweden, oil and gasoline prices in nominal dollars rose through the 1980s, but they did so gradually and as a result of tax increases rather than scarcity. Between 1982 and 1994, natural gas increased in cost by only 5 percent in nominal dollars, but even this modest rise annoyed some Foleyans who had converted from oil to natural gas furnaces when oil prices jumped in the late 1970s. (Nominal price trends are reported here because they shape outlook among consumers, who do not take inflation into account when discussing price histories.)

HOUSEHOLD FUEL CONSUMPTION

In order to compare fuel consumption totals for Foley and Munka Ljungby households, the joule (the international unit of energy) was used as a common denominator. All fuel totals were converted to MJs (megajoules) or GJs (gigajoules) based on equivalents shown in Appendix 2. Procedures used to distinguish heating fuel from household fuel appear in Appendix 3.

In both 1980 and 1993, Foley households used more household fuel (that is, fuel for all household purposes other than space heating) than did Munka households. Further, the gap between their averages widened from 6 GJ to 10 GJ over time, as shown Table 2.5.

Table 2.5
Average Household Fuel Consumption during Measurement Year
(Foley and Munka Ljungby Household Fuel Samples*)

	1980	1993
Foley	52.0 GJ	51.8 GJ
Munka Ljungby	45.6 GJ	41.8 GJ

Consumption mode was tied in the categories of 40–49.9 GJ and 50–59.9 GJ for
Foley and in the 30–9.9 GJ category for Munka.

*Household Fuel Consumption sample Ns:
    1980s: Foley, 91; Munka Ljungby, 63
    1990s: Foley, 106; Munka Ljungby, 36

Munka's average household fuel consumption was 88 percent of Foley's in
1980, decreasing to 81 percent of Foley's in 1993. Whereas the Foley average
stayed nearly level between 1980 and 1993, Munka's average decreased by
nearly 4 GJ, or 9 percent. To put this reduction in perspective, 4 GJ is about one
fifth of the energy used for all household purposes other than heating water for a
family of four in Sweden (*Ängelholms Energiverk*).

FACTORS CONTRIBUTING TO MUNKA LJUNGBY'S LOWER
HOUSEHOLD FUEL CONSUMPTION

A detailed analysis of why Munka Ljungby's household fuel consumption
is less than Foley's cannot be totally precise, given the impossibility of distinguishing fuel used to heat water from heating fuel and adding it to the household
totals (see Appendixes 3 and 4). However, certain contributing factors may be
noted.

These include Munka's

- slightly smaller average household population (2.6 persons versus Foley's 3 in the
  1980s; 2.6 persons versus Foley's 2.8 in the 1990s)
- greater number of houses with showers only (precluding baths, which are more
  energy intensive)
- universal use of electricity for cooking (50 percent less energy intensive at point of
  use than gas, because there are no combustion losses)
- smaller refrigerators (and earlier, no duplicate ownership)
- smaller freezers and fewer upright models
- absence of air conditioners, humidifiers, or dehumidifiers
- fewer clothes dryers

WATER HEATERS

Water heaters demand more fuel than any other appliance. They account for
18–23 percent of total (heat and household) residential fuel consumption in the
United States and Scandinavia (Schipper and Meyers et al. 1992), and for fully

40 percent of household fuel consumption (Schipper and Sheinbaum 1994). Yet, water heaters are overlooked by householders, who focus on lights, televisions, and other visible forms of consumption. Patterns of household operations and activities influencing energy demand for hot water imply that Munka Ljungby-ans use more than Foleyans. Though Foley had a smaller proportion of electric water heaters (more efficient at point of use than natural gas or oil heaters), average volume was smaller and temperatures were lower than in Munka Ljungby. Swedish national averages for water heater consumption had to be used in Munka calculations, because it is impossible to distinguish heating from household fuel using summer bills there (see Appendix 3).

Water Heater Volume and Setting

In the 1980s I was surprised to discover that Munka's water heaters were much larger, on average, than those in Foley. Water heaters of 60 gallons or more were the mode in Munka (owned by 70 percent of the questionnaire sample), but a rarity (4 percent) in Foley. Even though a shift toward smaller water heaters (30- or 40-gallon size) has occurred, nearly 40 percent of the 1990s Munka sample had 60-gallon or larger models. In Foley, heaters this large continued to make up just 4 percent of the sample.

In Munka and Foley alike, most core householders do not know their water heater settings (usually the choice of the installer). After determining these, core group comparisons revealed that Foley heaters were set at low or medium, and most in Munka were set at medium-high or high. By the 1990s more Foley water heaters were set at low. Munka households also lowered their settings, but nearly one third of their water heaters remained set at high. (Settings are categorized according to manufacturer guidelines: low = 120° F; medium = 140°; medium-high = 150°; and high = 160° F.)

HEATING FUEL CONSUMPTION

In order to make meaningful comparison of fuel consumption by the Foley and Munka Ljungby heating samples (Table 2.6), differences in climate had to be taken into account. Fuel consumption totals for heating samples in Foley and Munka Ljungby were adjusted for differences in degree-days Fahrenheit (°F-day), procedures described in Appendix 5.

MJ/°F-day comparisons do not take into account differences in total area to be heated, however. To determine "thermal integrity," energy consumed per square foot adjusted for °F-days must be calculated. Such figures are usually reported as BTU/°F-day • sq. ft. (BTUs per degree-day Fahrenheit per square foot of heated space). The lower the number, the less energy is being consumed, and the more efficiently the area is being heated.

Table 2.6
Average Heating Fuel Consumption for Heating Samples, MJ/°F-day

	1980	1993
Foley	13.7 MJ/°F-day	11.0 MJ/°F-day
Munka Ljungby	15.6 MJ/°F-day	16.5 MJ/°F-day

From Table 2.7 it can be seen that average thermal integrity in both locations has improved greatly since 1980. Whereas Foley and Munka alternated for better thermal integrity in various area categories in 1980, Foley's thermal integrity is better for all sizes of housing in 1993. (This relationship mirrors national trends. Schipper and Meyers et al. [1992] report that nearly twice the reduction in heating energy intensity occurred in the United States than in Scandinavia between 1973 and 1988.) Of course, even with good thermal integrity, more fuel is needed to heat a large house than a smaller one—and overall, Munka's houses are larger than Foley's.

Table 2.7
BTU/°F-day • sq.ft. Averages, Foley and Munka Ljungby Heating Samples

House Area	≤1100 sq. ft.	1101–1400	1401–1700	1701–2000	≥2001 sq. ft.
1980					
Foley	13.1	13.6	16.2	14.6	15.0
Munka	13.6	16.8	15.6	12.4	16.2
1993					
Foley	9.3	8.4	6.4	6.0	6.2
Munka	12.8	9.7	10.2	7.7	7.4

FACTORS CONTRIBUTING TO FOLEY'S LOWER HEATING FUEL CONSUMPTION

A mixture of infrastructural and behavioral variables contributed to Foley's lower heating fuel consumption average. The necessary exclusion of Munka homes where heating fuel could not be isolated (that is, all-electric houses and those with combination furnaces) advantaged Foley in several ways.

Necessary Exclusion of Munka's All-Electric Houses

In calculating residential fuel consumption, measurement begins with point-of-use consumption; that is, within the boundaries of the household. From this perspective, households having electricity as their primary fuel are more efficient than those with natural gas or oil because electric heating systems and appliances have no conversion losses. Energy losses incurred in the production and distribution of various fuels are excluded from analysis here. However, electricity is a highly energy-intensive fuel because it requires another fuel for its production (with the exception of solar energy or hydropower) and because it incurs losses in distribution along grids. As an end-use fuel, electricity was nearly three times as energy intensive as oil or natural gas for end uses in the early 1980s and is currently twice as intensive as these fuels—however, electricity from nuclear or large coal plants remains three times as intensive.

Electricity, therefore, is more energy intensive than reflected in household kilowatt-hour consumption totals. Sweden's substantial number of all-electric houses—58% in 1994 (Swedish Institute 1994)—works to its advantage in international comparisons of residential energy consumption, which are typically based on point-of-use measurements. Including generation and transmission losses when calculating Swedish residential consumption would increase its per capita demand statistic by 20 percent, and Swedish demand would then lie just under that of the United States (Schipper 1996b).

Very few Foleyans heat their homes with electricity (5% of the Foley 1980 heating sample and 4% in 1993). Natural gas predominated over oil in the Foley sample, giving it a slight energy efficiency advantage over the Munka sample, which contained no natural gas, but only oil and wood heating systems.

The exclusion of all-electric houses has consequences for Munka in addition to a lost low-intensity advantage. As a result, newer homes (and newer heating systems) were excluded from Munka's heating sample, since all-electric construction began fairly recently (in the mid-1970s). Roughly one quarter of homes in Foley's 1990s heating sample were built during the 1980s or 1990s, but none in the Munka sample was. However, roughly one quarter of homes in Foley's 1980 and 1990 heating samples were built before 1920, but only one tenth of Munka's samples were. And it should be noted that one heating fuel consumption advantage *conferred* by the exclusion of Munka's electrically heated homes from the sample is that these newer homes are typically larger.

Both structural and behavioral factors contribute to lower heating energy demand in Foley. These include Foley's thicker insulation, smaller average house area, more frequent closing off rooms from heat in winter, lower average nighttime temperatures, turning down the thermostat when houses are empty, not airing out houses by opening doors or windows, lesser use of wood, and fewer fireplaces.

Thicker Insulation in Foley. Surprisingly, Foley reported having thicker insulation than Munka, in both attics and walls. This can be explained partly by the wave of retrofitting in Foley during and after the 1980s research: people panicked over rising fuel costs and were well aware that their houses were drafty. In the 1980s, 30 percent more households in Foley had wall insulation of 4 inches or more; 20 percent more in Foley had attic insulation of 6 inches or more; and twice as many in Foley had attic insulation of 10 inches or more.

Even though insulation thickness had increased markedly in both communities by the 1990s, Foley still led in all categories. This unexpected finding is explained in part by the tightening of the Minnesota State Energy Code in

1985, to 6-inch wall and 12-inch attic insulation mandates for all new houses. The stricter Swedish building code R-values of the 1980s were probably satisfied through the use of other construction materials with good insulating property. (Also, over one quarter of the houses in Munka's 1980 and 1990 heating samples were built before 1950, when the first Swedish national codes were introduced.)

Foley's Smaller Average House Area. Contrary to stereotype, houses in Munka Ljungby were larger on average than those in Foley, both in the 1980s and the 1990s. Almost twice as many Foley houses as Munka houses were 1100 square feet or less, and more Munka houses (50 percent more in the 1980s, 100 percent more in the 1990s) were 2001 square feet or larger. Swedish building trends in the 1980s were toward larger houses; currently, this trend is waning.

More Foleyans Closing Off Rooms in Their Houses in the Winter. More Foleyans reported closing off rooms in their houses from heat during the winter than did Munka Ljungbyans, both in the 1980s and the 1990s. In the 1980s, more than three times as many Foley heating sample households reported closing off rooms from heat: 43 percent, versus 13 percent in Munka. This practice declined somewhat over time in both communities, but was still reported by more Foleyans: 33 percent, compared to just 6 percent in Munka. Further, 80 percent in Foley closed off more than one room, but only 0.5 percent in Munka did so.

Foley's Lower Average Nighttime Temperature. Another variable contributing to its lesser heating fuel consumption is Foley's lower average nighttime temperature. Foley heating sample households in the 1980s averaged two degrees lower at night than did the Munka households: 65.4° F versus 67.3° F in Munka. In the 1990s, Foley's nighttime average continued lower than Munka's average, but lower by one degree rather than two: Foley's average stayed essentially the same at 65.5° F, and Munka's average decreased very slightly to 66.8° F.

More Foleyans Turning Down Thermostats when Houses Are Empty. In contrast to Foley's lower nighttime averages, Munka's daytime temperature average (occupied houses) was roughly one degree lower than Foley's in both the 1980s and the 1990s. The Foley 1980s sample averaged 67.9 °F during the day, compared with Munka's slightly lower 67.1° F. In the 1990s the average temperature for each town increased slightly, and the relationship is essentially the same, with 68.5° F for Foley and 67.5° F in Munka.

Contrary to stereotype, Swedes maintain the highest average indoor temperatures in Europe. The average daytime temperature in Sweden in 1982 was 69.8° F (21° C). The 1981 Minnesota statewide average temperature of 65° F was nearly five degrees lower than this Swedish average. (Munka's average temperature was 2 degrees higher, and the Foley average 3 degrees lower, than the national and state averages.) Sweden's 1994 average daytime temperature remained at 21–22° C (69.8–71.6° F). The 1993 daytime temperature median for the Midwestern United States was 67–69° F, up from Minnesota's earlier average (Munka's 1994 average was 3 degrees lower than the national figure;

Foley's average of 65.5° F was lower than the Midwest range.) (NSP 1981, Marknadsföring AB 1980, U.S. DOE 1993, and Schipper 1996b).

Whereas the Munka daytime temperature average was slightly lower, more Foleyans lowered their thermostats at night. And five times as many Foley as Munka households turned down thermostats when their houses were empty: 65 percent versus 13 percent in Munka. In the 1990s this practice had declined somewhat in Foley but had increased in Munka. However, twice as many in the Foley questionnaire sample turned down their thermostats before leaving home: 47 percent, compared to 24 percent in Munka. Foley's average temperature among those turning down their thermostats before leaving was 64.6 degrees, four degrees lower than its daytime average for occupied houses. Savings from this practice are substantial, because a decrease of only one degree can reduce heating fuel demand by 5 to 6 percent.

Munka's Ventilation Practices. Ventilating or airing out homes by opening doors or windows (*vädring*) is practiced widely in Sweden. All 20 of the 1980 core households reported ventilating, and 17 of the 20 did so daily. The remaining 3 households ventilated two or three times per week. Surprisingly, two thirds in Munka ventilated without adjusting their radiators, despite intensive 1980s government reminders to do so. Ventilation time ranged from 5 to 20 minutes, with no relationship between duration and whether or not thermostats were adjusted.

A smaller proportion, 12, of the 1990s core households ventilated daily. Slightly more than two thirds (14 of 18) who ventilate said they do so without adjusting radiators. Duration ranged from 5 to 60 minutes, with an average of 24 minutes. Interestingly, those who said they turned down the heat reported ventilating the shortest times.

Greater Use of Wood in Munka. Although wood burning has declined in both communities since the 1980s, a greater proportion of households in Munka than in Foley burned wood, and these households burned more cords of wood as well. Further, wood is a fuel with considerable energy intensity (see the joule conversion chart in Appendix 2). Burning one cord of wood increases heating fuel consumption by 20.3 GJ—or about one sixth of the average heating fuel consumption for a Munka household in the 1990s measurement year.

More Fireplaces and Fewer Fireplace Improvements in Munka. In the 1980s twice as many households in the Munka heating sample owned and used a fireplace; in the 1990s nine times as many in Munka did. If used without improvements, fireplaces can be highly inefficient or even cause a loss of household heat. Use of doors, vents, and blowers in conjunction with fireplaces was common in Foley during both fieldwork periods but was much less frequently found in Munka Ljungby.

Chapter 3

Household Activities

MAGNITUDE OF RESIDENTIAL ENERGY DEMAND

Residential energy consumption forms one quarter of total national demand in both Sweden and America (Schipper and Meyers et al. 1992). Underscoring the importance of behavior in determining that demand, early studies such as that of Robert Socolow (1978) documented dramatic (by a factor of two, and even three) variation in energy consumption among structurally-similar households. Even small changes in behavior can have substantial consequences. For example, Louise Gaunt and Ann-Margret Berggren (1983) concluded from their survey of all-electric homes in Sweden that variations in fuel use amounting to as much as 17,000 kWh (61.2 GJ) annually resulted from choice of indoor temperatures and patterns of use of household appliances. Also, they found that variations in electricity consumption as great as 3,500 kWh (12.6 GJ) were due to differing use of clothesdryers and kitchen fans and different ventilation practices.

The question which originally precipitated this study was the role daily energy-using routines played in determining Sweden's lesser demand for household operations. Munka consumed 88 percent of Foley's average household operations energy in the 1980s, decreasing to 81 percent of Foley's in the 1990s. In this chapter, patterns of energy-demanding household activities and appliance use recorded by Foley and Munka core households are compared. I found routines in Foley and Munka to be similar for most tasks, and here I discuss exceptions or significant energy dimensions of certain tasks. A striking range of patterns and diversity of personal preferences characterizes use of household technology in both communities.

ENERGY DEMANDS OF EVERYDAY LIFE

Checklist Methodology

In order to compare everyday life in Foley and Munka Ljungby, groups of "core" households in both communities kept daily records of engagement in specified energy-using activities for four weeks. (In the 1980s, 22 core households in Foley and 21 in Munka completed all four weeks of records; in the 1990s, 20 in each location did so.) Eighteen activities were recorded in the 1980s; microwave oven use was added for the 1990s. Records were in checklist form, on which additional information—such as duration or temperature—was also requested. Selected checklist activity findings are shown in Table 3.1.

Table 3.1
Weekly Averages of Checklist Activities (Core Households, Foley and Munka)

Activity	Foley		Munka Ljungby	
Oven Use	1980s:	4 times	1980s:	3 times
	1990s:	3 times	1990s:	3 times
Range Use	1980s:	12 times	1980s:	12 times
	1990s:	7 times	1990s:	10 times
Microwave Oven Use	1980s:	8 times	1980s:	2 times
	1990s:	8 times	1990s:	10 times
Dishwashing (hand or machine)	1980s:	13 times	1980s:	12 times
	1990s:	6 times	1990s:	6 times
Loads of Clothes Washed	1980s:	9 loads	1980s:	4 loads
	1990s:	8 loads	1990s:	6 loads
Loads of Clothes Dried in Machine*	1980s:	12 loads	Numbers of loads not available	
	1990s:	11 loads		
Iron Use	1980s:	1 time	1980s:	2 times
	1990s:	1 time	1990s:	2 times
Showers and Baths**	1980s:	14 showers 5 baths	1980s:	12 showers 1 bath
	1990s:	13 showers 3 baths	1990s:	12 showers 3 baths
Shower and Bath Durations	1980s:	shower = 9 min. bath = 19 min.	1980s:	shower = 11 min. bath = 39 min.
	1990s:	shower = 10 min. bath = 26 min.	1990s:	shower = 9 min. bath = 24 min.
Vacuum Use	1980s:	3 times	1980s:	3 times
	1990s:	2 times	1990s:	3 times
Television Watching	1980s:	27 hours	1980s:	13 hours
	1990s:	37 hours	1990s:	30 hours

* by Foley dryer owners who "never" use lines (N = 6 in 1980s and 8 in 1990s)
** in households with facilities for both

All household members aged seven or older filled in personal sets of checklists, reporting daily engagement in activities. Activity records were kept by 61 persons in each community in 1993–94. In 1981–82 they were kept by 75 persons in Foley and 74 in Munka. Foley's average core household size was slightly larger than Munka's in the 1980s (4 versus 3.4 persons), but in the 1990s average sizes were nearly identical: 3.5 in Foley and 3.4 in Munka Ljungby. Core households were selected randomly from the pool of question-naire respondents, but the final selection was guided to ensure that the spectrum of life-cycle stages was represented in each sample.

Parallel seasonal data were obtained for fall and spring. Foley core house-holds kept records for one week during each of the months of March, May, October, and November 1981 and during the same months in 1993 (October, November) and 1994 (March, May). Munka households kept their records during the months of May, June, August, and September 1982 and April, May, September, and October 1994. A research assistant in each locale distributed and collected activity records when I was not in residence.

Other checklist activities include using a minor kitchen appliance, electric hair dryer, or power tool; listening to radio or stereo; engaging in a sport or exercise; doing yard or garden work; and eating a restaurant meal. Shopping, another checklist activity, is discussed in conjunction with consumerism in Chapter 8.

Microwave Oven Use

In Foley in the 1980s, half of the core households owned microwaves, but just one Munka core household did. By the 1990s ownership grew to 19 of the 20 Foley core households, and 16 of 20 in Munka. Although microwave ovens were introduced later in Sweden, Munka Ljungbyans reported using their microwaves two times more per week than Foleyans: 10 versus 8 times.

Heating water for and rewarming beverages were the most frequently-reported microwave tasks in both communities. The next most popular function of the microwave in Foley was reheating of leftovers; in Munka it was thawing frozen bread or meat, and then warming leftovers. Other moderately reported microwave uses in Foley include popping corn, cooking frozen prepared entrées, and making snacks. Munka Ljungbyans often used their microwaves to cook cereal and to warm bread or rolls. A microwave oven saves the most energy when it replaces a conventional oven for cooking meat or bread rather than for snack preparation or the thawing or reheating of foods. Further, 23 percent *more* energy is used by the microwave than the range for boiling water for beverages (Berry 1978). These non-energy-saving microwave functions are the most popular in both Foley and Munka.

Dishwashing

In the 1980s Foley households washed dishes, either by hand or by ma-chine, an average of 13 times weekly. In the 1990s this average shrank by about half, to 6 times weekly. Munka's averages are closely parallel. In the 1980s

Munka core households washed dishes 12 times per week; by the 1990s this average also was cut in half, to 6 times per week. This decrease in number of dishwashing episodes probably reflects less time available to householders, resulting in increased use of pre-prepared or take-out food and therefore fewer cooking dishes, or letting dishes accumulate before washing. Dishwashers were owned by approximately two thirds of both the Foley and Munka cores in the 1980s. In the 1990s core groups, dishwasher ownership was the same in Munka but slightly less in Foley: 11 of the 20 households. (Saturation differs for the larger communities, however. As has been reported, dishwashers are more common in Munka than in Foley.)

In the 1980s most machine owners in both Foley and Munka used their machines almost daily. This use decreased to 4 times per week in both Foley and Munka in the 1990s. Informants in both locales chose to wash dishes by machine instead of by hand about half the time, citing time savings as the reason for their choice. Hot water used for hand dishwashing can range from 5 to 30 gallons, depending upon whether constant running water, intermittent running water, or basins are used. Contrary to expectations of conserving behavior, half of the Munka core reported washing and rinsing dishes under hot running water in both the 1980s and the 1990s. Only 10 percent of the core members in Foley washed and rinsed dishes in this manner. The prevalent method in Foley was a basin wash and an on/off rinse under the tap.

Most Foleyans and Munka Ljungbyans stipulated using warm water for washing and rinsing. Four in Munka, however, said they choose very hot running water to rinse dishes in order to get the dishes "really clean," to avoid lime residue on glassware, or so that the dishes would dry faster.

Clotheswashing

Foleyans wash more loads of clothes each week than Munka Ljungbyans. However, Munka's average number of loads rose from half to three quarters of Foley's average over time. Programs of Swedish clotheswashers are longer than their American counterparts. A prewash phase of 30 minutes in length is automatic unless programmed out by the user. Munka informants choose the regular white cycle (140 minutes at 90° C, or 194° F!) only for very dirty white cotton or linen items, selecting the energy-saving white cycle (125 minutes at 65° C, or 149° F) for the rest of their whites. The color wash program takes 75 minutes at 40° C (104° F).

In Munka in the 1980s, no core households reported washing or rinsing clothes in anything but hot water. In contrast, Foley households at that time most frequently selected warm washes and warm rinses, though a few rinsed with cold. Lower water temperatures were selected in both Foley and Munka over time, but no Munka households reported washing their clothes in cold water, while half the Foley households did, all or most (80%) of the time. Additionally, more Munka households continued to select hot rather than warm temperatures for laundering. Munka Ljungbyans emphasize that hot water is needed to achieve the whiteness they desire. The strong value they place on very white and very clean laundry overrides considerations of energy saving. Foley-ans tried all-temperature detergents, found their results satisfactory (not having to meet Swedish standards!), and continue selecting lower temperatures.

Clothesdrying

In both the 1980s and the 1990s, all except one of the Foley core house-holds owned a clothesdryer. In the 1980s half of Munka's core households owned dryers, but ownership rose to 13 of the 20 by the 1990s. Swedish dryers are of two types, the *torkskåp* (or "drying cupboard") and the *tumlare* (tumbler). The *torkskåp* is 50 percent more energy intensive than the tumbler, which is the same style as American dryers. In the 1980s 9 of the 10 Munka dryer owners had a *torkskåp*; the remaining household had a *tumlare*. In contrast, the majority (9 of 13) of households in the 1990s had a tumbler, and 3 had a *torkskåp*. Additionally, 1 household owned both types of dryers.

Foley core households in the 1980s chose to dry their clothes in the dryer instead of on the line 78 percent of the time; Munka households chose the dryer just 8 percent of the time. I had anticipated that with increased saturation of the tumbler in Sweden, Munka families would choose to dry their clothes by tumbler instead of on the line—because earlier, households had expressed dissatisfaction with the stiffness of clothes dried in the *torkskåp*. A dramatic switch to the machine was not the case, but Munka core households reported using their dryers 28 percent of the time. Foley core households continued to choose dryer over line more than three quarters of the time. It should be noted, however, that whereas one third of the households used dryers exclusively, another third reported supplementing dryers with lines. Additionally, two Foley households chose the line exclusively, even if they owned dryers.

What influences Foley owners to choose the dryer over the line? In Foley, climate is a major factor: some households use their dryers when it rains or during the winter. Other Foleyans feel the flexibility offered by the dryer to be a major advantage. One informant commented, "You can wash any time, day or night, and when *you* want to." Some households use their dryers exclusively for towels, socks, underwear, and fabrics that, if tumble-dried, do not need ironing. A few other households stated that they use their dryer because they do not have clotheslines hung. However, one informant added that even if she had lines she probably wouldn't use them "because of the *time* involved in hanging clothes. Especially socks—*ugh!*" Foley dryer owners said that when they use lines, it is because they like the resulting freshness of the clothes. Others cited money-saving as an advantage. Drying clothes on the line was said to be nostalgic of childhood or of a "simpler time."

A smaller number of Munka dryer owners gave bad weather as the reason they chose dryers over lines. Some said that they use their machines when time is short or when they need some item quickly. Munka Ljungbyans praised line-dried clothes for their fresh smell. Some informants stated that dryers are "a waste of electricity" and therefore undesirable; others said that they do not need dryers because they have clotheslines already hung.

Bathing and Showering

Most of Foley and Munka's core houses contain facilities for both bathing and showering. Those Foley houses with facilities for one or the other have bathtubs only; in Munka it is showers only. Per household, Foleyans took more baths and showers than Munka Ljungbyans, but these averages converged over time. The weekly average number of combined baths and showers for all Foley core households was 16 in both the 1980s and 1990s. In Munka Ljungby the average number of combined baths and showers per week rose from 12.5 in the 1980s to 14 in the 1990s.

Over time, shower frequency stayed about the same in both communities. Bath frequency declined in Foley but rose in Munka Ljungby. Baths are more energy demanding than showers, which take on the average about one fourth as much energy (Harrysson 1981). That Munka Ljungbyans took fewer baths in the 1980s probably reflects the influence of energy conservation campaign messages. Where the choice of bath or shower existed, Foleyans chose showers 83 percent of the time, but Munka Ljungbyans still chose showers slightly more often, 92 percent of the time.

Longer showers and baths in Munka Ljungby in the 1980s contradicts the image of Swedes as vigilant energy conservers. However, the fact that Munka Ljungbyans are more likely to choose showers over baths, and to shower and to bathe slightly faster than Foleyans in the 1990s is to Munka's advantage regarding household energy consumption. It can be concluded that Foleyans demanded slightly more energy than Munka Ljungbyans for bathing and showering on the average in the 1980s and substantially more energy in the 1990s.

What prompted people to choose baths over showers, and what influenced the duration of each? Those who preferred showers said that they are cleaner (Foley: "I don't want to sit in my own dirt"; Munka Ljungby: "really get the soap off."). Showers are favored because they take less hot water than baths, and both Foleyans and Munka Ljungbyans revealed that their concern was not about saving energy but rather to ensure a hot water supply for other family members. In both Foley and Munka, those who said that they take showers that were "longer than really necessary" feel that these are relaxing or fun. Teenagers in both locales praised long showers but could not articulate why they favor them. Using hair rinses and conditioners and shaving legs all increased time in the shower.

Those in Foley who preferred baths said that it was because they find them more relaxing or more soothing to aching muscles. Some Munka informants said they like baths—and long ones—during the winter months. Some in both locales gave reasons of illness as the basis for choosing baths over showers. Others said that their children prefer baths because they like to play in the bathtub. Two Foley informants identified the bathtub as a place to relax and think, one bringing her radio in for company during long soaks.

Television Watching

All core households own television sets, but Foleyans use their sets more. Foley households watched television an average of 27 hours per week in the 1980s; Munka averaged less than half that time, 13 hours per week. Viewing time increased in both locations in the 1990s, but Foley still leads with an average of 37 hours compared to Munka's average of 30 hours. (Averages reflect combined activity record reports from all members of each household. Two individuals may have watched TV together one evening for an hour, for example, but two hours would be added to their household total. Determining combined and separate viewing would require a study in itself, because most core households owned more than one television. However, it can be reported that individuals watching the most television in each household averaged 17.2 hours per week in Foley, higher than Munka's average of 13.6 hours.) The energy demand of televisions is much less than most people would assume. Operating a color set for 5 hours consumes only one kWh of electricity (NSP), costing 5 cents in Foley and 10 cents in Munka in 1994.

Why do Foleyans watch so much more TV? They could choose from among five channels, and nearly round-the-clock broadcasting in the early 1980s. At that time Swedes selected from two state-owned, non-commercial channels and one Danish channel. Scandinavian broadcast days averaged 8 hours during the week and 10–12 hours on weekends. Several Munka Ljungby-ans complained about dull (tråkigt) Swedish programming, which largely featured discussions of social issues and nature documentaries. They much preferred the Danish channel and American series and specials when they appeared.

Now, Foleyans can choose from among nine channels on regular broadcast networks and two dozen more on cable. Twenty-four-hour broadcasting is the norm. In Sweden, two commercial stations have joined the two state-owned channels, broadcasting many more American programs and Swedish versions of American talk and game shows. Broadcasting hours are expanded. Even though TV watching is something core households in both communities lament, time spent watching increased since the 1980s, and the satellite dish is an important status symbol in Munka nevertheless. Core households expressed surprise and embarrassment over the total viewing hours they logged. Watching TV is stigmatized as a nonproductive activity. Yet, people are so enervated from their workday that this is sometimes all they can manage in the evenings. Watching sports is largely exempt from stigma, since this is considered vicarious activity.

Some Foley core households leave their sets on all day "for company," but no one in Munka reported this habit. One household in the 1980s and one in the

1990s left a television on throughout our interview. Many Foleyans stated that they use their TVs to "unwind," and one household said it uses its television to generate white noise in order to sleep better. Televisions, radios, CD players, and stereos are listened to more in Foley and are more likely to be kept on continuously there.

SUMMARY: ENERGY DEMANDS OF EVERYDAY LIFE

Several heating and household operations patterns in Munka Ljungby are more energy intensive than those in Foley. Specifically, these patterns are choice of slightly higher nighttime indoor temperatures, rare downward adjustment of thermostats at night or when leaving home, and heating the entire house all winter long. Additionally, Munka Ljungbyans engage in frequent and year-round ventilation of their houses and often neglect to adjust radiators during this process. Munka Ljungbyans keep their water heaters, usually larger than those in Foley, set at higher average temperatures.

Overall, however, it is evident that Foley household activity energy demands are greater. Although Foleyans more carefully monitor heating energy consumption, they own and operate several appliances more frequently and longer than Munka Ljungbyans do. Notably, these appliances are clotheswashers, clothesdryers, air conditioners, and dehumidifiers.

It can be concluded that for the laundering of clothes, Foley core households require more energy than those in Munka. This difference is due primarily to Foley's much more frequent use of clothesdryers; canceling factors were in operation regarding washing: Foley wash more loads of clothes, but at lower temperatures. Though Foley's cooking patterns demand less energy, natural gas appliances there demand more energy than Munka's electric versions. Wide ownership of microwave ovens in Foley does not decrease cooking energy significantly because the functions delegated to microwaves are those which are just as efficiently, or more efficiently, done on the range. In both the 1980s and 1990s, Foleyans took a greater number of both baths and showers than Munka Ljungbyans, although totals were closer for the two communities in the 1990s.

Household activity patterns reveal some higher-energy-demanding choices made in Munka Ljungby, however. In contrast to Foleyans, Munka Ljungbyans prefer hot water for clotheswashing and often wash dishes under hot running water. Their 1980s showers and baths were longer than those in Foley, and in the 1990s they averaged more baths than their American counterparts. Although numbers of episodes are essentially the same in the two communities, Munka Ljungbyans vacuum and iron slightly longer than Foleyans (about seven minutes longer for each activity). They also use their kitchen fans daily, a habit requiring a small amount of direct energy but which can result in the loss of significant amounts of heated air. (By the 1990s, however, most fans cleaned and recycled heated air back into kitchen.)

In the next chapter, rationales given by individual informants to explain these and other energy-intensive choices are related to broader cultural factors. A major strength of ethnographic fieldwork is its holism in obtaining the background to behavior, its cultural context. For example, Americans may be quick to read energy-conserving motives or the expression of a cultural ethos of frugality into Swedish choices. Munka Ljungbyans do not choose clotheslines over the dryer primarily to reduce energy consumption. Rather, they choose the line because they do not have a dryer, or because drying clothes outside conforms to beliefs about the health benefits of airing, or because they are dissatisfied with the stiffness of clothes coming out of the *torkskåp*. They choose bicycling or walking over driving mainly because it is "beautiful to exercise" or because 10-speed bicycles are part of the latest assemblage of status symbols rather than to save fuel or the environment.

Chapter 4

Consumer Awareness: Energy, Self-Image, and Conservation

In this chapter, the circumstances, energy awareness, self-images, and conservation strategies of consumers in Foley and Munka Ljungby are contrasted. As shown, the period following the 1970s oil crises was marked by alienation in Foley but by solidarity in Munka. In both Foley and Munka, energy awareness emerged from and is maintained by price. Munka Ljungbyans define energy more comprehensively than do Foleyans. In the 1980s Foleyans' awareness was largely bounded by their households or immediate region, in contrast to broader frames of reference in Munka: energy, environment, economic, temporal, ethical, and sociopolitical. Although perspectives opened up somewhat in Foley by the 1990s, Munka's outlook remains broader and more holistic. Munka Ljungbyans are well aware of both Sweden's energy-efficient technology and its small energy demand relative to other countries. Ironically, this awareness discourages energy conservation in Munka: Foleyans make more-extensive structural retrofits and engage in more energy-conserving behaviors. Core households in both towns, however, point to other demographic groups and communities as being far more wasteful than their own. Additionally, they perceive the residential sector as lower than most others in terms of energy demand and waste.

Fuel conservation is handicapped in both communities by lack of knowledge of the relative energy demand of household appliances and functions. Informants place undue emphasis on lights and televisions and small appliances. When asked about obstacles to energy conservation, both communities identify economic considerations, hectic pace of life, force of habit and human nature, inhibiting infrastructure, and lack of information about energy-saving techniques. In addition, householders do not conserve because of cognitive blocks, fear of regression, and feelings of entitlement to energy and to certain comfort levels.

SITUATION OF THE CONSUMER

Confusion and Anger in Foley

The 1980s were a confusing and frightening time for most Foleyans as they struggled to make sense of conflicting reports about energy supplies and projections of future trends. Further, each household stood alone, lacking both the economic support and the type of authoritative, disinterested information provided by the Swedish welfare state. Dependent upon the products and services of oil and utility companies, Foleyans scrambled to do the best they could for themselves. However, a theme of powerlessness pervaded their interviews.

Contradictory estimates of energy supplies confused and irritated Foleyans, and anecdotes from friends testifying to oil abundance further muddied the situation. Additionally, informants said they resented what they called "treading water," their intensive conservation efforts just keeping fuel bills level.

We don't know what to believe any more. You hear one story from the companies, another on TV, and so forth. . . . Our friends tell us that there's *plenty* of oil: They saw capped wells in Oklahoma.

It costs us just as much to heat now as it did before we fixed up the house. Due to rising prices. So we end up not saving a thing. And we're *tired* of doing it [monitoring behavior].

Resentment that conservation efforts led to no obvious cash savings was compounded by Foleyans' dim views of energy companies. Two thirds of the 20 core households expressed frustration with the "huge" profits made by exploiting customers, and one third stated flatly that conservation only led to price increases due to the continual demand for corporate profits. Foleyans conveyed feelings of helplessness in the face of power wielded by corporate interests and the improbability of the emergence of a consumer movement:

I'm cynical. Big oil companies control the country, and utility companies pay off to stop research on things that might hurt them [alternative fuels], that might loosen their grip on the customer. Everybody knows it.

To be honest with you, I figure there's nothing I can do about it because they're just too big for us. Other than if we'd all band together. . . . But what are the chances of that happening? Zip. Zee-ro.

Other themes in Foley were the failure of consistent government leadership and the suspected complicity of government and big business to exploit consumers. Irritation with government and corporations for failing to anticipate fuel shortages was also evident there. Formerly "penny cheap" (one utility's motto) and abundant fuels became costly and in unpredictable supply, with no reasons for these reversals apparent to Foleyans. Further, future price hikes and rationing were rumored. Foleyans reacted with hostility, many reasserting a sense of personal power through claiming that they would refuse to conserve or even declaring their intentions to increase fuel consumption. Informants legitimated such statements with their ability to pay for whatever they consumed. Such rebellious stances are illustrated by the following quotations:

I'm paying my bill. *They're* not. So I'll do what I damn well please.

Other people can walk to work if they want to. Not me. I'm no sucker, jumping just because somebody tells me to. Like they say, "It's all jive—Drive eighty-five!"

Solidarity in Munka Ljungby

The 1970s oil crises did not lead to comparable stress and resentment in Munka Ljungby, where residents largely trusted their government and the equity of its policies. Munka Ljungbyans knew that economic aid would be available to them if needed. They expressed greater confidence and a sense of personal power as well, part of the legacy of a history of strong and effective folk movements in Sweden (Hallin 1994). By the 1990s, however, Munka Ljungby-ans questioned changes in oil reserve estimates and their government's stance on conservation:

In the eighties, they were saying "In ten years, there will be no oil left." And now, new reports on oil reserves are contradicting the earlier reports. I am disillusioned by all this.

In the eighties, we waited for the renewables. Nothing happened. There is no real energy policy today. Alternate energy prototypes proved too costly. The government now says that we don't need to save, that there's lots of electricity: "No problem!" Can I trust that?

ENERGY AWARENESS IN DAILY LIFE

Emergence of Energy Awareness

Clearly, prior to the energy crises of the 1970s, neither Americans nor Swedes thought much about energy: it was plentiful, cheap, a given. When asked how they first became conscious of energy, Foley and Munka Ljungby households responded in terms of economics. The majority cited the oil price hikes of the 1970s as initiating awareness; others spoke of first home or car ownership. Additionally, some in each location emphasized the importance of a farming background. Only one Foley household alluded to public messages urging conservation as shaping its outlook, but six households in Munka identified either the government conservation campaign or the nuclear energy debates as initiating their awareness.

The Primacy of Price

Even when Foleyans and Munka Ljungbyans say they are aware of energy and energy issues, such awareness does not necessarily lead to conservation. In both communities, price is dominant in heightening awareness and shaping behavior. Typical quotations from Foleyans in the 1990s underscore this primacy of price:

Our level of concern follows the price of gas!

There's not the same carefulness about driving—people just pick up and go. We know there's a need to conserve, but gas prices lead to more driving.

Munka Ljungbyans also speak of price as central to their awareness:

If prices rise, you shrug your shoulders and pay, especially if they rise slowly. I don't think so much about it [energy] these days. A hefty price-hike would make me more aware and more saving.

We think about energy when the electric bill comes, when the gasoline statement comes. We don't think every day, "How can we save energy?"

Munka informants report a decline in pleasure driving since the 1980s and attribute this to higher gasoline prices. Findings from the Foley-Munka comparison clearly indicate that consumers do not attempt to conserve energy in the absence of market signals. Even the most-aware consumers find it hard to conserve when there is no economic incentive.

Definitions of Energy

In both the 1980s and the 1990s, core households were asked to define energy. The difficulty that most had with this task reflects the recent emergence of this concept into popular awareness. Informants in both communities resorted to body language and sound effects when formulating their answers: arms outstretched, swooping hands, buzzing sounds, and so forth. Foleyans blocked more often than Munka Ljungbyans, who were instead frustrated by their inability to incorporate all they wanted into their definitions. Definitions from Munka were usually comprehensive, such as the following:

Energy is everything. Without it, one cannot do anything. I think first of gasoline, electricity, and oil. Then there are the renewables: trees, solar, hydropower. We have energy ourselves, of course, our own physical power. Food crops, fuel, the sun—it's all tied up together. Energy is what maintains life.

It's hard to define because it's so common. So all-pervasive. All that can be transformed to motion or warmth. Energy takes an endless number of forms.

In the 1980s twice as many Foley households couched their definitions of energy in terms of a source of power replacing human effort or as an energy servant. For example:

Energy is an important part of our way of life. What we use for our living. A product that makes things work . . . allows us to flip the switch on. [Energy is] . . . that which is used to make life a little easier.

Energy is a source that runs all the things we have. It's like getting a hired man!

Foley definitions in the 1990s continued the emphasis on energy replacing human effort. Further, one household implied that "energy" was strictly a product of modern times:

Something that does something for you without you having to do anything. . . . In the olden days there was not a thing called energy. No electricity . . . Horse and buggy. Now, with *everything* in our everyday life, we're using energy.

Overall, however, Foleyans provided broader definitions than they had earlier, such as the following:

Energy creates virtually all we have on earth. The sun provides heat, wind, water, weather. It's all-encompassing.

Munka's definitions, though continuing to be more inclusive than Foley's, are somewhat less elaborate, probably because of diminished media attention to energy. Summary statements from Munka Ljungbyans include: "everything . . . the foundation for all life," "Without it nothing can function," and "indestructible . . . and there's always the same amount, but some forms are more usable than others." Munka Ljungbyans conceptualize energy more broadly and are more likely to incorporate food, renewable fuels, and natural resources into their definitions. Whereas a holistic orientation characterizes Munka responses, power and need fulfillment themes dominate Foley definitions of energy.

Its invisibility removes energy from user consciousness. Energy in the form of fuels is most often an unseen entity, flowing magically through appliances, from tanks to furnaces, and from pumps to auto tanks. Fueled machines seem to take on independent life. As one Munka Ljungbyan commented, "It's funny. I never think of the vacuum cleaner as using electricity. It doesn't seem to be connected to anything." Energy is invisible, and therefore its waste is intangible and seems unreal. One Foleyan said, "Waste of energy is unreal . . . not like a person *starving*."

Paul C. Stern and Elliot Aronson (1984) outline four common ways of perceiving energy: as commodity, ecological resource, social necessity, or strategic material. Findings from Foley support their conclusion that energy as commodity is the dominant view in America. Further, many Foleyans were frustrated by price hikes because they saw fuel as a special commodity which should be protected from market dynamics and rising prices. Statements from the 1980s reflect this attitude but also reveal awareness of its irony:

They should decide on the price of fuel and should put it out, and that's what it should *be*.

If oil companies make us mad, we see a conspiracy. But if food or clothes prices go up, we accept it.

People get all steamed up about paying $1.27 a gallon of gas so that they can drive in to St. Cloud and buy $40 designer jeans. We're used to cheap energy—but not cheap status symbols!

The controversy over natural gas deregulation in the United States in the early 1980s reflects this view of fuel as a protected commodity. If consumption is sacrosanct in American society, as sociologist Michael Sobel (1981) declares, fuel consumption is even more hallowed, regarded by most Foleyans as a need and a right.

ENERGY FRAMES OF REFERENCE

In the 1980s Munka Ljungbyans placed energy in much broader frames of reference than did Foleyans. In Foley, energy was viewed chiefly as an internal, household budgetary problem. Energy costs also concerned budgeting Munka Ljungbyans, but they linked energy to the national economy as well, stressing the need for national solidarity. Further, Munka Ljungbyans conveyed an international awareness and a global solidarity that Foleyans did not.

Although Foley perspectives expanded somewhat by the 1990s, Munka Ljungbyans still evidence greater awareness of energy and its relationship to environment and economy, as well as its international context. Their time frame is longer, and they are quicker to identify moral dimensions of energy use. Chapter 7 traces the expansion of Foley's environmental awareness and reports informants' comments on moral aspects of energy use and the environment.

Economic

Foley and Munka core households were asked to describe connections between energy and the economy. All Munka households responded to this question, but some Foley households could not. Though answers from Munka varied in complexity and detail, most 1980s responses centered around oil and the health of the national economy. In the 1990s the focus is on the costs of fuels for industry and commercial operations. Typical 1980s Munka answers about energy-economy links include the following:

Yes, of course. [smiles at such an obvious question] Energy steers the economy. . . . Oil also influences the electricity supply and prices. All the fuels are bound up in complicated economic relationships.

Decidedly. Sweden depends on cheap energy to thrive. Otherwise, the whole economy "tilts." Taxes increase. Industrial competition in the world market weakens, for industry is particularly dependent on oil and energy.

In contrast, Foley households spoke nearly exclusively in terms of their household economies rather than the national economy. Even those who linked energy to larger economic trends assessed these in terms of their consequences for individual consumers. Typical is this comment:

High energy bills lead to economic troubles. If energy prices go up, the prices of lots of things go up. Recreational expenditure is the first thing to go.

In the 1990s Foleyans are somewhat more likely to convey a sense of the intertwining of energy and the economy. As one informant commented,

Our economy is basically energy-driven. Fuel availability and prices affect all aspects of it. Industry, agriculture, transportation, the stock market.

However, primary focus remains on consequences for consumers, as illustrated by the following:

The better the economy, the more money, the more vehicles people will buy, and the more fuel they'll use. When recession comes, that's the end of weekend drives.

Clearly, Munka Ljungbyans see their society more holistically, especially regarding the dynamics between energy prices and the national economy. Furthermore, they show greater awareness of the international political dimensions of energy than do Foleyans.

International

Unlike Munka Ljungbyans, Foleyans rarely make international or global references when discussing energy. In the 1980s Foley's resentment towards Middle East oil producers was high, and Third World countries were most often mentioned in terms of their potential threat to American energy supplies. Additionally, three Foley core households posited that the inability of Third World countries to use refined fuels argued against reducing American consumption. Other countries were viewed as competitors, not just for fuels, but for survival. Quotations from Foley illustrate these perspectives:

There's no worldwide shortage of energy. But our access to it might be limited. They said they're [OPEC nations] making so much money on oil that they're driving big cars and building big buildings . . . living high on our money. We're really paying. They got wise, I guess.

Well, they can't use the gasoline over there. They aren't developed enough. So we might as well have it, since we need it.

One Foley informant described a plan he had heard for guarding U.S. oil wells in foreign countries:

Loading satellites to the gills with explosives. If anything goes wrong, you get the men out and the satellite blows everything to bits. That way no one else will get it.

Another provided this new interpretation of Darwin's principle:

We want to get everything we can, you know, to be sure that we survive even if nobody else does. That's human nature, I guess: Survival of the fittest . . . the ones who have got the most.

Such aggressive statements would shock most Swedes, and those who might agree would not dare to express such opinions openly. Some Foleyans did, of course, express concern for the welfare of others and disapproval of America's disproportionate consumption of energy and other resources.

Temporal

Sweden adopts longer time frames in its policy and planning than the quick-fix United States, as seen in the contrast of energy policies in Chapter 1. Some Foleyans expressed frustration with America's shortsightedness and with the way in which immediate demands obscure a longer focus:

We never put anything *back*, not even a tree. You can't put coal back. We're very good at taking. Our great grand-kids will come along and there'll be nothing left to take. I don't think too many people think that far ahead, though.

I think that people have a commitment to future generations, that they feel it, deep down, but that they are distracted by their immediate needs and pressures.

Typically, Munka Ljungbyans conveyed genuine feeling for future generations:

It's a *cursed* inheritance that we will leave if we destroy everything.

The longer Swedish time frame leads to consideration of moral or ethical aspects of energy use. As one Munka Ljungbyan emphasized:

You must take the *longer* perspective in order to discuss the moral aspects of energy and resource use. Our generation has been so destructive in such a short time. We take a disproportionate amount of people's share.

SELF-IMAGE

Perceived Vulnerability

Sweden's history of energy resource vulnerability is much a part of Swedish consciousness. In both the 1980s and the 1990s, Munka Ljungby core households underscored how very vulnerable they were to potential energy shortages. In contrast, Foleyans in the 1980s portrayed themselves as invulnerable to such shortages because of their community's small size, its strong ties to agriculture, and local abundance of fuelwood. Also, few Foleyans voiced concerns about national vulnerability, given plentiful domestic energy supplies in the United States. In the 1990s, however, Foleyans communicate slightly greater vulnerability. A minority continue to emphasize wood as an alternative, but others look beyond the bounds of their community. They speak of ties binding them to the larger society and acknowledge the high fossil-fuel dependence of agriculture, an economic activity formerly seen as conferring independence.

Self-Image and the Relativity of Waste

In both the 1980s and the 1990s, core households were asked to rank sectors of society in terms of magnitude of energy demand and energy waste. Both communities ranked other sectors of society—specifically, government, industry, and business—as demanding and wasting more energy than the residential sector. They ranked education and agriculture as demanding less. One Munka Ljungbyan spoke for Munka and Foley about the bad energy reputation of industry:

Industries are bad. Their energy use has increased and increased. They just let the heat go out; they don't shut their doors. They leave the lights on all night, and the machines running, too.

Foleyans share a self-image of people living carelessly in abundance and confessed to being "spoiled," "wasteful," and "taking things for granted." However, many say that other Americans use more residential energy and other resources than they did; for example, wealthy urbanites. Foleyans see waste in relative terms, stating that all Americans ("even the poor") waste—it is just a matter of degree. Though they lament the amount of energy and resources consumed in America, Foleyans place themselves at the lower end of the consumption continuum, and this identification does not motivate conservation.

In contrast, the Swedes are self-satisfied about their relatively low consumption. Awareness of their country's small size and population, compact and efficient technologies, and modest scale of living dampens conservation urgency. Though some Munka Ljungbyans confess that they "have it too good," others compare their way of life favorably with that of other communities, especially the fashionable seaside towns nearby. The following quotations reflect Munka's satisfaction with the status quo and willingness to rely on technology as the chief means of achieving low energy consumption:

Swedes think our way of life is good. We don't have to do anything about it. We don't use much energy.

We have a well-insulated house and tight windows. Most Swedes do. We don't need to try to reduce our energy consumption.

We don't try to conserve any more than we do because we have a heat pump.

ENERGY KNOWLEDGE AND CONSERVATION STRATEGIES

Knowledge of Household Appliance Energy Demand

Most consumers are uncertain about the relative energy demands of appliances and fixtures, and as a result, waste their efforts to conserve. For example, many Foleyans emphasize turning off lights and televisions, where consumption is most visible but relatively negligible, in order to save energy. (A 60-watt bulb lit for 16 hours or a color television on for 5 hours each demands only one kilowatt-hour of electricity [NSP 1993].) These misconceptions also appear in Munka Ljungby, but to a lesser extent than in Foley. Additionally, consumers in neither society realize how little energy is demanded by small electrical apparatuses. For example, the average *annual* consumption for blenders is 0.9 kWh; for electric can openers, 0.2 kWh; and for hand-held electric mixers, 10 kWh (Berry 1978). Less energy is required for a daily four-minute shave with an electric razor for one *year* than is used to shave daily with hot water and a blade for one *week* (Ibid.).

Attempting to conserve in the 1980s, Foley informants bombarded me with questions about the relative energy costs of different appliances and the relative effectiveness of different energy-saving strategies. These included the lowest water temperature at which one may safely use dishwashers and the relative energy demand for the care of natural versus synthetic clothing. Foleyans were frustrated by the lack of accessible information with which to guide energy decisions and having to rely on hearsay. Just as Foleyans put their conservation efforts into areas offering negligible savings, they also attempted torturous comparisons of energy demand—for example, that of a toaster versus a toaster oven and keeping coffee hot in a coffeemaker versus reheating each cup in a microwave oven. State energy conservation campaigns provided Swedes with guidelines, but these were usually the same repeated tips: Don't wash dishes under running water, shower instead of bathe, and carpool. There were no water temperature reminders from the Swedish government similar to those for space heating temperatures. Munka Ljungbyans were largely unaware of the ways in which their open fireplaces and kitchen fans consume heated air, features more common and used more often in Munka than in Foley.

Appliance Selection

In 1975 the U.S. Energy Policy and Conservation Act mandated appliance labeling, to become effective by 1980, in order to provide energy information to consumers. In Foley, hardware and appliance store managers emphasize that initial purchase price dominates decisions, even among the minority of customers who calculate the trade-off between cheaper models and costlier but more-efficient models. Initial purchase price was the determining factor in appliance selection in both Foley and Munka Ljungby over time. Similar findings are reported for Norway and Japan (Wilhite et al. 1996). Now improvements in efficiency narrow the range of annual costs of operation so that energy efficiency is a negligible influence—and may elicit choices resulting in greater net consumption. As one Foley hardware merchant recounted: "Customers think, 'Well, for $8 more per year, I'll get the 19-cubic-foot refrigerator instead of the 17-cubic-foot model.'" Though both models use half the energy they did a dozen years ago, consumer preferences and manufacturing trends are toward ever-bigger refrigerators and freezers. Refrigerator doors are now built deep to accommodate one-gallon milk containers and large cartons ("suitcases") of soda. The latest Swedish refrigerators and freezers feature such extras as ice makers and beverage dispensers.

Likewise, and despite intensive government energy-conservation campaigns, energy factors are not primary considerations when Munka Ljungbyans purchase household appliances. Appliance store managers related in 1982 that most customers did not inquire about energy efficiency. Price was the leading factor, followed by noise level and *finess* (appearance and diversity of options). Swedish dealers in the 1990s report that a few customers ask about operation costs of appliances and water heaters after electricity prices began to increase. They say, however, that customers first want easy and effective functioning, and second, low purchase price. Appliance advertisements emphasize interest-free purchase and freon-free manufacture, rather than the energy efficiency that they touted earlier.

Conservation Strategies

Foleyans are more concerned about reducing heating fuel than fuel used for household operations, due to dramatic winter peaks in utility bills. Despite their earlier bluster against conservation, many Foleyans lowered their thermostat settings accordingly. They placed primary emphasis on structural rather than behavioral changes to save heating fuel, however. Foleyans needed to make more changes in their housing to save heating fuel than did Munka Ljungbyans, due to tighter Swedish construction practices. Nearly half of 1980 Foley questionnaire respondents added roof insulation, and one quarter added wall insulation. In contrast, in Munka only 14 percent added roof insulation and 14 percent added wall insulation.

Given the costs of retrofitting, many in Foley took a patch-and-repair approach. Caulking of seams and cracks, weather-stripping of doors and windows, and covering windows with plastic sheets were the cheapest and most popular technical means employed to conserve energy. (Of the Foley questionnaire sample, 45% reported caulking and weather-stripping, and 23 percent put plastic on their windows.) Banking foundations with bales of hay or with plastic bags filled with leaves was a strategy used by about one tenth of homeowners. In addition, 15 percent in Foley reported adding storm windows; 16 percent added storm doors. (Highly energy-efficient primary doors and windows make storm doors and windows unnecessary in Munka.)

Caulking and weather-stripping were popular procedures in Munka Ljungby as well. Like Foley, nearly one half of the Munka questionnaire sample reported taking these steps. Munka Ljungbyans, however, were more likely to caulk only in spots, whereas Foleyans caulked overall.

In the 1990s, when asked to give examples of ways in which they conserve energy, the most frequent response in both Foley and Munka continued to be monitoring lights and televisions. Next was operating dishwashers and clothes-washers only when filled. A few in each town mentioned baking more than one dish when using the oven. Munka Ljungbyans continued to emphasize choosing showers over baths, and some spoke of capturing passive solar energy.

Foleyans did not mention any new technologies, but Munka informants spoke enthusiastically about heat pumps and the significant savings they offer, quoting the number of kilowatt-hours they save by using them. Munka Ljung-byans also reported fireplace improvements and energy-saving outdoor light-bulbs. (No one in either town mentioned energy-saving *indoor* bulbs, however.)

OBSTACLES TO ENERGY CONSERVATION

Core households were asked, "Why don't you conserve more than you already do?" They identified tangible obstacles such as economics, lack of information, and infrastructural barriers. Also, they emphasized pace of life, the force of habit, and human nature—and revealed cognitive and psychological blocks to conserving, such as fear of regression and feelings of entitlement.

Economics and Infrastructure

The cost of retrofitting or purchasing new energy-efficient technology was declared a block to further energy conservation by several households in both communities. Most focus on initial purchase cost rather than calculating pay-back time, but even when they do so, they conclude that they do not have the money. Conversely, some households in each community said they do not conserve because they have the means to pay for all the energy they want.

Core households were asked how much more fuel would have to cost in order to get people to conserve. In both communities, the dominant response was that prices would have to double, because people are now accustomed to the levels set by earlier hikes. Illustrating this view:

It would have to get a *lot* more expensive to get conservation, probably double. Energy has become one of those costs which people accept. [Foley]

When prices first went up, all were going to bicycle, and so forth. Then, we got used to them, and kept on driving. Energy would have to double in cost, now [to motivate conservation]. [Munka]

More than Foleyans, Munka Ljungbyans referred to infrastructural blocks to energy savings. Such comments focus on the need for a car and lack of access to fuels other than electricity:

You *must* have a car to live here; there are lots of activities in Ängelholm and Helsingborg. Bus connections aren't good at night, and it costs as much to take the bus as to drive.

We don't have access to any other fuel than electricity; all we can do is lower the temperature.

Lack of Information

As reported earlier, informants lack information about relative energy demands of household appliances by which they could direct efforts at saving energy most effectively. They were unable to identify any energy-saving techniques additional to what they were already doing. "I don't see how we could cut down any more," was the response from the great majority of households in both Foley and Munka households in the 1990s. These comments are typical:

I suppose there is some place we could cut down, but I really don't see it. [Foley]

Where could we cut down? One can't stop washing clothes, cooking, and so forth. [Munka]

In Foley some basic questions about relative energy demand continued into the 1990s. These include whether it takes more electricity to turn lights or the TV off and later on again than it does to leave them on continuously. Also, informants wonder whether it costs more to raise the indoor temperature to the desired level after dialing down at night or before leaving an empty house than it does to leave the setting alone.

Pace of Life, Force of Habit, and Human Nature

Pace of life relates to economics, the increase in two-salary households, and scarcity of time at home in both Foley and Munka Ljungby. One Munka couple noted that today, "people's jobs leave them *psychologically* exhausted, not physically exhausted. Either way, it is going to be hard to save energy." Another Munka household said:

Looking at the questionnaire, I realized we could cut back more. But then, it's another thing to actually change behavior to reduce electricity. It's a question of will, more than anything else.

Informants stressed that they are creatures of comfort as well as habit, children of their cultures:

Despite everything, we want a little comfort. [Munka]

Why don't we conserve more? Because it would "hurt" . . . and we're children of a society that doesn't like to hurt. [Foley]

Hallin (1994) found that environmentally-inactive households stress choosing comfort and convenience. One quotation from Munka he cites presents a "human nature" rationalization for such choices:

Man does whatever is easiest . . . the simplest. . . . This is certainly human nature.

Cognitive Blocks

In both Foley and Munka Ljungby, informants revealed cognitive blocks to energy conservation. One example from Foley is the informant with a malfunctioning thermostat who could not bear to set it below 65 degrees, even though the resulting actual indoor temperature would be several degrees higher than the setting. One Munka Ljungbyan keeps his water heater temperature set very high because he believes that was one way to conserve: "With water that hot, you need to take less from the faucets." And one Munka couple reported that they maintain a high water heater setting because the installer told them that anything lower "gives the water heater 'more work,' and it is therefore less efficient."

The theme of "my little bit" (of trash, of waste) not mattering characterizes both towns but is voiced more often in Munka. Conversely, informants in both towns say that their "little bit" of conserving would not make a difference either—a theme more widespread in Foley. One Munka Ljungbyan summed it up:

People think: "It doesn't make any difference if I throw this away, or use this energy, or throw batteries out in nature, because this bit is so little, it's nothing."

Fear of Regression

A psychological block to conservation in both towns is the association of conservation with regression, with generally lowering one's standard of living and "going back." Informants defend against change by exaggerating it and then rejecting such suffering and sacrifice:

What should we do, quit *showering*? [Munka]

We don't want to sit and *freeze*. [Foley]

We'd have to break our patterns totally: take away our freezer, microwave, coffeemaker, lower the temperature . . . lower our living standard! [Munka]

One informant went even further, shuddering, "We'd live at the 1800s-level." All stoutly reject regression to, for example, totally-manual labor and outhouses.

You don't know how long energy will last, but you also don't want to go back to the old days, with no electricity, no hot water. [Munka]

I won't ever go back to doing dishes, mixing dough, and such things by hand. [Foley]

Entitlement

In Foley especially, feelings of entitlement discourage conservation. Those in or near retirement feel that they have "got it coming" or "earned it" at their stage in life. They report using the clothesdryer because of arthritis, using a riding lawn mower because of bad knees, and running their air conditioners because they like it cool. "The U.S. thinks it's due the energy resources. Anyway, how can we take what we might save and give it to some other country?" asked one Foley couple. In the 1980s another Foleyan declared:

I'm *not* putting a sweater on. I have a *right* to comfort, inside my own house.

Conflicts with Deeper Values

Although informants did not cite values conflict as an obstacle to energy conservation, it is clear that when conservation conflicts with deeply-held values, the latter wins. Such sanctions for consumption are presented in the next chapter.

Chapter 5

Energy Consumption: Cultural Mandates and Individual Rationales

Sociologist Loren Lutzenhiser (1992) writes in his incisive article on cultural analysis of household energy use that even though individuals make choices, they are "culturally-sensible and collectively-sanctioned" choices. Patterns of energy use in Foley and Munka Ljungby were contrasted in earlier chapters. Here, rationales given by informants for their choices are placed in context and related to cultural values and mandates. Certainly, these uses are culturally legitimated. No Foleyans challenge, for example, using energy in order to save time or to "unwind" from stress-inducing schedules. Neither do they question energy consumption justified by the argument that one is entitled to as much as one can afford. Likewise, Munka Ljungbyans do not question the use of energy to meet culturally mandated standards of housekeeping, appearance, and entertaining or to compensate for an oppressive climate.

Core sample households vary widely in their daily routines and energy use choices, even within the community. Rationales for energy-intensive choices provided are also diverse. Yet, certain cultural themes emerged during discussions of activity records and from responses to such interview questions as, "Sometimes people choose to act in a way that is less saving of energy than another. Are there such choices in your lives? What are the reasons for your decisions?"

In addition to these themes, trade-offs among time, energy, and money which underlie consumption decisions are explored here. As is documented, energy considerations had diminished, and were largely ignored, by the 1990s. Saving time was the most frequently cited rationale for energy consumption in Foley, both in the 1980s and the 1990s. Demands for time economy are much stronger in Foley than in Munka Ljungby, often outweighing the countervailing 1980s goal of reducing fuel bills.

Economic rationales for consumption cited in both Foley and Munka are that the household economy can afford it and that it contributes to the health of the national economy. Social imperatives requiring energy consumption exist in both locations and include such factors as social relations and obligations, home orientation, self-image, and patterns of conspicuous consumption. In response to the question "Are there some times or circumstances when you are less saving of energy than others?," informants in both communities identify holidays, especially Christmas, as their least-saving times. Energy is consumed in both communities through higher indoor temperatures when entertaining guests; Munka Ljungbyans stress using energy to meet expectations of punctuality as well. Folk beliefs and traditions play strong roles in fostering energy consumption in both communities. Climatic inducements to consume energy are stronger in Munka than in Foley, both winter and summer.

Although Munka Ljungbyans face stronger sanctions to meet social standards, these sanctions are sporadic, and their fulfillment is clearly bounded. For Foleyans, however, social expectations regarding consumption are continuous, and their satisfaction is open-ended. In the words of one Foley informant, "Here, the sky's the limit!" Foleyans more readily criticize stinginess than waste, and Munka Ljungbyans feel freer to make value judgments, readily labeling waste and excess—as demonstrated in the next chapter.

ECONOMIC FACTORS FOSTERING CONSUMPTION

Household Economy Permits Consumption

Economic and utilitarian considerations influence energy-intensive choices in both Foley and Munka Ljungby. However, Foleyans more often express these decisions in direct monetary terms. "Why should I be cold for two dollars?" is a question raised in Foley typifying this economic rationale. Several Foleyans defend higher temperatures by saying they were "cheaper than kids' medical bills." Some say that they chose higher temperatures because they could afford them. "It doesn't pay" is a phrase often used in Foley to explain rejection of energy-conserving choices. One informant driving to the grocery store declared, "It doesn't pay to walk. I don't want to spend thirty minutes for milk." Two Foley informants said that if they joined carpools, they could not put in lucrative overtime hours when they wished to: "So there's no way *that* could pay." These examples illustrate the time-energy-money trade-offs typical of Foley. There, money remains the most important consideration; energy has nearly disappeared as a factor. Time, however, has increased in importance and is sometimes chosen over money.

Economic considerations also shape choices in Munka Ljungby, of course. Two Munka core households stated that they would cycle to work if they had no money, and one said that they choose higher indoor temperatures because they can afford them.

Consumption Bolsters National Economy

Foleyans and Munka Ljungbyans alike justify consumption because it stimulates the national economy. Demand for fuels and products is believed to maintain employment and to keep money circulating. In the 1980s Swedes tempered such consumption boosterism with concern over reducing both oil dependency and the national debt. By 1994, however, Sweden was experiencing its highest unemployment rate in decades, and the consumption-provides-jobs argument was stronger than ever. Reduction of imported oil eased the fuel component of the national debt, but other factors caused it to rise again in the 1990s. Debt was another in a list of economic and social problems Sweden faced, and not one to be assuaged by energy conservation.

The same argument is used more often regarding the consumption of embodied energy in the form of goods. Both Foleyans and Munka Ljungbyans lament planned obsolescence and the rapid turnover of goods in their societies, and especially the proliferation of disposable products. Foleyans referred often to their "throwaway" or "plastic" culture, and Munka Ljungbyans drew my attention to the vast number of *engångsartiklar* (literally, one-time items) in their *köp-slit-släng* (buy-use-toss) society. However, the continued consumption of such items is defended as functional in that it provides employment.

INCREASING SCARCITY OF TIME

Time as Commodity

Time is viewed as a commodity in increasingly short supply in Foley and Munka. In the 1980s more Foleyans than Munka Ljungbyans reported a continuous struggle with time shortages. Foleyans said they were "always on the run." Most Munka Ljungbyans, in contrast, stressed their "rational" use of time and reported hurrying only occasionally to clear time for special events or outings. In contrast, Foleyans gave the impression of struggling just to keep abreast of their schedules. Munka Ljungbyans planned, but Foleyans *schemed*, in order to save time.

Tight scheduling and time shortages extend beyond work to Foleyans' leisure hours, which are filled with civic and recreational activities. Most Foley informants complain about the "hectic" pace and the social demands that community life thrust upon them. A plethora of social clubs and activities, as well as civic organizations and activities, volunteer work, church involvement, hunting and fishing, and children's lessons compete for time. Additionally, a steady increase in the number of two-income households further exacerbates time shortages experienced by Foleyans and leads to increased energy consumption. "When two people work outside the house, you go for convenience rather than what's most economical or most saving on energy," related one Foley informant.

Economist Staffan Linder (1970) describes the scarcity of time resulting from the transfer of the workplace goals of productivity and efficiency to all facets of life in his book, *The Harried Leisure Class*. This scarcity, combined with the consumption of more than one product at the same time, acquiring more-expensive versions of a commodity, or successive consumption (enjoying one commodity at a time, but for a shorter period) has obvious consequences for energy demand, both direct and embodied. Swedish ethnologists Jonas Frykman and Orvar Löfgren (1987) concur with Linder, writing in their study of the transition of Sweden from a peasant to a bourgeois society that people came to feel under a "tyranny of time," oppressed by the new and pervasive goal of maximum efficiency.

These trends were much more evident in Foley than in Munka in the 1980s. By the 1990s the pace of life in Munka Ljungby had accelerated noticeably, although it still has not reached Foley's. Munka informants complained about fitting in all their activities and the difficulty of scheduling meetings. As in Foley, several commented on the impact of two-wage-earner households. These quotations are typical:

Life is stressier now than in the '80s. People are much more active now. It's really hard to find a time when everyone can get together. People don't have time for much.

We have many more activities now [than in the 1980s], especially sports. Parents are more involved with their children's lessons. And of course, one always has "a thousand things" to do in the yard. Spring is an especially stressy time.

We say that "we have it too good" in Sweden, but that depends on *both* working. With one adult working, they don't have that standard. . . . And they don't have that *stress*, either!

Supporting Linder's intensification of leisure hypothesis, another informant wearily concluded, "Free time certainly *takes* lots of time!"

In Munka Ljungby as in Foley there are many social organizations and children's activities. As Hallin (1994) points out, there is less church but more political involvement in Munka. Munka Ljungbyans of all ages are also more involved in sports. The Swedish tradition of study circles and courses is strong in Munka. Cleaning and yard and garden work engage Munka Ljungbyans for longer periods, and they also spend more time in the woods and on the beach. Expanded television broadcasting consumes more time as well. In an April 1994 *NST* article on "*Sköna maj*," the headline reads: "Get up and get going: spring is short!" A photo shows a man seated under beech trees, among the wood anemones, with pen and calendar in hand. In addition to being a month with several holidays "which you must somehow work in" (Walpurgis April 30, Ascension Day, Monday after Pentecost), the article enumerates such May requisites as work ("unending garden preparation"), school exams, spring parties, outings to enjoy the greening beech forests and wildflowers, first trips to the seashore, making rhubarb pie and nettle soup ("from nettles which you pick yourself, of course"), and starting a suntan before the swim season begins. The article concludes, "Welcome to the month of stress!"

A 1991 survey conducted by *Time* magazine and CNN revealed that 69 percent of Americans polled said that they would like to "slow down and live a more relaxed life" (cited in Elgin 1993). That life in Munka is not as harried as life in Foley is reflected in responses to the questionnaire item: "I would like to live a simpler life, with fewer activities and appointments." Fully 70 percent of Foley Q sample agreed with this statement; slightly fewer, 59 percent, of the Munka sample did. Even fewer Munka Ljungbyans would have agreed with this statement in the 1980s.

More Munka than Foley informants continue to express skepticism about time-saving efforts through such comments as:

People drive all the time to save some time. But it's self-deception. You have to find a parking place, and so forth.

Other folks buy prepared foods to save time. I wonder how much they *really* are saving?

Nearly all Foleyans lament the pace of their lives, but only two expressed more fundamental doubt in interviews:

What are we really saving time for? I see autos on the highway. How many of them know *where* they're going and what *for*?

People think when you're "busy" you're doing something productive. *Ha!*

Saving Time through Spending Energy

Foley informants reported choosing to spend energy in order to save time; for example, they drive faster or more often, or use power tools and appliances. Munka informants described making similar choices, although such reports were not as numerous. Nor are Munka Ljungbyans as scrupulous about calculating down-to-the-minute savings.

Households were asked, "What connections do you see between energy and time?" In the 1980s two thirds of Foley core households and one third of Munka households said that they used energy in order to save time. By the 1990s nearly all of the Foley core households and two thirds in the Munka core group said that they did so. These Foley responses illustrate the connection:

The use of energy gives you more time, something we can all use. In the old days, time was spent acquiring energy. Quite a switch, isn't it? Now, our easy energy gives us free time for "extra-curricular" activities.

You could cut energy usage tremendously if you had lots of time to spare. But who does?

Typical responses from Munka to the energy-time connection question:

We use energy to save time. It's demanded in today's society that all goes fast, starts on time. The boss won't accept, "I'm late because I cycled." So, I drive.

Anything which takes a shorter time needs more energy. Driving versus cycling, for instance. If you take more time, you use less energy.

Saving time is the most usual rationale for decisions to use household appliances and power tools. It is the reason for dishwasher use in both Foley and Munka Ljungby, as well as for using running water when doing dishes by hand, rather than turning water on and off as needed. Clothesdryers save time otherwise spent hanging and ironing clothes, Foleyans feel. Munka Ljungbyans use their dryers when time is generally short or when they need a particular item fast. Informants in both towns praise the electric mixer for getting the job done quickly; likewise, the power mower is said to save time for Minnesota and Swedish operators. Some Munka Ljungbyans say they choose to preheat their ovens because baking then goes "faster." The microwave oven's principal advantage is said to be its speed. The most extreme example of using energy to save time was given by one Foleyan, who said she chooses to use "really hot water" to rinse dishes because that way they dry faster. (It should be noted that these dishes were left to dry in a dish rack!)

Speed is the chief reason given by both Foleyans and Munka Ljungbyans for driving their cars on in-town errands. This habit was much more common in Foley in the 1980s, when core household members drove on 81 percent (144 of 177) of local trips made over four weeks of record-keeping. In contrast, Munka Ljungby's core group members used their cars for local errands less than half that often, 37 percent of the time (56 of 153 reported trips).

In the 1990s Munka Ljungbyans drove more frequently on local errands: 54 percent of the time (93 of 172 trips). Foleyans drove slightly more than they did earlier, on 88 percent (698 of 797) of local trips. It should be noted that though the total number of trips made by all core households was comparable for Foley and Munka in the 1980s and rose slightly in Munka over time, Foley's trips increased dramatically, from 177 to 797. This increase reflects greater time scarcity and less effort to combine trips to save fuel, as Foleyans had reported doing earlier.

In *The Joyless Economy: An Inquiry into Human Satisfactions and Consumer Dissatisfaction*, economist Tibor Scitovsky (1976) describes what he calls "the economy of care and bother." Care and bother involve the expenditure of mental effort in thinking, planning, and remembering. Scitovsky writes that our capacity to care in these ways is limited. Further, because we believe that the good life should be carefree as well as leisurely, we try to economize on caring as much as we do on time and physical effort. Care and bother irritates residents of both communities, but Foleyans see it as especially aggravating. Planning ahead to combine shopping trips with other errands or outings is something Foleyans engaged in much less often than Munka Ljungbyans, in either the 1980s or the 1990s. Five times as many Foleyans and Munka Ljungbyans bothered to turn down the thermostat before leaving home in the 1980s, but only twice as many Foleyans did this later on—reflecting the importance of price as motivation for bother.

Time stress and intolerance for care and bother have as their consequences "poor planning" and "lack of organization," reasons given by both Foleyans and Munka Ljungbyans for various energy-intensive choices, although more frequently in Foley. "Disorganization" is said to result in such choices as using the microwave rather than planning meals in advance or remembering to take items out of the freezer; driving to grocery shop daily instead of weekly; not planning ahead for all-oven dinners; washing one item of clothing needed for a special event; and using the power mower because grass had grown too tall for the hand mower. Affirming Scitovsky, one Munka informant declared, "No time to *think*—that's the villain in this drama!"

Simultaneous accomplishment of various household tasks is seen as desirable and efficient by Foleyans and underlies decisions to use dishwashers and clothesdryers. With the dishwasher, said one informant, "you can rinse and load the dishes and then be free to go off and do something else. It's really efficient, time-wise." Clothesdryers free up another user from constraints of both time and weather: "This way I can do things in between loads, rather than commit all that time to the line. Also, you can dry when *you* want to, not just when the weather allows." Other examples of multitasking favored by Foleyans are ironing while drying clothes, typing while washing clothes, and talking on portable phone while cooking. In Munka, the 1980s emphasis on prioritizing and arranging tasks rationally persisted, but in the 1990s emphasis on simultaneous activities appeared as well: cooking and cleaning, for example.

Accelerating Pace of Life and the Prestige of Being Busy

Residents pointed out that an increase in households with two wage-earners intensifies time scarcity in both Foley and Munka Ljungby. Even though the loss of one person in the household undeniably shrinks available time there, much activity is taken on voluntarily. Some of this activity is enjoyable, of course, but being busy is being needed and assuages fears of being left out, Foleyans and Munka Ljungbyans told me. They also said that keeping busy also satisfies the work ethic and demonstrates that one is not lazy. I asked core households whether being busy in some way confers prestige. Households in each community confirmed this, though a greater number in Foley than in Munka said that it did. Quotations from Foley reflect a variety of motivations to be busy, and also convey feelings of being trapped:

Yes, being busy is a "good" thing to be in Foley. Everybody gripes about it, though. We've lost control of over how busy we are.

The number of organizations you're in can mean how needed a person is. My wife is more busy than I am. I hate to admit that!

Yes, it is still important to be busy, to be involved in church, with your kids' activities, and so forth. You feel obliged to volunteer for things. It's a curse to be so busy, though. You're doing what you're supposed to be doing. But inwardly, you're going crazy.

Being busy confers prestige in Munka as well, as the quotations that follow affirm. The relative newness of this busy state is reflected in informants' comments from 1994 that it was currently "in" to be busy and their references to the new importance of date-books. One of the latest status symbols in Sweden is cellular telephones, called "yuppies' teddy bears" by some. The phones had made their appearance in Munka Ljungby also.

It's "in" to say you are stressed. You have got to be stressed.

Yes, those with their datebooks all filled in feel very important.

This "busyness" has a little something to do with status. One creates one's status.

Feelings of obligation pervade and influence life in Munka. Anxiety over being left out or failing to meet others' expectations is expressed more frequently there than in Foley. The following Munka comments convey this pressure:

You have got to keep up. You have a certain anxiety about not keeping up. There's *enormous* pressure to have a perfect yard and garden, for example.

We take this thing with time seriously. Swedes are time-fixated: "Come on time, Eat at this time, Go home at this time," and so forth.

One Munka informant succinctly summed up the trend toward increased activity he perceived: "It used to be: 'Do the *right* thing.' Now it's: 'Do *some*thing!'"

Even the Munka couple living the closest to voluntary simplicity reported difficulty with over-commitment: "We really wish that the week had one more day. It's really hard to say no [to political and environmental activities]." However, Munka Ljungbyans contrast themselves favorably with the residents of large cities, whom they see as much more harried.

TRADE-OFFS OF TIME, MONEY, AND ENERGY

Reference was made earlier in this chapter to the deliberations both Foleyans and Munka Ljungbyans engage in when making everyday energy- using choices. In both communities, informants compare and consider the relative benefits of saving time, money, and energy. Earlier, economic factors dominated, but time considerations are gaining in priority. More than one Munka informant said, "Time is money *and* energy."

One Foleyan spoke of the time-money-energy triangle and the predominance of time:

Energy gives me more time for doing what I enjoy. It takes more time to conserve energy. A lot of people would rather spend the money [for energy to gain time], especially working couples.

A Munka informant clearly articulated the trade-off, and the primacy of time for him:

I save time by flying to Stockholm instead of going by train. I sometimes try to save time with the car, also. One pays for time with money and with energy. It's worth it.

Additional Foley statements reflect the primacy of time in energy use decisions:

It's more important to save time than to save energy. It really should be the opposite, if I look into my conscience.

While we don't constantly try to save time, it's more precious to us than energy. . . . If we need to be somewhere on time, we'll speed . . . or take two cars if necessary.

Why do we drive uptown, two blocks away? To save time. Saving time has become more important than saving fuel or money, because there's so much going on, and we try to do it all. I think, 'you're down forty minutes' if we walk to piano lessons and back.

The above reference to being "down forty minutes" in particular affirms the Linder hypothesis about how economic calculations have pervaded daily life. Even when actual time saved is negligible, the inclination to hurry persists, as one Foley informant related:

You go over the speed limit by ten miles to St. Cloud—You save about *three minutes*! But I'll still do this. I don't know why.

Time versus Money

Like respondents in the larger surveys cited in the introduction, Foleyans and Munka Ljungbyans theoretically value time more than money. When asked on the 1990s questionnaires which they would choose, a raise in pay for working the same number of hours per week or working fewer hours for the same pay, a majority in each community said they would opt to work fewer hours. However, the faction choosing time over money was somewhat larger in Munka: 70 percent, compared to 61 percent in Foley.

Although time seems to be gaining priority in trade-offs of time, money, and energy, money continues to dominate. For example, some families choose to live in Foley despite a long drive to workplaces in the Twin Cities, due to lower costs of living and tax rates in Foley. For them, monetary savings outweigh the time and energy consumed in commuting. Money is the final arbiter in Munka as well. "Economy steers," chorus Munka Ljungbyans.

Often, energy is excluded from calculations altogether. For example, one Munka man told me about his parents making several round-trips to a rural acquaintance's home in their car, "using lots of gas to get 'free' wood. They just don't think about 'energy' at all."

CULTURAL SANCTIONS FOSTERING CONSUMPTION

Housekeeping Standards

The home is an especially important environment to Swedes. It provides refuge from both an inhospitable winter climate and a social arena in which the potential for criticism is constant. Yet, as Orvar Löfgren (1982) stresses, the Swedish home is both shelter and stage (*skydd och scen*). The stage is always set for drop-in visitors, "who, of course, would never dare to transgress the rule . . . but just in case, the home is kept ready." Munka Ljungbyans keep both their homes and their yards in meticulous order, the few exceptions glaringly apparent. Maintaining high standards of cleanliness and order is a common theme of the Swedish energy use rationales just discussed. (Harold Wilhite and Richard Ling [1992] report similar findings for Norway.) The phrases "*Rent ska det vara*" (It must be clean) and "*hålla i ordning*" (keep in good order) are heard often in Munka. Munka Ljungbyans use very hot water to "get the dishes *really* clean," vacuum longer to "get the house *properly* clean," and use their kitchen fans often in order to keep the air clean and to avoid grease spatters. One Munka woman told of a hostess who once got out her vacuum and cleaned up crumbs on the carpet while her dinner guests were still at the table! The dishwasher was cited as desirable by several Munka informants because it prevents a clutter of dishes in the sink or on the counter.

The term *städmani* ("cleaning madness") was used by several Munka informants to describe the local penchant. One informant said, "People here vacuum every day and feel guilty if they don't. Or they feel guilty if they leave their cleaning and go to town first." Such painstaking tidiness can be interpreted as a defense against social censure. It is an attempt to compensate for feelings of inadequacy fostered by real or imagined social criticism and guilt over failure to fulfill the ideals put forth by what Löfgren (1982) calls "the society of the 'shoulds.'"

Standards are more casual in Foley, where drop-in guests are not only a possibility but a probability. A ritual apology "for the mess" does the trick, and a visit can then be conducted freely. Further, the range of what constitutes a "mess" is broad in Foley, in contrast to Munka's strict standards. Fastidiousness extends to yards and gardens in Munka, where residents say they favor using electric tools (like electric hedge-trimmers) as much for their meticulous results as for the time savings they offer.

Concern with quality of performance, though not absent in Foley, was not as central to informants' statements. Some Foleyans believed that preheating ovens gives "more accurate results," but more Munka Ljungbyans stressed the importance of preheating to assure baked goods of "*excellent* quality." Likewise, some Munka core informants said they choose to use their electric mixers to insure against a "failure" of some sort, something that they are able to dismiss much less easily than are Foleyans.

Folk Wisdom

Many Foley cooks follow conventional wisdom, some of which was inherited and some of which comes from contemporary authoritative sources. Several Foleyans reported preheating ovens and using electric mixers because their mothers did so. After saving time, the most frequently cited reason for using electric mixers was "because the recipe says so." The advice given by technicians is influential in both communities. One Foley woman justified her frequent use of the self-cleaning option on her oven by saying, "The repairman was here . . . and said that it takes only a little more energy than it does to bake a cake. So I use it." One Munka couple recounted that the installer of their water heater declared that by keeping the water at a hot (160° F) temperature, it "makes less work" for the appliance, and so they follow this strategy.

Beliefs about resultant health benefits are accepted energy use rationales in both communities. Some Foley households feel that lower indoor temperatures directly compromise their children's health. One Foley woman was told by her in-laws that she should not open a garage door when pregnant, so an electric opener was acquired. The theory that eyestrain results from reading or watching TV without bright lighting flourishes in Foley. A pervasive health-related belief in Munka is the essential need for fresh air, resulting in frequent airing of houses and use of kitchen fans.

Punctuality

Punctuality is mandated in Munka, for both formal and informal events. Whereas Foleyans stated that they drive fast in attempts to *save* time, Munka Ljungbyans reported driving fast in order to *arrive* on time. One Munka couple, active in environmental organizations and the anti-nuclear power movement, reported driving long distances at high speeds to avoid being late to such meetings! Norms are much more relaxed in Foley. Though punctuality is appreciated, harried Foley hosts said that they are sometimes "relieved" if guests come a little late.

SOCIAL RELATIONS

Conspicuous Consumption

Veblen's concept of conspicuous consumption applies more directly to embodied energy in the form of goods, and such consumption is described in Foley and Munka Ljungby in Chapter 8. Certain consumption choices obviously influence direct energy consumption, however, such as model of car or size of house. And, as is shown, fear of being thought of as poor or stingy by reducing heat or light drives consumption in both communities.

Individual versus Group Demands

Both Foleyans and Munka Ljungbyans said they often choose higher indoor temperatures when entertaining guests, especially older persons. The Swedes verbalized concern that *no* one be uncomfortable. As has been emphasized, social demands for conformity to standards of house and yard maintenance and canons of hospitality are much stronger in Sweden.

Whereas Swedes conform more strictly to group standards, Foleyans accede to the wishes of other individuals more frequently. An example of the weight of individual interaction in Foley is that of one informant who told of how, when he first moved to Foley, he would walk the mile across town from his home to his job. He said, "Now, I drive. People kept stopping and offering me rides. When I didn't accept, one guy said, 'What's the matter? You too good to ride with me?' So now I drive myself, because it's not worth the hassle to walk." This same informant added that he is careful not to leave for work at the same time his merchant neighbor walks the three blocks downtown to open his store so that he will not be tempted to press a ride on him!

In contrast, Munka Ljungbyans are not subject to such personal confrontations, because most Swedes avoid them at all costs (a theme of Swedish culture stressed by ethnologist Åke Daun [1994]). Rather, they are fearful of not meeting collective standards, and what might be gossiped about them.

Holidays and Entertaining

Holidays, especially Christmas, were cited as less-saving times by both Foleyans and Munka Ljungbyans. Christmas is seen as a time of extra lights and more cooking and baking. That these extras are culturally mandated is illustrated in the words of one Foley woman (emphasis added):

I do this enormous Christmas baking, even though I know we'll never use it all. *Somebody out there tells you you should.* It's not rational. But I feel guilty if I don't.

Probing revealed her mother and holiday issues of family magazines to be the sources of these standards. In Sweden, similar probes revealed fear of censure by guests or neighbors.

Christmas is a long event in Sweden, the season beginning December 13, St. Lucia's Day, and lasting a full month, until January 13, St. Knut's Day, when Christmas trees are dismantled. Its importance is evidenced by that fact that over half of Munka core households cited Christmas as their prime example of a "less-saving time."

Christmas is the time of lights. We have guests more and bake and cook special foods.

We use energy to make our home environment extra cozy. Also, everyone cleans more. Everything must be *completely* clean.

About one third of the core households in each community said that they are less saving of energy when entertaining. Some reported turning up their thermostats when guests were coming. Said one Foleyan, "Some people just aren't used to it. Earlier, *we* froze." In Munka: "It would be *terrible* if *anyone* were cold. Besides, guests come in their fine clothes, which aren't at all warm." In addition to raising temperatures, both Foleyans and Munka Ljungbyans say they use more lights when entertaining. Additionally, a few Munka households reported starting to heat their ovens about thirty minutes earlier than necessary to be sure that meals are served on time.

Extra care is taken with meals for guests and at holidays and celebrations. In Sweden, aesthetic norms require the use of flowers; candles; and special linens, dishes, and glassware. More than one Munka informant spoke of the importance of creating the properly festive mood. In Foley, emphasis was placed more on quantity and richness of food than on creation of a special dining atmosphere. Clearly, norms of hospitality demand increased consumption of both direct and indirect energy.

PERSONAL NEEDS

Need to Unwind and Have Fun

Not surprisingly, Foleyans said that they consume energy in order to unwind from their pace of life. They relax with long showers or baths, for example. Men take fishing weekends to relax, often a couple hours' drive each way. Some Foleyans stated that they use energy in order to "put some fun" in their routines. One woman said she chooses to use her microwave and a variety of specialized kitchen gadgets (such as a sandwich maker) even though "one electric fry pan could really do all those things—but that's no fun!" Another said she uses her electric mixer because it is "fun, something you don't get enough of in the kitchen—or anywhere else!"

Health Needs

Some Munka Ljungbyans said they use energy because of health problems. One bathes rather than showers because of a bad back; one drives to work because of a hip problem; one uses an electric trimmer for lawn borders because of arthritis in the hands; and one keeps her waterbed heated higher than usual because of fibromyalgia. Likewise, one Foleyan reported using her clothesdryer because of arthritis in her hands; another, a riding lawn mower because of bad knees.

INFLUENCE OF CLIMATE

In Foley, long, cold winters and frequent hot summer days result in increased energy consumption. Several Foley informants reported turning up their thermostats immediately upon coming in from the winter cold. Weary of months of being bundled in layers of woolens, some Foleyans shed them and turn up the heat. Two Foley households named winter as a less-saving time due to greater heating needs, greater use of lights, and more frequent use of clothesdryers. Even though Minnesota summer heat waves are neither common nor lengthy, heat and humidity prompt many Foleyans to use air-conditioning.

Munka Ljungbyans spoke often of the need for compensation for the long, dark winters that they endure. Compensation through energy use takes the forms of higher indoor temperatures, lots of lights ("light *therapy*," said one woman), fires burned for aesthetic purposes, and long hot baths. For some, "Lapp sickness" (cabin fever) is relieved by getting out and driving. A universal goal is creating a cozy (*mysigt*) and pleasant (*trevligt*) indoor environment. (Wilhite et al. 1996 discuss the importance of coziness to Norwegian lighting energy consumption.)

Interestingly, a few Munka households identified summer as their less-saving time, because it is then that they compensate for winter:

We drive out and around a lot more in the summer and use much more gas. The weather is so glorious—and so is the sea!

We take advantage of every good day we can in the summer. Go on many more expeditions. We eat ready-made food more in summer, to free us up to spend more time in the yard.

In the 1980s I was startled to discover Munka Ljungbyans prolonging summer by attaching radiant heaters to the roofs of their open back porches! This enabled them to sit outside after dinner even as fall arrived. Just one Foley household named summer as a less conserving time:

Because the bills are down and we're less aware of how much energy we're using. Also, we're not tending wood—that makes us more aware of "energy" in general.

As seen, the factors fostering consumption in both Foley and Munka Ljungby are diverse and pervasive. They reflect and are reinforced by dominant cultural values and largely overwhelm the forces fostering conservation, which are presented in the next chapter.

Chapter 6

Energy Conservation: Cultural Sanctions and Individual Motives

If Foleyans are subject to multiple and continuous pressures to consume, limited only by their budgets, Munka Ljungbyans are subject to equally diffuse sanctions for moderation. Chief among these restraints are a pervasive moralism and *lagom*, the Swedish principle of moderation, coupled with demands for conformity of good citizens and members of society in all aspects of life. In addition, personal bonds with nature and concern for the environment, stronger in Munka than in Foley, foster conservative attitudes. In both communities, residents who came from farming families share a dislike of waste of any kind; in Foley a fairly widespread conserving orientation can be traced to the 1930s depression.

Economics proved to be the strongest motive for energy saving in both Foley and Munka Ljungby. In the 1990s, core households were asked why they thought people in their town conserved energy and then were asked to rank the conservation motives of money, energy supplies, and environment. Money ranked first in Foley, with energy supplies and environment tied for second place. In Munka, money was also first, followed by environment, with energy supplies a distant third. The low ranking of energy supplies by Munka Ljungbyans reflects greater faith placed by Munka Ljungbyans in technology and their awareness of ongoing experiments with alternative fuels, whereas Foleyans are still shaken by events of the 1970s and fear future shortages.

ECONOMIC MOTIVES TO CONSERVE

Saving money was reported as the chief motive for conserving energy in both Foley and Munka Ljungby through time. In the 1980s, Foleyans worked to reduce fuel bills, but by the 1990s they had grown accustomed to the prices that had shocked them earlier. They did not focus on fuel costs, but rather emphasized using the money they would save through energy conservation for other things. In contrast, Munka Ljungbyans felt the steady rise of fuel prices during the 1990s, and several focused explicitly on cutting fuel bills in discussions.

Inflation and unemployment rates were high in the United States during the early 1980s, but they had decreased and did not concern most Foleyans in the 1990s. In Sweden, these problems eased through the second half of the 1980s only to return with greater force later on.

Foley households are much more vulnerable to economic hardship than their Swedish counterparts. Without such financial aids and securities as those afforded the Swedes by their welfare state, Foleyans felt directly the brunt of rising fuel costs beginning with the oil embargo. Furthermore, because these prices were unprecedented and the Middle East was unstable, uncertainties about the future added to their stress. So, even though Foleyans expressed rebellious and defiant attitudes, they engaged in conserving behaviors.

Foleyans' concerns centered on their own household budgets, whereas Munka Ljungbyans expressed the need to conserve oil in the interests of both the national and their personal economies. By the 1990s, however, Munka's primary emphasis was also on the personal. Quotations from 1990s Foley and Munka Ljungby reflect the importance of personal financial motives for conserving energy:

Most of our friends aren't trying to conserve. They say that there's no sense in conserving . . . until there is *financial* reason to conserve, of course! (Foley)

If you use less energy, you get more money in your pocket. Why else would you really want to do it? (Foley)

I'd like to say my motive for using less fuel is conserving resources, but it's not that. It's m-o-n-e-y. (Foley)

Why do we try to use less energy? Money. That's the way people are; they think of themselves first. (Munka)

Money. Energy is really very expensive. You can have a lot more fun for those crowns [saved through fuel conservation]. (Munka)

Economics can also forestall conservation, however. Americans move more frequently than Swedes, and Foleyans are more likely to calculate the length of payback for energy-saving improvements. Many conclude that some improvements, such as solar panels, are too expensive relative to the value of their homes. Likewise, the end of tax rebates marked the end of investing in alternatives for some Foleyans. Initial purchase cost stops others. As one Foleyan commented:

They [compact fluorescent bulbs] cost a *fortune*! Down the road you get paid back, but the initial investment, people can't afford. Same thing with high-efficiency furnaces.

Although budgetary limits are unarguable for some households, Foleyans' shock over the initial costs of energy-efficiency improvements and alternative systems sounds like their earlier resentment about having to pay more for oil-based fuels. Foleyans balk at using discretionary income—for which there are dozens of other, more exciting options—for energy-related purchases. They continue to regard cheap energy as an entitlement.

SOCIAL AND CULTURAL MOTIVES TO CONSERVE

Conformity, Moralism, and the Principle of *Lagom*

The conformity of citizens to state mandates is more easily achieved in Sweden than in America. This is largely due to the Swedish conviction that there is only one right position on every issue and to the confidence Swedes have in their government to identify that position because of its inclusive consultative process and goal of consensus, described earlier. In contrast, Foleyans have no such assurance, given the adversarial nature of their political system and the power of lobbyists. In 1980s Munka, solidarity in support of national concerns such as reducing oil dependence was frequently named as motivation for fuel conservation. In the 1990s, however, only one household named good citizenship as a motive. (Solidarity remained a declared motive for pro-environmental behavior, however, as will be seen in Chapter 7.)

Swedish society is imbued with a heavy moralism and an unremitting sense of failure and guilt. The films of Ingmar Bergman convey the inner conflicts of Swedes, people struggling between egoistic desires and moral dictates, feeling self-reproachful. As elaborated in Chapter 7, more Munka Ljungbyans than Foleyans believe that energy issues have moral dimensions. The Swedish imperatives originate not only from teachings of the state Lutheran Church (now greatly attenuated) but also from the humanitarian philosophy underpinning the welfare state. Because the Swedes have the sort of government to arrive at the "right" decisions, Swedes endow policy not only with political authority but also with moral weight. When the Swedish state began its energy conservation campaign in the mid-1970s, Munka Ljungbyans readily adopted the official stance. Moreover, they labeled wasting energy as *fult* (ugly, offensive). In contrast, Foleyans hold diverse political philosophies and varied opinions on moral issues. Energy use is regarded by most as a purely utilitarian concern without moral overtones.

Although solidarity as rationale for energy conservation may have declined, the principle of moderation (*lagom*) remains a strong force. The *lagom* concept pervades Swedish life, buttressing social ethics. Translatable as "just right," "moderate," or "appropriate," this yardstick has a variety of applications. It can be used with regard to the properties of objects: *lagom sött* (just sweet enough) or *lagom bred* (just wide enough), for example. *Lagom* is also used in conjunction with personal characteristics (such as friendliness) and social or aesthetic atmospheres (festive, elegant). *Lagom* provides parameters within which Swedes should operate in order to satisfy the social and moral requisites described here. It connotes both a quantity and a moral judgment on that quantity (Ruth 1984). Individual desires and impulses are brought into conformity with the common spirit, for the common good. Energy and resource use is tempered by *lagom* in delimiting one's fair share. This restraint prevents any "tragedy of the commons" (Hardin 1968) from taking place in Sweden. Avoidance of excess is judged desirable in all areas of Swedish life in order to maintain social harmony. Consideration for others is expected, and Swedes carefully avoid encroaching on others and thereby eliciting criticism. The preservation of tranquil environments is also a concern, reflected in a newspaper article berating noisy lawn mowers and electrical tools in general as "excessive, since they disrupt peaceful neighborhoods" (*Sydsvenska Dagbladet* 1982).

No guiding principle like *lagom* is found in Foley. Foleyans' definitions of waste or excess were always highly relative and identification of instances of excessive consumption tentative and apologetic. Foleyans admit to being more wasteful of energy than they would "like" to be but contrast their consumption favorably with others in America. Munka Ljungbyans claim to use just as much energy as they "needed" to live—and because their way of life is within so-cially-approved bounds, who can fault them?

Two institutions represent contrasting approaches to consumption: the American "all-you-can-eat" restaurant and the Swedish coffee party (*kafferep*). At the latter, a festive atmosphere is created with special tableware, napkins, and flowers. Foods accompanying the coffee are rich, usually a variety of pastries and cookies. Each guest, however, takes only one of each type of baked goods offered. (This assurance of conformity simplified planning and saved the budget when I hosted thank-you parties for Munka core household members!) Such restraint contrasts with the multiple trips to laden buffet tables in the all-you-can-eat restaurant, where the goal for many is eating to the point of pain. Even private celebrations emphasize quantity, and rather aggressively offered, as one Foley host showed in reflections on a party:

When I invite people over, it's done *right*. . . . We had a huge party, and we *champagned* everybody! Tons of food, and tons of leftovers, but everybody still talks about it. God, what a time!

The Instinct of Workmanship

Conspicuous consumption is easily recognizable in each community, but Veblen's countervailing force, the "instinct of workmanship," is also in opera-tion, if less overtly. This instinct generates the desire to create or construct, intrinsic valuing of work, and dislike of futility. Workmanship is a conserving force, venerating human efforts, and is antithetical to wasted efforts or materials. Both Foley and Munka informants testified to the joy of creation and the intrinsic satisfaction of work. From Foley came such comments as the follow-ing:

I like to cut wood by hand . . . to feel the power of my own hands . . . to get a job well done, and know *I* did it.

I much prefer baking "from scratch" than buying it or making from mixes. It's more satisfying, somehow. I really can't explain it.

Munka Ljungbyans pronounced it beautiful (*skönt*) to make something by hand or to dig up one's own potatoes. Much of what decorated and serviced Munka homes is handmade. Munka women have multiple craft skills, most commonly weaving, knitting, embroidery, and crocheting. Baking is an integral part of Swedish home life as well. Foley women are less versatile and tended to produce purely ornamental and craft items, with the exception of the minority who sew clothing. However, Foley men in the core households are more involved than their Munka counterparts with home repair and remodeling projects.

Dislike of Waste

Waste is defined in both Foley and Munka Ljungby as unnecessary consumption. It is equated with use in excess of what is needed and is labeled careless, poorly planned, and goal-less. Socially-infused definitions of waste predominate over economically- or ecologically-oriented definitions in both communities.

In Foley, veterans of the 1930s depression had passed on their conserving attitudes to their children. References to the depression were common in Foley interviews but rare in Munka. The depression more directly threatened survival in America, for social security was already established in Sweden at that time and the ethos of solidarity was strong. Also, Swedes were familiar with hardship, having experienced famine just a few decades earlier. But the depression came as a shock to people in America, the land of plenty.

Although all informants reacted negatively toward the idea of waste, they also consider it to be inevitable, pervasive, and relative. The following quotations reflect this resignation:

No one is free from waste. It's just all over. Everyone wastes power and stuff. You can't get away from it. (Foley)

It's human to waste . . . to have a little pleasure. One must allow oneself to be careless, occasionally. (Munka)

Part of the pervasiveness of waste, informants said, is due to a lack of awareness. Waste of energy was described by one Munka informant as unnecessary use of energy out of force of habit rather than by conscious choice. As one Foleyan stated, "I think we all waste our share, one way or another, without really intending to. You think back later, 'Well, *boy* . . . .'" Lack of thought was associated with lack of care by several Munka Ljungbyans, one of whom cited the failure of owners to maintain possessions properly, thereby needing to acquire new ones, as a prime example of waste.

Many informants in both communities called unnecessary use of energy wasteful. Yet, most commented as well on how fast luxury or convenience items or habits became necessities. And when asked to cite examples of wasteful behavior, either their own or others', Foleyans were reluctant and retreated into statements about the relativity of waste. After it was made clear that such identification would not imply heavy value judgments, Foley informants could begin, but typically prefaced examples with "Well, it's only because I'm so conservative that . . ." or "Maybe I'm cheap, but . . . ." Even extreme examples were qualified, as illustrated by two accounts from Foley. One informant said that her neighbor:

Just can't sit still. It's back and forth with the car all day long. He even takes his dog for a car ride. Of course, it [driving constantly] must serve some purpose for him.

Another Foleyan told of nearby ranchers who heated their horses' water troughs in winter. She concluded, "But isn't that affluence, rather than waste? Who's to say?"

The feeling in Munka that people occasionally need some recreation and luxury (and inevitably waste in the process) exists in Foley also. In a syllogism of legitimization, Foleyans stated that energy used towards these ends was therefore not wasted, because human needs were being met. Tolerance for idiosyncrasy also exempts certain behaviors from being labeled wasteful. One Foley woman declared, "Some people vacuum every day. I call that waste, but some people can't live with dirt."

Fewer Munka Ljungbyans than Foleyans hesitated to identify wasteful practices. Those cited most frequently in the 1980s were pleasure driving, airing out houses by opening doors or windows without adjusting radiators, and lighting unused rooms. In the 1990s, airing out and lighting were joined by streetlights, idling parked cars, and driving on errands within the village. Also, Munka Ljungbyans began to speak of material items in this context—items such as packaging, appliances (frequently, clothesdryers and electric toothbrushes), and convenience items (pre-prepared food and disposable utensils). Not recycling was also said to be wasteful. Although some of these examples reflect environmental more than energy concerns, it is as one Munka Ljungbyan said: "Take care of excessive packaging and you save both energy and the environment." Informants expressed disapproval of disposable mugs and utensils in particular and their increasingly *slit-och-släng* society in general. "Sweden doesn't repair any more so much as throw away," lamented one resident.

In Munka more than in Foley, informants exempted acts involving small quantities of resources from wastefulness. One Munka woman, commenting on her use of hot running water to clean a few pans, declared "It's so small, you can't really call that waste." Other Munka Ljungbyans cited power mowers or trips to Ängelholm as demanding so little energy that they could never be considered wasteful. However, Munka Ljungbyans are also more likely to link waste and social responsibility, illustrated by the following quotations:

If you're aware that something is limited but you continue to use it, that's waste . . . true irresponsibility.

I think it's waste if you use more than you need of something, even if there's plenty. The size of your fair share is not unlimited: Waste is spoiling for others.

Although most Foleyans and Munka Ljungbyans said that waste occurred even when the commodity being wasted is plentiful, a minority stated that waste applies only when resources are scarce. One Munka informant declared, "If there's a *shortage* of water, then it's waste to let it run, to water your lawn, or to wash dishes under running water."

Most informants decried waste, but few take the initiative to reduce waste in their own lives. They apologize for and express guilt over their inertia in overcoming habit and their preference for convenience but make no changes. Is waste censured by Foleyans and Munka Ljungbyans because it represents inefficiency, pricking at either bourgeois standards of productivity or at the instinct of workmanship posited by Veblen? Or is there some intrinsic moral or ecological precept that waste transgresses? These questions cannot be explored here, but they are interesting areas for future research.

In contrast to relativistic discussion of wasting other commodities, the idea of wasting food triggered strong and absolute negative responses, infused with moral overtones. No informant hesitated to condemn or to give examples of this practice. If the moral weight ascribed to the waste of food could be transferred to the waste of fuel and other resources, the consequences for conservation would be enormous. Much of the greater negative impact of wasted food stems from its immediacy, of course. One must act to dispose of unused food. Food can be seen going to waste, and spoiled food is offensive, unlike invisible fuels. Further, food is regarded as a universal human need, transferable to foreign contexts in the minds of informants. The following quotations reflect these dichotomies:

Fuel is worse to waste than food—Something can always eat food. (Munka)

Nobody *dies* from lack of electricity! When I was a kid, I was taught not to waste food, that people were starving in other lands. But no one said, "If you light two lamps, someone can't light one in Africa." (Munka)

Waste of energy is "unreal," not like a person *starving*. (Foley)

ENVIRONMENTAL MOTIVES TO CONSERVE

Influence of Farming Heritage

Informants from core households in both Foley (five) and Munka (three) attributed their conservative bent to ties to the environment originating in their agricultural backgrounds. They sadly predicted the demise of this legacy of awareness and appreciation. Foleyans related:

You grow up being aware of your surroundings when you are on a farm, even if you take them for granted when you are young. Crop farming makes you appreciate the need for soil conservation, because of crop rotation . . . but also makes for stronger ties to the earth.

We're definitely going to lose this conservative, agricultural heritage. The younger generation don't know what conserve really *means*—They just know what's in the media. Now they have external controls, not internal ones.

People are not thankful for what they have. There's no grace before dinner, now. In the forties and fifties, more people worked in farms, factories . . . were more involved in production. We're far removed from that part of it now.

Munka Ljungbyans said:

I came from a family interested in nature, out in the country. It gives you a different outlook on the world, and your place in it, I think: more humble, more careful.

I was born and grew up in the country, where you don't waste. We raised our own animals. You don't raise hens, take their eggs, see where it all comes from, and then *waste*. You just can't do it. Those who live in town or have money don't have the same feeling. Our kids are different—they toss what they don't eat!

Farming mores against waste have both economic and environmental dimensions. The farm and the household together comprise a family enterprise, adversely affected by any kind of waste. Respect for the environment as a source of food and appreciation of natural surroundings would also inhibit wasteful practices. As a farm-based community, Foley has long acknowledged the need for soil and water conservation. However, Foleyans rarely recognize agriculture's high dependence on fossil fuels (and therefore could state that Foley was not very vulnerable to energy shortages, as recounted in Chapter 4) or the environmental impacts of fuel production. Not all farmers show ingrained respect for the environment, of course. Only families residing in town were included in this study, but children of Foley farmers told of the earlier practices of plowing under old machinery and disposing of oil or pesticides by dumping them in fields.

In the 1980s few Foleyans expressed concern over the consequences of fossil fuel exploitation. While a very few said that they expected a depletion of local wood supplies due to increased household wood-burning, no one spoke of resultant atmospheric pollution. As described in Chapter 4, most Foleyans did not articulate a sense of ecosystem at the local, regional, or global level—any more than they conveyed awareness of larger political dynamics. Hence, environmental concern exerted little influence on household fuel consumption in Foley. In Munka at that time, thought was not so compartmentalized. Rather, greater fluidity existed there among the entities of food, fuel, money, and natural resources.

Swedish Bonds with Nature

Jamison and his co-authors (1990) describe Sweden's long traditions of communing with nature. Because Sweden was transformed from a rural to an industrial society within one generation, they surmise that returning to nature served an important function for newly-urbanized Swedes. Earlier, Sweden saw itself as a province of Europe and regarded Paris and Berlin as culture arbiters. Sweden still has a nature, and not an urban, orientation and culture, these authors conclude.

Orvar Löfgren (1992) argues that the often cited Swedish "love" of nature developed fairly recently as an antidote to industrialization and urbanity—nature representing the authentic and unaffected, in contrast to the artificial and commercialized. Frykman and Löfgren (1987) describe the sentimentalization of nature that took place as Swedish bourgeois culture emerged. Löfgren (1994) declares that the Swedish right of common access to land (*allemänsrätt*) has nothing to do with love of nature but rather was medieval common law in a sparsely populated country with common rights to outfields. However, he agrees (1994) that this legal heritage helped to shape a deep appreciation of natural surroundings among the Swedes.

The stereotype of Swedes as closer to nature than Americans was affirmed to me during fieldwork in various ways. Nature articles and programs saturated newspapers, magazines, and radio and TV programming. Signs of spring were celebrated on radio programs and on the front page of the Ängelholm newspaper. They also featured in conversations, both among customers in the Munka grocery and among academics during coffee breaks at Lund University. Names are another dimension of Swedish culture infused with nature. Many Swedish surnames are composed of words for natural entities: *Björk* (birch) and *Lind* (linden), for example—and such suffixes as *gren* (branch), *berg* (mountain), *holm* (island), and *dal* (valley).

A favorite activity of Munka Ljungbyans is to be out in nature, hiking, cycling, fishing, mushroom- or berry-picking, swimming, or simply savoring the woods. Bicycle or hiking tours are popular ways to spend vacations. Such contact with the environment is more than merely a pastime or a recreation for most Swedes. It seems intrinsic to their sense of place, self, and well-being. These ties create and maintain respect for the inherent worth of natural elements, as well as the obligation to care for them, as typical quotations from Munka reveal:

If you see and appreciate the beauty, you take care not to destroy it.

All has its place and its rights, in the balance of nature. Money certainly can't dominate or control *everything*!

Concern for the environment also factors into Munka Ljungbyans' consideration of energy alternatives to oil. A primary criterion in both the 1980s and the 1990s was how clean or environmentally friendly (*miljövänlig*) a fuel is.

Proponents of nuclear power cited cleanliness and nondisruption of the environment as arguments for its continuation.

In the 1980s personal bonds with and feelings of moral responsibility for the environment and government campaigns designed to stimulate such awareness combined to make environmental concern a much stronger motive for energy conservation in Munka Ljungby than in Foley. In the 1990s government energy conservation campaigns are gone, but deep-seated environmental ties remain. Munka Ljungbyans have shifted their focus from conserving fuel to preserving the environment, as is shown in the next chapter.

Chapter 7

The New Environmental Focus

THE SHIFT FROM ENERGY TO ENVIRONMENT

By the 1990s environmental concerns had displaced energy concerns in both the United States and Sweden. Even though environmental awareness has expanded greatly in America over the last decade, Swedes continue their lead. With typical Swedish rigor about research and dissemination of information, pervasive government messages in the media heighten popular awareness of the need to care for the environment. Newspapers are filled with environmental stories and ads. An environmental motif tinges public space as well: Large posters at bus stops instruct proper battery disposal methods, and billboards on train platforms tout the environmental advantages of train travel. In 1980s Sweden, an upstanding citizen (*ordentlig medborgare*) was one who conserved energy. Now, it is doing your part for a cleaner environment "for all Munka Ljungby— actually, for the whole world," as one Munka informant expressed it.

Kommuner and the Natural Step organization position environmental information specialists in grocery stores. After training courses, these specialists advise customers on which products are most desirable from an environmental viewpoint—products like laundry and dish detergents, various cleaning agents, shampoos, and paper goods. They also hand out brochures offering brand-name guidance. One Swedish grocery store chain, ICA, provides "green lists" of least-damaging products for its customers. In some ICA and other Swedish grocery stores, environmentally friendly (*miljövänlig*) products are grouped under a banner on certain shelves, with less-friendly products on others! Lead batteries are now sold with an added environmental fee of 40 SEK ($6) each. For several years, merchants have been obliged to accept used batteries.

A quotation from Munka Ljungby reflects the shift from energy to environment and heightened awareness resulting from saturation with information:

In the eighties, we got daily propaganda, all about energy. Now, it's the environment we are faced with at every turn. We are *drowning* in information!

Environmental awareness is said to be taken to an extreme by a few individuals, however. The phrase "environmental fanatic" is not uncommon in Munka, applied to people who structured all aspects of their lives based on environmental considerations. Informants told of one woman who became so environmentally oriented that it was a plague (*pest*) to have anything to do with her, as she was always challenging others' habits as being environmentally damaging. It is said that she was divorced because of her environmental obsession!

PERCEIVED ENERGY-ENVIRONMENT LINKS

Core households were asked, "What connections do you see between energy and the environment?" In 1980s Foley, most households were unable to describe *any* energy-environment links, although four expressed concern over air pollution created by fossil fuel use and over depletion of local wood supplies by increasing numbers of wood-burning households. In contrast, all Munka households at that time cited various types of environmental damage caused by energy use and placed their examples in broader contexts than Foleyans did. By the 1990s all but three Foley core households could describe some environmental consequences of energy consumption, and a few conveyed a systemic perspective as well. Every Munka household at that time cited a variety of energy-environment interactions. However, despite the broader perspective Munka Ljungbyans maintain, they do not relate their personal energy use choices and behavior to environmental problems. Harold Wilhite and his colleagues (1996) found similar dislocation of personal activities from larger problems among Norwegians and Japanese.

Foleyans themselves describe their energy-environment awareness as recent and limited. Much of the concern they express is of a utilitarian nature, that environmental damage will result in problems of energy acquisition and problems for energy users. Those seeing the larger picture stress that others do not:

If we overdo on the environment, we lose out on energy supplies.

I don't think most people realize that it's all connected. We're going to have to deal with this [environmental damage] later in life. People don't think about the fact that it's a closed system. Once you ruin it, unless something is done in research, we'll never get it back.

Seven Foley core households provided more-general statements about energy use and its effects: that any type of fuel is damaging to the environment in its procurement and combustion, and in consequent problematic waste. Illustrating this broader outlook:

Any time you use energy you hurt the environment . . . even nuclear energy. Burn coal, and you got to mine coal. Burn wood, and you're cutting down trees. It's cause-and-effect. There's not a truly clean source of energy. Well, maybe solar. We need research to see if it is enough to run industries.

We'll be in disharmony with each other until we clean up the fuels and figure out how to mine without doing *too* much damage. . . . Fuel use destroys the environment, causes smog. Major environmental problems are not here now, but possibly in the future.

Production and use of energy creates heat. The Sherco coal plants add pollution, despite their scrubbers. And nuclear plants: what to do with their waste? Any combustion produces waste materials and acid rain.

Foley informants confuse the greenhouse effect and ozone depletion. A few are skeptical about the reality of these phenomena or their link to human activity.

Just as Foleyans displace the causes of environmental damage and pollution to industry, they also place the locus of any such problems far away from Foley. They refer to environmental problems in distant locales, such as the destruction of South American rain forests, threatened whales, and Los Angeles smog. Foleyans perceive their area to be unaffected by environmental pollution:

Gasoline pollutes, but in the Foley area, air pollution disperses.

It's tougher for us to understand this because we still breathe clean air. The kids hear about "toxic"—but don't get the connection to their own lives.

However, Foleyans cited as well a few indicators of regional environmental damage—for example, warnings that pregnant women should not eat fish from Minnesota lakes more than once a week because of high mercury content.

Munka Ljungbyans were overwhelmed by the energy-environment question during the 1990s research because they see so *many* connections. Responses encompass pollution of various sorts, global warming, depletion of the ozone layer, increased allergies and health problems, and harm to other species. That the Munka outlook is more sophisticated than that in Foley, revealing greater awareness of pervasive and subtle dynamics, is shown by these quotations:

The more energy one uses, the more pollution results: of the forest, air, and water. It's pervasive. The less energy you use, the better it is for the environment. Right now, we are doing uncontrolled damage everywhere.

Critical are auto emissions and the burning of oil. Factories burning their fuels do damage, of course, but so do motorists—and even the pleasure cruises along Finland's coast leave poisons which kill the birds.

No matter what fuel you choose, carbon dioxide is given off. You can't be really sure what the effects are. Even some alternative form of energy won't solve our environmental problems if we have a society like this, just consuming and consuming.

Some confusion and doubt about environmental problems exist in Munka as well as in Foley, however. Although no core household expressed skepticism about the reality of a hole in the ozone layer, many confessed bewilderment about it. Additionally, one Munka couple related that they had read in the newspaper that there was just as much sulfur in the atmosphere "long ago, that environmental damage has always gone on. You don't really know who to believe."

Munka, though it shares global concerns, also faces more-immediate problems. Northern Sweden received radioactive fallout from the Chernobyl accident of 1986, and Swedes are aware of proscriptions on reindeer meat and northern milk, mushrooms, and berries. Likewise, many Swedes have seen in their beloved forests what they believe to be the consequences of acid rain or auto emissions and are aware of salmon dying in the Baltic, believed due to pollution.

MORAL ASPECTS OF ENERGY AND ENVIRONMENT

In the 1980s more than twice as many Munka Ljungby as Foley core households responded positively to the question, "Do you think that energy use has moral or ethical dimensions?" Thirteen Foley and four Munka households were puzzled by the question and could not address it. Of these, some Foleyans responded with "No comment," implying that discussions of ethics are sticky and better avoided. Munka Ljungbyans interpret the moral dimensions of energy use in a variety of ways. Their responses encompass responsibilities to the environment, to future generations, and to other peoples.

Yes. Oil burning is destructive to the environment. We have a moral responsibility to our surroundings, to nature.

The energy resources could end with our generation. And what will the next do then, those poor things?

Absolutely. Globally, we have to think of our brothers. Even if we are stingy, we still squander compared to other lands. If I waste, it hurts us all.

Although most Foleyans in the 1980s did not identify a moral dimension to energy use, two households stressed the stewardship of resources, which they feel to be an ethical responsibility. Foleyans speak of responsibility to future generations rather than nature protection. For example:

Yes. The misuse of energy, or waste, could endanger future generations. They wouldn't have enough resources to keep them alive.

By the 1990s more core households in each community affirmed moral or ethical dimensions of energy use: three quarters in Foley (up from one third earlier) and all but three in Munka (up from two thirds earlier). The stewardship theme expanded in Foley, along with expressions of concern for future generations, typified by these quotations:

Yes. We are only here for a short time. We should try that our effects won't last for eons and eons. We're God's caretakers—and doing a *lousy* job, too!

Yes, we have a responsibility to the earth. Natural resources are a gift [from God], not to be wasted. We have a responsibility to others coming after us also.

Energy use only has moral dimensions if you feel we have any obligation to future generations. It isn't ethical to eat the whole pie. It used to be immoral *not* to develop this country. Now it's our moral duty to save old growth forests and the rain forests.

One Foleyan spoke of resistance to the behavioral changes implied by the acknowledgment of existing environmental problems:

Yes, we have a moral responsibility to help take care of the world and to not do things to it that are not recoverable. . . . In the past, we were ignorant about the consequences of our activities. Now, people resist changing their activities, so they deny that there really are problems, and therefore don't have to make a moral decision on it. You have to, if you realize that everything is based on everything else.

This realization that "everything is based on everything else" and its moral corollaries is a rare perspective in Foley, and though expressed more frequently in Munka, it is not the dominant view there either. Ethics was a common theme of environmental discussions with informants in Munka Ljungby, where it is believed that it is ethical to be a good citizen, following government directives and considering others. In Sweden these ethics are based on humanism rather than religion. As reflected in the following statements, Munka Ljungbyans recognize the complexity and intrinsic value of nature, deeming its care a human responsibility. Munka Ljungbyans also say it would be wrong to destroy nature, because it is enjoyed by so many, and they refer to ethical obligations to future generations and (unlike Foley) to others on the globe as well.

Nature has been here forever. Every element in nature has worth in itself. It is our ethical responsibility to recognize and respect that.

We don't know what consequences will result from losing a species. We don't know what runs the whole system, keeps it in balance. It is *awful* that we hurt nature and pollute the air.

It's wrong to destroy the environment with pollution from energy use. Everyone wants to go out in the forest, to go fishing . . . to breathe clean, fresh air.

Yes, the ethical dimensions involve the next generation. . . . Most of all, nuclear waste. How can we build up something that we cannot handle, when it can be *lethal*?

ENVIRONMENT VERSUS ECONOMICS

In the 1990s a few Foleyans worried about their government's constricted view in choosing economics over environment:

Our government should see things a little broader than just money, or they'll regret it later.

If you have a good economy and you're ruining the world, I don't know about that either.

Munka Ljungbyans also expressed frustration with the increasingly high priority given economic considerations in their society, reflected in their responses to the 1990s questionnaire statement "Economic growth should be more important than environmental protection." An overwhelming majority disagreed with this statement in both Munka (89%) and Foley (92%). These findings corroborate a trend identified by large-scale surveys: the affirmation of environment over economics. OECD polls in industrial consumer societies show that in 1991 more than half of those surveyed preferred protecting environmental quality over economic growth (cited in Durning 1992). Cambridge reports show that in 1990, 64 percent of Americans surveyed said they would choose to sacrifice economic growth in order to protect the environment (cited in Kempton, Boster, and Hartley 1995). And in a 1992 Danish study, 77 percent of respondents said that environmental considerations are more important than economic growth (reported in Nørgård 1993).

Sweden has a universal carbon tax. Foleyans were asked in their questionnaire, "What do you think about the energy tax on all fuels proposed earlier, the Btu tax?" A very strong majority (82%) of respondents disagreed with such a tax. Distrusting government, they voice skepticism over whether tax moneys actually would be used as promised for environmental betterment. Foleyans were also asked what they thought of the 4.3-cent-per-gallon gasoline tax. A majority of respondents also disagreed with this tax, although a smaller proportion (64%). Their chief objection is that such a tax is unfair to truckers and others whose livelihoods depend on gasoline.

Dislocating their lives from larger trends, respondents in both Foley and Munka affirm the sacrifice of economic growth for environmental protection, but they also imply that such sacrifices have nothing to do with them personally. A few Foleyans and Munka Ljungbyans described environmental concern as a luxury of the well-off. Further, no core household in either community identified capitalism or consumerism as underlying the predominance of economics over environment. Personal economics versus environment trade-offs were stated plainly during discussions of environmentally friendly products in Munka. One couple said that if it were a choice between a discount product and an environmentally friendly product, they would "always take the cheaper, which is worse for the environment." A few Munka informants expressed frustration that environmentally friendly detergents cost more than others.

ENGAGEMENT IN PRO-ENVIRONMENTAL ACTIVITIES

Human geographer P. O. Hallin visited Foley and Munka Ljungby during my fieldwork period in the 1990s to compare environmental concern and pro-environmental behavior. His questions about informants' engagement in specific pro-environmental activities appeared on my Foley and Munka energy questionnaires, and Hallin has given me permission to present responses to these questions here. Whereas I asked core households about energy-environment connections already in the 1980s, later collaboration with Hallin led to my participation in interviews with households additional to the core groups and with key informants from environmental fields.

On the basis of questionnaire self-report, Munka Ljungbyans can be said to be more environmentally active than Foleyans. They regularly recycle more commodities and are more likely to compost yard and kitchen waste. Munka Ljungbyans are also less likely to use chemical pesticides, are more likely to walk or bicycle on in-town trips, and are more likely to bring their own shopping bags to grocery stores.

Interestingly, Hallin found no statistically significant correlation between environmental concern and pro-environmental behavior. However, he did find that environmental actors in both locations emphasize the ethics of natural resource use and are motivated by altruism. In contrast, nonconservers do not recognize ethical aspects of natural resource use. Although they criticize "throwaway society," their criticism is largely couched in monetary considerations and not in waste of natural resources (Hallin 1995b).

Recycling

Both Foley and Munka Ljungby are situated in areas that lead in recycling participation. Minnesota is the top state in the country in recycling solid waste (38%) and in number of yard waste composting programs (*Minnesota Monthly* 1995). And of all *kommuner* in 1993, Ängelholm had the second-highest level of participation in paper recycling (ÄRAB). Whereas only 5 percent of packaging was recycled in Sweden in 1994, the government has set the ambitious goal of 70 percent for 1997. Additionally, packaging is to be cut in half by the year 2000. Following Germany's example, Sweden in 1994 adopted measures aimed at reducing packaging materials. These laws stipulate that manufacturers must collect and reuse or recycle most packaging materials, including cardboard, paper, plastic, glass, and metal. *Kommuner* are no longer responsible for collecting packaging from households. Further, these regulations include newspapers, magazines, catalogs, and direct advertising. In 1994 packaging could be left by customers at some grocery stores in Malmö and Lund and was collected in big cartons to illustrate unnecessary packaging. Consumer pressure in the United States has led to packaging reduction in certain instances, such as fast-food containers, cardboard deodorant boxes, and compact disc boxes.

Although Foley consumers complain heartily about "excessive packaging," no comprehensive packaging control legislation has been enacted in America.

Recycling Opportunities

Recycling is currently the pro-environmental topic and activity of choice in both Foley and Munka, and many informants brought up recycling at the mention of energy or environment during 1990s interviews. In the 1980s both Foleyans and Munka Ljungbyans claimed to be one step away from active recycling: Foleyans said that if they did not have to take their recyclables into St. Cloud, they would recycle; Munka Ljungbyans said if they did not have to take theirs to the center of Munka, they would recycle. Munka Ljungbyans currently have a more supportive infrastructure for recycling, and a program accepting a wider range of commodities. In 1988 Ängelholm's *kommun* established a recycling program offering both curbside pickup and a drop-off center in Ängelholm. A private company, ÄRAB (*Ängelholms Renhållnings AB*), contracts for operation of both these services. Curbside pickup in 1994 included magazines and newspapers monthly, and yard waste twice monthly in season, when residents display their *källsorterat* (source-separated) sign. Household goods can also be indicated for pickup. ÄRAB distributes free calendars highlighting pickup schedules and procedures to all households.

Most glass bottles and aluminum cans have deposits and can be returned to grocery and liquor stores for redemption. A deposit of four crowns (60 cents) is also returned on bottles of PET (hard) plastic. Containers for batteries are prominent in grocery stores. Hazardous waste may be dropped off at the Munka gas station or at nine other locations within the *kommun*. Paper and glass collection sites have been retained in Munka's center as well. At the recycling center, residents can leave all commonly recycled commodities (such as glass, paper, cardboard, and aluminum foil), and also polyethylene (soft) plastic, household hazardous waste, batteries, fluorescent lights, styrofoam, electronics, clothing and shoes, lumber scraps, and yard waste. No hard plastic or tin cans are accepted, however. Recycling center personnel said that the plastics are too complicated to separate, even if their burning leads to emissions. Likewise, some tin cans have lead in their welding, which is considered too expensive to separate out. Patrons receive no money for any of the commodities they leave, and pay a fee for leaving leftover building materials. ÄRAB also sells composters at subsidized prices at the center. One can buy composted soil and get tips on composting from an expert on duty there as well.

In Foley a rural cooperative established a recycling center in town in the mid 1980s. Residents say they are dissatisfied with this center because they have to pay fees to drop off commodities for which they earlier received compensation. The exception is aluminum, which still brings cash. Bimonthly curbside pickup run by the City of Foley was introduced in April of 1994, and residents are billed a nominal monthly charge on their water bills to cover program costs. In 1995 city officials reported a participation rate of 75 percent, with an additional estimated 5 percent doing independent recycling at facilities paying them for commodities. As in Munka, recycling reduces garbage volume and thus hauling fees for households. In the early 1990s, recycling bins for paper, glass, and cans appeared in Foley schools and in government buildings. The Foley grocery has a container for recycling plastic grocery bags but none for batteries, about which there was much less propaganda than in Munka.

The City of Foley operates a yard waste collection center and composting site, established in 1991 after a new state law excluded yard waste from landfills. The center is located a few miles southeast of Foley. Foleyans have access to a household hazardous waste drop-off center in St. Cloud, operated by the Tri-County Solid Waste Management Commission. Additionally, Foley runs an annual Clean-Up Day in which household goods to be discarded and household waste, including hazardous waste, are picked up at residents' homes. A Tri-County Commission planner stressed the importance of economic factors in recycling participation:

People want to do the right thing for the environment. That'll motivate a certain segment of the population. But not all. Recycling programs around here are driven by economic concerns more than environmental concerns. . . . And people have this perception that their garbage is valuable to somebody else [and therefore should be paid something for it].

He related that recycling participation in St. Cloud doubled after the city began charging by the bag for garbage removal ($3), but added, "It's still relatively cheap to throw things away here," because increased tipping fees have not been passed on to residents. Providing recycling bins also increases participation, because they act as reminders of recycling days and generate peer pressure among neighbors.

Recycling Participation

Given these differences in recycling structure, how do levels of recycling participation in Foley and Munka compare? Table 7.1 displays participation frequencies for various commodities reported by questionnaire samples. The most striking differences are found in paper and glass recycling. Of questionnaire respondents, roughly 80 percent in Munka reported that they always recycle these commodities, while only half as many in Foley always do. Further, only 1 percent of Munka respondents never recycle paper or glass, compared to a respective 22 percent and 21 percent in Foley who never do so.

The percentage of Foleyans always recycling aluminum rises to 75 percent, nearing Munka's 83 percent participation and reflecting the strong incentive that payment represents. (Munka Ljungbyans return aluminum cans to stores to recoup deposits of about 8 cents per can; they are not paid for aluminum by the recycling center.) The same percentages in each community occasionally, seldom, or never recycle aluminum.

Foleyans recycle plastic more often than Munka Ljungbyans: 34 percent always do so, compared to 21 percent in Munka. Also, 38 percent never recycle plastic in Munka, compared to 23 percent in Foley. (As reported earlier, the Ängelholm recycling center takes only soft plastic.)

Why don't people recycle? According to a Minnesota Extension Service Educator in Foley, the most frequent reason given is that recycling is messy. Informants also said that the "hassle" of sorting commodities and having to handle bulky bundles and bags discourages participation. No time to spend on recycling was a common response, though one informant added, "But I'm sure if it [a landfill] was in my back yard I'd *make* time to recycle." Most Foleyans who do not recycle stressed the inconvenience of making the trip to St. Cloud. The new curbside pickup has removed the travel barrier now, of course.

Although many more Munka Ljungbyans recycle, certain rumors there dampen motivation for some. These rumors include the idea that recycled glass goes to the garbage dump if the *kommun* cannot handle the volume, and that garbage pickup puts batteries and paper in with other trash ("So even if *you* do right, others do wrong."). Also, it is said that the *kommun* blends clear and colored glass ("after we've gone to all the trouble of sorting it") and that Sweden buys recycled paper from Germany because it is cheaper, while Swedish paper "just lies there."

Table 7.1
Recycling Participation
(Questionnaire Households, Foley and Munka Ljungby)
(Curbside in Munka Ljungby, but not in Foley)

	Always	Usually	Occasionally	Seldom	Never
PAPER					
Foley	40%	18%	11%	10%	22%
Munka	82%	13%	3%	1%	1%
GLASS					
Foley	38%	15%	16%	11%	21%
Munka	80%	15%	3%	1%	1%
ALUMINUM					
Foley	75%	15%	2%	2%	6%
Munka	83%	7%	2%	2%	6%
PLASTIC					
Foley	34%	13%	16%	14%	23%
Munka	21%	6%	18%	17%	38%
TIN					
Foley	41%	18%	9%	9%	23%
Munka*	–	–	–	–	–

*Tin recycling was not available in Ängelholm's *kommun*.
Top to bottom, Foley's Ns = 129, 128, 135, 128, 128,
Top to bottom, Munka's Ns = 141, 137, 130, 115, n.a.
Where percentages do not total 100, it is due to rounding.

Use of Chemical Pesticides

One third of Munka Ljungby's households reported that they never use chemical pesticides (strictly regulated in Sweden) on their lawns or in their gardens, but only 2 percent of Foley's households said that they never use them. More than one half of Foleyans seldom use such chemicals, however. (See Table 7.2.) Emphasis on lawns of pure green grass in Foley is enforced by social sanctions. As one Foley informant related, "I'm forced to use pesticides by my neighbors' concerns. Creeping Charlie is 'ugly weeds,' in their eyes." The expanses of unbroken green that surround Foley homes are not found in Munka; yet, Munka Ljungbyans are subject to social pressures to meet high standards for gardens, which they spend hours grooming. Further, two Munka Ljungbyans reported to me instances of neighbors "sneaking" water at night (during sprinkling bans) to get fine green grass. A chief obstacle to adopting this and other environmentally benign behavior is the lack of change by others, for this makes it difficult to break established standards and undermines feelings of effectiveness as well. As one Munka informant said, "It doesn't help that I do anything different if everyone else does the usual. . . . The others haven't changed, so why should I?"

Table 7.2
Use Chemical Pesticides
(Questionnaire Households, Foley and Munka Ljungby)

	Always	Usually	Occasionally	Seldom	Never
Foley (N=129)	3%	15%	26%	54%	2%
Munka (N=135)	2%	3%	17%	44%	33%

Composting Kitchen and Yard Waste

Munka Ljungbyans are more likely than Foleyans to always compost yard waste or kitchen waste. They are also less likely to never compost: whereas nearly two thirds of Foley households never compost kitchen waste, only about one half of Munka households never do so. (See Table 7.3.)

Table 7.3
Compost Kitchen Waste
(Questionnaire Households, Foley and Munka Ljungby)

	Always	Usually	Occasionally	Seldom	Never
Foley (N=113)	12%	6%	11%	9%	63%
Munka (N=118)	21%	11%	10%	9%	48%

That fully 37 percent of Foley households always or usually compost yard waste likely reflects the establishment of the composting center outside town. In the 1980s yard waste was placed in plastic bags for pickup by garbage haulers. However, it should be noted that 44 percent of Foley households never compost yard waste. (See Table 7.4.)

Table 7.4
Compost Yard Waste
(Questionnaire Households, Foley and Munka Ljungby)

	Always	Usually	Occasionally	Seldom	Never
Foley (N=127)	24%	13%	11%	8%	44%
Munka (N=144)	38%	15%	9%	8%	26%

More Munka Ljungbyans than Foleyans reported having kitchen composts. Unlike other American towns, there are no ordinances prohibiting composting in Foley; rather, the chief objections given by residents are the smell and messiness in handling food wastes. Swedes responded so positively to promotions of composting by their government that Holm and Thunberg (1993) declare, "Composting is practically a folk movement in Sweden." Munka Ljungbyans stated that it "feels good" to compost, and that composting also yields the bonus of good soil for gardens. Some cited the additional advantage of reduced garbage pickup fees. One household added, "It's just not because of money, but it also saves unnecessary labor. And you say to yourself, 'Bravo! Well done.' It's so easy. If all make their little contribution, then all added up it becomes a *lot*."

Walking or Bicycling on Local Errands

On the basis of interviews and fieldwork observations, Hallin and I believe that both populations inflated their reports on walking or bicycling instead of driving on in-town errands. Yet, twice as many Munka Ljungbyans as Foleyans said that they always walk or bike, and six times as many said that they never take their cars on short errands—reflecting pretty accurately the proportionate engagement in these practices in the two communities we observed. (See Table 7.5.)

Table 7.5
Walk or Bicycle on Errands of Less Than Half a Mile
(Questionnaire Households, Foley and Munka Ljungby)

	Always	Usually	Occasionally	Seldom	Never
Foley (N=133)	11%	27%	32%	17%	13%
Munka (N=142)	19%	30%	23%	15%	2%

Typical of Sweden, Munka has a well-developed bicycling tradition. Bike paths link various parts of the village, underpasses afford safety in crossing the highway, and motorists respect cyclists. Flocks of bicycles are parked outside the Munka post office, banks, and food store—and most are outfitted with baskets, which testifies to utilitarian service. Greater importance of bicycling in Munka is reflected in greater saturation of bicycles there compared to Foley. Whereas 35 percent of Foley households reported owning no bicycles for adults, less than 1 percent of Munka's sample own none. In Munka, walking is also well established as an intrinsically desirable activity. Pedestrians there are not subject to the social pressure to accept rides described earlier for Foley.

Greater emphasis on driving in Foley is reflected in greater vehicle saturation there. Sixty-five percent of the 1993 Foley questionnaire sample own more than one vehicle, compared to 39 percent in Munka Ljungby. Earlier a rarity in Munka, the two-car household constitutes 34 percent of its 1990s questionnaire sample; and the three-car household, 5 percent. Two-car households were common in Foley even in the 1980s; but in the 1990s more Foleyans own trucks and vans, significantly more fuel-intensive than cars. Forty-eight percent of the 1993 Foley questionnaire sample own two vehicles, 15 percent own three, and 2 percent own four. Of these multiple vehicles, nearly 40 percent are trucks, and 10 percent are vans.

Bringing Own Bag to Grocery Store

Nearly half of Munka respondents always or usually bring their own bags with them to shop for groceries, compared to only 11 percent of Foley respondents who do so. Three quarters of Foleyans, compared with nearly one quarter of Munka Ljungbyans, never bring their own bags along. (See Table 7.6.)

Table 7.6
Bring Own Bag to Grocery Store
(Questionnaire Households, Foley and Munka Ljungby)

	Always	Usually	Occasionally	Seldom	Never
Foley (N=132)	3%	8%	7%	7%	75%
Munka (N=140)	24%	24%	14%	15%	23%

Cloth bags with a supermarket logo are available for purchase in Munka and at one time were available in Foley. I saw one Foley shopper with such a bag but found none on display for sale. I asked the store manager if they had sold out. He answered, "Nope, they sat there for a year, and we sold, what, *two*? So we got rid of 'em." Cloth bags cost the equivalent of $1.50 in Sweden, compared to twice that in Foley. Yet, $3.00 is not a steep price—and a nickel is subtracted from the bill with each use. Why is there this marked difference? Paper and plastic bags each cost a crown (about 15 cents) in Munka area grocery stores, but this is not sufficient incentive for all to bring their own bags, of course. Both paper and plastic bags are free in Foley.

Inertia clearly overpowers change of habit regarding bags. Having grocery bags provided to Foleyans is so automatic that it is out of awareness. Even those few Foleyans who own cloth bags said, "I always forget to bring them." Also, new bags are praised as being "clean" and "crisp," satisfying America's emphasis on the new—a theme addressed in Chapter 8. Interestingly, no one in either Foley or Munka mentioned using their own bags when shopping at other than grocery stores.

Paper versus Plastic

Because both paper and plastic bags are the products of energy-intensive and environmentally harmful industries, it is best to use bags of durable cloth made from natural materials. Petroleum-based plastic shopping bags, for which recycling options have recently been introduced, are still most likely to be filled with garbage and burned or deposited in landfills. The paper-versus-plastic issue is complex. Participants in archaeologist William Rathje's Garbage Project (Rathje and Murphy 1992) concluded that organics like food and yard waste were the only items truly vulnerable to biodegradation under normal landfill conditions. Paper was not degrading rapidly; in fact, newspapers were used to date garbage deposits decades old. However, plastic does not biodegrade or change in any way in a landfill, except to break apart.

Plastic bags predominated in Swedish grocery and retail stores already in 1981, whereas only paper bags were used in America at that time. In the 1990s core households in each community were asked which type of bag they chose at the grocery story. Foley responses indicate a slight preference for paper; Munka responses reflect one for plastic. Households in both communities give the same reasons for their choices. Most selecting paper indicated that they do so "for the environment"; that is, because paper is biodegradable. Those preferring plastic often said that it is because plastic bags will be used again for household garbage: all eleven of the plastic-preferring Munka core households cited this function. Importantly, a regulation of Ängelholm *kommun* stipulates that garbage must be bagged in plastic for pickup. Plastic bags from grocery stores fit perfectly into the Swedish wire garbage baskets, mounted inside cupboard doors. American garbage cans are usually three to four times as large as the Swedish baskets, and most Americans buy special plastic "trash bags" to put in them. Two Foley households, however, stated that they choose plastic bags for holding garbage before they go into trash bags. Five Foley households said that they choose paper over plastic bags because they can be recycled more easily; those preferring plastic bags pointed out that these can be brought back to the store for recycling. Paper bags are perceived in both communities as being more commodious. Paper bags are regarded by some Foleyans as being somewhat harder to carry, because they have no handles. (In Munka, both paper and plastic bags have handles.) Respondents in both communities clearly have second uses or recycling in mind which influence their choices.

Most expressing dissatisfaction with plastic emphatically attacked it as nonbiodegradable or damaging to the environment if burned. A Foley informant said, "I want my kids to have a clean Earth. The plastic lasts forever. If you can't get rid of a product, you shouldn't *make* it!" Her counterpart in Munka declared, "Plastic bags, plastic in general, is crazy, because it costs to produce and it costs to dispose of. If you burn it, you get pollution; if you bury it, it *stays* there. Especially those colored plastic bags with ads on them: What's in those dyes?" Some residents in each community erroneously stated that some plastic bags are environmentally friendly in that they disintegrate completely in water or underground.

Purchasing Environmentally friendly Products

Foleyans and Munka Ljungbyans reported similar levels of participation in purchasing environmentally friendly products. That Munka respondents are not more active than Foleyans is a little surprising, given specially designated sections and advisors for such products in Swedish supermarkets. Munka's pattern parallels national statistics, however: roughly half of Swedish households say they always or often buy environmentally friendly cleaning materials (SCB 1994). (See Table 7.7.)

Table 7.7
Purchase Environmentally friendly or Recyclable Products
(Questionnaire Households, Foley and Munka Ljungby)

	Always	Usually	Occasionally	Seldom	Never
Foley (N=129)	8%	41%	39%	10%	2%
Munka (N=135)	7%	42%	39%	10%	1%

Purchasing Environmentally friendly Detergent

Foleyans engage in only one activity more than Munka Ljungbyans: buying environmentally safe detergent. Twelve percent more Foleyans always buy such detergents. About the same percentages in each population seldom or never buy them. (See Table 7.8.) Why? As P. O. Hallin (1994) points out, when new environmental options and other more entrenched values conflict, the latter will likely win. Here, the dominant value is the Swedish standard of cleanliness. Swedes want *white* whites as proof that their laundry is truly clean. For this reason they choose to launder their clothes in hot water and hesitate in purchasing an environmentally friendly laundry detergent. (The Swedish Central Bureau of Statistics reports that only one half of households are satisfied with the performance of environmentally friendly products they have used [reported in *NST*, 1994].) Many Swedes prefer that other things be very white as well. One couple showed me and Hallin a cup with a brownish stain left after machine dishwashing with an environmentally friendly detergent. Another informant rejected unbleached toilet paper, repelled by its "truly *disgusting* brown color."

Table 7.8
Purchase Environmentally friendly Detergent
(Questionnaire Households, Foley and Munka Ljungby)

	Always	Usually	Occasionally	Seldom	Never
Foley (N=131)	31%	37%	17%	9%	6%
Munka (N=135)	19%	41%	28%	10%	4%

Driving Less to Protect the Environment

Foleyans and Munka Ljungbyans gave parallel reports about driving less to protect the environment. However, they also responded in similar low proportions to this questionnaire item: 109 and 100, compared to usual response numbers of 130 or more. (See Table 7.9.) Hallin and I posit that many who do not drive less to protect the environment did not answer this question. However, reports of driving less do not mesh with answers to interview questions on this topic and observed behavior, and Hallin and I further think that no one in Foley always or usually reduces driving out of environmental motives, and that only a tiny percentage in Munka does so.

Table 7.9
Drive Less to Protect the Environment
(Questionnaire Households, Foley and Munka Ljungby)

	Always	Usually	Occasionally	Seldom	Never
Foley (N=109)	10%	23%	29%	23%	15%
Munka (N=100)	11%	21%	20%	21%	18%

REDUCE, REUSE, OR RECYCLE?

Swedish historian Lars Lundgren (1992) characterizes recycling as an ecological indulgence (*avlat*), like those sold by the Catholic Church centuries ago. Engaging in recycling, a "small but symbolically conspicuous behavior," grants you forgiveness for all environmental transgressions and relieves you of the need for any further action. Foley and Munka's preoccupation with recycling bears out this hypothesis. Most Foleyans take no pro-environmental actions in addition to recycling (other than purchasing some environmentally friendly products). Further, Foleyans recycle mostly the commodities for which they say it "pays." Recycling is to environmentalism what busing was to integration: a stop-gap measure which ignores underlying causes of the problem.

This lack of awareness (or denial) of deeper connections appeared in discussions with informants about preferred environmental efforts. Core households in Foley and Munka were asked which they thought was the most important: to reduce, reuse, or recycle. Interestingly, two thirds of Munka households responded with "recycle," as might have been anticipated for both communities based on their recycling emphasis, but half the Foley households answered "reduce." Foleyans said that by reducing consumption, one would need to engage less in the other two activities. Reducing also was said to have the advantage of not requiring additional energy, often mentioned in the context of recycling. Reducing is perceived to be less expensive and more saving of the environment, yet the hardest strategy to accomplish.

Munka Ljungbyans are obviously influenced by government recycling campaigns. They stated that they selected recycle because this option creates jobs, saves the environment and forests, and reduces the growing "mountain of garbage" (*sopberg*). Reduction "can be hard," and reuse is "limited," whereas recycling has many possibilities, and new products can be created. Some informants expressed resistance to the idea of reducing, saying "We're accustomed to a certain level of consumption." Seven Foley households said they chose recycle because through recycling we can avoid extracting new resources. Recycling was judged paramount because "even if we reduce and reuse, eventually it all has to be disposed of."

Foleyans applied "reduce" chiefly to gasoline, electricity, or water—not to consumer goods. This was also the case for the three households in Munka who selected reduce. (Additionally, two Munka households said that all three are equally important.) Informants in both communities frequently confounded "reuse" and "recycle." Their frequent response to questions about what they recycled was plastic bags, because they use them for garbage.

ENVIRONMENTAL MATERIALISM

As described earlier in this chapter, Munka Ljungbyans were much more environmentally aware than Foleyans in the 1980s. Although awareness in Foley has grown over time, Munka Ljungbyans continue to provide more knowledgeable and systems-oriented responses to questions about the environment, thanks in part to the Swedish government's intensive environment information campaign. Yet, Munka Ljungbyans are no more likely (or willing) than Foleyans to link their personal energy use choices to environmental damage. And there is no association of consumer goods with environmental problems apart from those caused by the abstract entity of industry.

As with their energy-using activities, consumers do not place the things they buy in larger energy or environmental contexts. Foley and Munka Ljungby informants do not connect consumer goods to energy demand, as seen in the previous chapter's discussion of embodied energy. Neither do they link these goods to environmental degradation and resource depletion—with the exception of excessive packaging complaints, garbage and landfill site issues, and commodities that could be recycled directly. As Lundgren (1992) writes, we link environmental damage with production, not with consumption. Environmental protection laws are directed primarily toward emissions and not towards products. Lundgren urges that the cost of goods reflects their total actual cost, including collection, recovery, recycling, and disposal.

Further, what I call environmental materialism has emerged, especially in the United States. Like spiritual materialism (the inappropriate application of material approaches and measures to spiritual deepening), environmental materialism involves ineffectual attempts to mitigate environmental problems (or guilt) by buying environmentally benign products. Such products include handmade paper untreated by chemicals, shirts with tagua nut buttons (a rain forest product proposed as an alternative to clearing), and canvas shopping bags with prominent pro-environmental slogans or logos. Usually, these products are expensive and featured in upscale catalogs and shops. Patronizing companies that contribute a percentage of sales of certain products to environmental causes is also "environmentally correct"—for example, Ben and Jerry's Rain Forest Crunch ice cream. Like the indulgence conferred by the act of recycling, responsibility for deeper environmental involvement is also assuaged by the purchase of a few symbolic products. Durning (1992) shares this perspective, declaring that although green consumerism (what an oxymoron!) is a means to express concerns directly to manufacturers, it also functions as "a palliative for the conscience of the consumer class, allowing us to continue business as usual while feeling like we are doing our part."

Manufacturers have quickly capitalized on consumers' environmental concerns. "Environment sells" (*Miljö säljer*) is a refrain heard in Sweden, and marketers there identify environment and ecology as the central trend for the 1990s. Green attributes are emphasized and even falsely claimed for some products: environment advisors in supermarkets distribute pamphlets showing various symbols placed on products to imply environmental superiority but which are unrelated to official endorsement. Such symbols include a panda, a seal, and circular recycling arrows.

Although guides to the environmental qualities of products and manufacturers' social policy guides to products are appreciated, the title of one such guide, *Shopping for a Better World,* is ironic if not oxymoronic. It conveys the degree to which shopping has been institutionalized and the American delusion that we can shop our way out of environmental problems. We industrialists are caught in the cycle of applying materially based solutions to problems stemming from that very materialist orientation.

CONSUMPTION OF NATURE

The idea that consumers also consume nature has become widespread. Nature writer and cultural critic Bill McKibben (1989) concludes, "Nature has become a hobby with us. One person enjoys the outdoors, another likes cooking, a third favors breaking into military computers over his phone line." When the environment is regarded as another scenic resource through a perspective characterized by Kempton, Boster, and Hartley (1995) as utilitarian, environmental considerations do not enter into everyday awareness or choices. Such a utilitarian perspective is materialist, not deeply personally or spiritually based. As stated earlier, Sweden's environmental concerns were born of the pragmatic need to manage natural resources, although emphasis was later changed to the protection of nature, antidote to the discontents of industrial life. Orvar Löfgren (1992), skeptical of the idea of a love-of-nature ethos running through Swedish culture and aware of the gap between expressed ideals and actual behavior, cautions against assuming that declared love of nature will lead to environmental activity. He writes that environmental campaigns run the risk of producing more guilty consciences than actual change.

Consumers of nature are likely to be proponents of what Andrew McLaughlin (1993) calls "reactive environmentalism." He characterizes this concept as a "defensive response to the obvious excesses of industrialism" and its "technocratic elite" which emphasizes better management of nature as a collection of resources that we can control. "Ecological environmentalism" contrasts with reactive environmentalism in that it calls for a profound change in the ideology of nature implicit in industrialism. Ecological environmentalism recognizes that environmental problems are all interconnected, and that their origin can be traced back to the decision-making structures of modern society. Reactive environmentalism remains within the sociopolitical frame-work of the industrialism which generates ecological crises. "It assumes that management of the problems is possible, which leads to calls for technological innovation, more research, and more legislation and regulation by the state" (McLaughlin 1993). Consumers and reactive environmentalists alike, then, are bound by the industrial worldview. This outlook is the focus of Chapter 9, in which Foleyans and Munka Ljungbyans share their views on the energy future, how to solve energy and environmental problems, and quality of life.

Chapter 8

Consumerism

Consumer spending for goods and services represents roughly two thirds of GDP in both Sweden and the United States (U.S. Government 1994). Trends in consumer spending have critical implications for energy demand, as physicist and energy analyst Lee Schipper reveals in his longitudinal study of energy use in nine OECD countries (including Sweden and the United States). Schipper (1996a) reports that although technical improvements in energy efficiency have led to substantial reduction of energy intensities (energy demanded per unit of service) in both manufacturing and residential sectors of society since the 1970s, these improvements have now slowed. Further, changes in consumer activity have resulted in *increased* energy use, due to factors such as increased saturation of appliances and cars, larger homes, and a shift toward air travel and leisure services. Schipper writes, "Thus while many energy *uses* became less energy-intensive, *lifestyles* themselves became more energy-intensive, continuing a long-term trend well established before the 1973 oil crisis and subsequent declines in energy intensities." As a result of these changes in patterns of consumerist expression, energy demand is shifting away from manufacturers and towards consumers. Schipper dubs this shift "from production to pleasure."

EMBODIED ENERGY

The term embodied energy refers to energy used to produce and distribute consumer goods. It is also called indirect energy or energy cost. This concept parallels Marx's notion of embodied labor in that (for purposes of calculation) it assumes the fiction that the fuels dissipated in manufacturing and distribution processes remain embodied in products. Energy analysts Bullard and Herendeen (1975) underscore the pervasiveness of embodied energy, writing that "When you consume anything, you are consuming energy."

Embodied energy is a significant consideration in that rising household income is accompanied by a decrease in direct energy use, but by an increase in embodied energy demand (Hannon 1975). The decrease in direct energy is explained in part by the acquisition of more-efficient housing, heating and cooling systems, appliances, and automobiles. More determining, however, is the bounded number of uses for direct energy compared to the endless variety of goods and services available to those who can afford them. Marginal utility is a concept more meaningfully applied to direct than to embodied energy demand in consumer society, where redundancy of possessions is a goal. An additional concern about embodied energy consumption is that even though no product is as energy intensive as fuels, if consumers choose to spend the money they save through reduced fuel bills on goods and services of relatively high energy intensity, net energy savings are greatly diminished. Ultimately, this dynamic is important because it signals continued depletion of resources and environmental damage.

A Foley informant declared the conservation potential for direct energy to be greater than that for embodied energy:

People will conserve fuel more readily than they will buy less stuff. These things are really important to them. [Why?] Because they *show*, because they seem permanent, something you can keep and have around.

Of course, the manufacture of goods requires resources as well as direct energy, and all dimensions of the manufacture, distribution, and disposal of goods burden the environment. A familiar statistic is that the United States, with only 5 percent of the world's population, is responsible for more than 30 percent of annual global resource consumption. Danish physicist and sustainability analyst Jørgen Nørgård writes (1993) that providing even a modest European standard of living for the current world population would require 5–10 times ongoing production levels, which are already greatly damaging to the global environment.

Consumers interviewed in Foley and Munka Ljungby made no reference to global resource limits. Only one Munka Ljungbyan addressed this issue, saying, "Think if China and India consumed as much as we do. Where would all that come from? There are not that many resources on the earth." Nevertheless, majorities of questionnaire respondents in both towns said that there were not enough resources in the world to enable all to attain the American (or Swedish) standard of living: 79 percent in Foley, and 86 percent in Munka Ljungby.

Reducing direct energy consumption will only partially alleviate energy supply and environmental problems as long as there is no reduction of consumption of material goods and energy-intensive services. We need to look at material goods in new ways, to acknowledge the true energy and environmental costs of their manufacture, advertisement, distribution, maintenance, and disposal. We must recognize that "industry" is us, existing to serve our easily triggered desires to consume. Additionally, we should have greater awareness of the international implications and inequities of industrial consumerism.

The focus on direct energy and efficiency in energy research reflects the dominance of techno-economic over ecological orientations. Most energy research agenda are conservative in that they support the perpetuation of current living patterns and economic processes by making them more energy efficient rather than question lifestyle in any fundamental way. Further, most energy research does not take into account the social forces that constrain efficiency achievement. Addressing these factors, sociologist Loren Lutzenhiser (1992) writes:

The engineers and natural scientists in the energy community may only be required to ask "How can we be more efficient?" Social scientists are also bound to ask "Why are we not more energy-efficient, when clearly that has been possible?" . . . The social sciences tell us that cultures are organized in social structures, by means of which political and economic interests find expression. It follows, then, that an approach which inquires only at the site of consumption will overlook political and economic dynamics that contribute directly to the creation and maintenance of that consumption . . . the institutional sources of high levels of energy demand in the U.S.

Economist Nicholas Georgescu-Roegen (1971) eloquently communicates the significance of embodied energy, urging the redress of what he calls the false dichotomy of economics and energy. Emphasizing that all economic activity is anchored to a natural base and therefore cannot elude entropy and other laws of thermodynamics, Georgescu-Roegen advocates an economy based on the flow of solar energy and on slowing the depletion of natural resources. It is telling that three of the eight tenets of his proposed "bioeconomic program" for achieving these goals stipulate reductions in embodied energy demand, but only one addresses the need to reduce direct energy consumption.

AWARENESS OF EMBODIED ENERGY
IN FOLEY AND MUNKA LJUNGBY

No Foley or Munka core household, either in the 1980s or the 1990s, recognized the term "embodied energy." After the concept was explained, households were asked to give examples of products that they thought would contain relatively high amounts of embodied energy. Plastic goods was the most frequent response in both Foley and Munka in the 1980s, mentioned by half of the core households in each community. In Foley the second most frequent response was prepared or convenience foods, followed by canned or frozen foods, dairy products, aluminum, and packaging. After plastics, the second most frequent example given by Munka Ljungbyans was aluminum, then greenhouse vegetables or flowers; steel, meat, and frozen foods; and processed or convenience foods, metal wares, paper goods, and packaging. Encouragement to reduce use of plastic was part of the Swedish campaign to decrease oil dependence and had made an obvious impact on Munka Ljungbyans. Also, some Munka informants referred to 1980s media emphasis on the energy-intensive nature of aluminum production.

Foleyans linked embodied energy chiefly to food and food packaging, and to the grocery or restaurant business. They did not recognize the pervasiveness of embodied energy in the plethora of other products they purchase. Compartmentalized thinking characterized Foley in the 1980s, and informants did not make connections between energy and environment. Although awareness had expanded somewhat by the 1990s, few Foleyans relate their own consumer activity to energy and environmental demands.

When asked in the 1980s to give examples of wasteful consumption of embodied energy, half of Foley's core households answered emphatically, "Packaging!" Next most frequent was food: prepared, convenience, and "junk." Plastic wares was third. One household each responded with clothing, toys, paper products, nonreturnable containers, home decorations, dishwashers, cleaning products, disposable diapers, cigarettes, cars, and recreational vehicles. Most of these examples were cited by their self-confessed consumers. As in Foley, packaging was the most frequent example of wasteful embodied energy use in Munka, cited by one third of core households there. Tied for second were disposable items and the general "over-choice" of products. Third was plastic bags, followed by canned food, clothing, and mail advertisements. Aluminum cans, plastic toys, televisions, and videocassette recorders were each mentioned by one Munka household.

In Foley the question of embodied energy waste in packaging elicited angry comments and anecdotes about confrontations with fast-food restaurant staff. Again the image of the trapped consumer, without alternatives, was vivid. Foleyans expressed anger at the notion of planned obsolescence ("Now, isn't *that* a waste of energy?!") and at perceived inconsistencies of society:

They talk about the oil shortage and then they keep making these plastic bags to throw your garbage out in. Everyone goes overboard with packaging, too. Boxes are filled with products encased in plastic, and then the *boxes* are covered with plastic wrap! Also, there's lots of nice and colored packaging. So, if you don't know what *macaroni* looks like....

Despite such frustration, U.S. per capita consumption of heavily packaged and frozen foods doubled during the 1980s. Europe experienced a similar rise, although from a lower starting point (Durning 1992).

Some Foley consumers try to make choices that are intelligent in terms of economy, energy, and environment. However, lacking guidelines, they become discouraged by such attempts—as one informant recounted:

Some choices are more economical ones but end up being conservative [of natural resources], too. Others are more economical but less conserving, like when I buy generic cereal in a big plastic bag instead of a box. On the other hand, I think wood is more expensive than plastic. Think of the economic and energy costs of printing those boxes! I'm not even sure now, which is really the best way to go, or even the least harmful!

Discussions in Munka were not marked by the extreme exasperation and resentment toward commerce expressed in Foley. Yet, the Swedish system can also impede consumers' attempts to conserve. For example, several Munka Ljungbyans complained about lack of evening bus service to Ängelholm, and also about carpool members not being allowed income tax deductions for their commutes, whereas solo drivers are. Others objected that *Systembolaget* (the state-operated liquor store monopoly) does not accept returns of some bottles it sells. One Munka informant who considered plastic bags to be wasteful was irritated by *kommun* regulations stipulating that garbage must be contained in plastic for pickup.

In the 1990s Foley and Munka consumer focus remains on packaging, and there is no increase in awareness of embodied energy. No one mentioned plastics as being high in embodied energy—perhaps because the oil supply is seen as plentiful and secure, and people now view plastic as recyclable, even biodegradable. When discussing waste of embodied energy, two Foley households specified "not recycling" because of "the energy it takes to create these things." Such comments signify greater consciousness of embodied energy than earlier. Concern about landfill limitations is the primary motivation for recycling, however, and conservation of energy and resources is secondary.

CONSUMPTION OF GOODS

Conspicuous Consumption

Conspicuous consumption is much in evidence in both Foley and Munka Ljungby over time. This "specialised consumption of goods as an evidence of pecuniary strength" (Veblen 1899) is manifest in possessions, of course, but also through meals and entertaining, and in the appearances of homes and yards. Foleyans are caught up in emulation. Several Foley core households spoke of "keeping up with the Joneses," one informant declaring "When one guy gets something, the whole *block*'s gotta have it." When I described Veblen's ideas, another informant responded, "Boy, was *he* right!" In the 1990s Foley informants confirm conspicuous consumption dynamics:

Foley's a competitive little town. People lead their lives by comparison and raise their children by comparison. "The Joneses" are worse than ever!

People are not working now for what they used to: taking care of their families. Now they're working for the new carpet, or the RV [recreational vehicle] . . . for a lot of *stuff*, which they make sure everyone knows they've got!

That status and emulation are equally important to Munka Ljungbyans is illustrated by these typical quotations:

Man will always want to increase his status. It's fun to have something to show to your neighbors and acquaintances . . . and maybe feel a little higher [than them].

I'm influenced by the crowd. I have a tumble-dryer that I don't use but got just because it's "cool" to have.

In Munka, social demands for "pecuniary decency" (Veblen's concept of socially acceptable financial outlay) are more powerful than in Foley, but standards are also more modest, and upper limits set by considerations of *lagom*. It is important for Munka hosts to have sufficient food, but exceeding the socially defined range is considered bad form. The atmosphere created is as important as the food and drink served, so embodied energy is consumed to create "coziness" and "well-being" (*trivsel*) with special tableware, napkins, flowers, and candles. It is a common Swedish practice to leave the small labels of prestigious manufacturers on functional as well as decorative glassware.

As will be recalled, hosts in both Foley and Munka often turn up their thermostats when entertaining to ensure guests' comfort, but also to avoid being judged "cheap" in Foley or "stingy" (*snål*) in Munka. Also, informants   turn on more lights for guests. In Munka, pride in home decor is such that several informants reported the pattern of leaving lights on in unoccupied living rooms so that passersby can see the fine furnishings. The importance of an attractive home environment is reflected in the report that Swedes spend more money on home furnishings than do other Europeans (Löfgren 1990).

Status Symbols

Prominent status symbols in Foley in the 1980s were microwave ovens, recreational vehicles, and pickup trucks. Additionally, gold surpassed $600 an ounce at that time, and a rage for gold jewelry ensued. Pecuniary decency was at its most blatant in the form of necklaces with centerpieces of wafers of gold bullion issued by Swiss banks! Another tale of pecuniary decency is that of one woman who wanted a Christmas gift costing her husband one month's salary. When I asked what that was, I was told, "She doesn't care what it is, just that it *costs* that much." Teenagers wanted "label" jeans, just entering the market at that time, and the "Cities style" of clothes; children lobbied for Hot Wheels tricycles and certain brands of sneakers and bicycles.

In 1990s Foley, status symbols for adults are vehicles (trucks, cars, recreational vehicles, and motor homes), large homes in the new development, boats, snowmobiles, hunting guns and sports equipment, clothes, and deluxe sewing machines. Teenagers aspire to cars, label clothes and football team starter jackets, electronics equipment and the latest tapes and CDs, "cool" haircuts, and "the best" sports equipment. Children want computer and video games, Ninja Turtle shoes, Barney paraphernalia, B.U.M. sweatshirts, and certain brands of bicycles.

In 1980s Munka, VCRs and small backyard greenhouses led as status symbols for adults. Ownership of two cars also conferred distinction. Teenagers wanted famous-label clothing (*märkeskläder*). Informants were stumped by my request for children's status possessions, but by the 1990s they readily named

TV games and mountain bikes. Adult status symbols cited in the 1990s include leather sofas, satellite television dishes, enclosed glass porches, cars, boats, house-trailers, clothes, and impressive yards. Teenagers want certain label clothes and shoes, bicycles, computers, and electronics equipment, emphasizing "the latest" CDs and players.

In the 1990s just over half of Munka's core households could not identify a current status symbol in their community, but all in Foley could do this readily. Consumption traps are perceived and lamented by Foleyans, however:

People won't, can't, stop. The more they make, the more they spend . . . on whatever is "in." Having "the latest" means you have to *keep doing it.*

It's a losing battle, trying to impress people that way. You hate to think that what you put on your back determines your value, either to yourself or to anybody else.

One young Foley informant illustrated the theme that others had voiced, that purchasing one thing invariably leads to another:

I want a china cabinet because it will look nice in the house. I don't really *need* one. I have nothing to put in it. So I'll have to get dishes, too.

Munka Ljungbyans also stressed the trap of perpetual consumption:

The more you have, the more you want. You will never be satisfied.

People are interested in "the latest." They have money, and if they have it, they must spend it. It's never-ending.

Yet, despite consumers' expressed frustration with entrapment, the dynamics of conspicuous consumption, emulation, and pecuniary decency show no signs of abating, in either Foley or Munka Ljungby.

SHOPPING

Shopping persistently ranks higher in popularity among Foleyans than Munka Ljungbyans. Eight 1980s Foley core households cited shopping as one of their favorite free-time activities, making it the third most popular activity. In contrast, shopping took ninth place in the Munka listing, named by only 2 households as a favorite thing to do in leisure hours. "Malling" was a verb heard frequently in Foley, as in "Let's go malling on Saturday." In the 1990s shopping was named as a favorite activity by fewer households: down from 8 to 3 in Foley and from 2 to 0 in Munka. Foleyans' favorite activities, named by at least 10 households each, are sports, reading, and watching television. In Munka, sports also rank first, followed by walking. No Munka household reported watching TV as a preferred activity.

Time spent shopping has diminished for many. In the 1990s fewer all-day or all-afternoon shopping trips appeared on core household activity records than in the 1980s. Informants emphasize the new trend of knowing exactly what you wanted to buy and getting it, rather than browsing for entertainment. Informants say shopping is now more of a "hassle" than in the 1980s, because of increased traffic and more and widespread shops. Several identified the time-consuming nature of shopping as a drawback. Although long shopping expeditions are now less common in both communities, Foleyans continue to shop longer than Munka Ljungbyans: records of core household shopping trips reveal that shopping episodes of 90 minutes or longer are four times as frequent in Foley as in Munka, both in the 1980s and the 1990s.

Has social consensus started to turn away from shopping? Alan Durning (1992) notes that the consumer splurge of the 1980s "was halted more by hard times than by concern for the earth. For whatever reasons, as of early 1992, public opinion in the United States had swung against crass materialism." Durning quotes a public opinion researcher: "We're moving away from shop-till-you-drop and moving toward dropping shopping." Yet, he also reports that on average, Americans visit shopping centers once per week and spend six hours per week shopping—and that the time Americans spend shopping is second only to that spent watching television as categories of time use having the fastest growth over the last fifty years.

Although activity records kept by core households support the contention that the intensive shopping of the 1980s has diminished, interviews and partici-pant observation indicate that shopping continues to be popular for many Foleyans and Munka Ljungbyans. How do informants explain the appeal of shopping? Foleyans say that shopping is an inexpensive entertainment which remedies boredom and fills time for many. Some women shop when their husbands go hunting or fishing. Shopping is often combined with eating out, another favored and relatively inexpensive entertainment. Additionally, shop-ping is how one sees what is new and thereby "keeps up." Shopping can also be a way to avoid the unpleasant, like housework or family arguments. And some residents of small-town Foley said that they like the anonymity of malls and escaping local confines.

Foleyans told me about acquaintances who maintain a regular weekly shopping day and about "shopaholics" they know ("She just fills that cart up and feels so good"). Informants volunteered examples of people who they feel take buying to an extreme. One woman was said to have two hundred pairs of shoes, and another, fifty coats. Intensive and redundant consumption is not exclusive to women, however. According to his wife, one Foley man buys "*anything* for fishing and stuff. He has so much junk I can't get into the garage. There's one three-wheeler, one snowmobile, and *six* fish houses with stoves!" I heard of no such local legends of acquisition in Munka Ljungby.

Shopping continues to appeal greatly to younger adults and the next generation. One Foleyan declared with exasperation that female coworkers in their twenties have shopping as their chief conversation topic, take vacation time in order to attend garage sales, and "would shop constantly if they could."

Teenagers say that they like to shop with their friends for clothes, accessories, and audiotapes. If they don't spend their own money, they find things for their parents to buy for them. And during interviews with two core households, small children recited "Shop 'til you drop," giggling.

American trends and fads (such as jogging or brunch) inevitably diffuse to Sweden, which increasingly resembles the United States materially. Swedes are heavily exposed to American television broadcasting, the prime socialization agent for consumerism. Since the early 1980s shopping centers based on the American model have multiplied in Sweden. One major new center, Väla, is just 30 minutes away from Munka. Though the large warehouse-style IKEA furniture centers existed earlier, they have not been incorporated into the "mastodon" (as one Munka Ljungbyan put it) complexes that exist now. Large discount meccas have also become well-established. Shops in nearby Helsingör, Denmark, draw Munka Ljungbyans with a different variety of merchandise and cheaper liquor, meats, and cheeses. Brännborn's, a warehouse-style grocery and variety store in Ängelholm, is now open seven long days per week, compared with five and a half shorter days in the 1980s. Reflecting the 1990s view of shopping as an intrinsic recreational activity, the Brännborn's ad appears in the excursions (*utflyktsmål*) section of the local newspaper.

Like Foleyans, Munka Ljungbyans are divided in their reactions to shopping. Some stated that they enjoy it as a diverting and relaxing activity, but others expressed distaste at the very idea. As in Foley, Munka informants, especially teenagers, emphasize the social dimension of shopping, the chance to meet acquaintances. (One shopping center in the city of Örebro is called the meeting place—*Träffpunkt*.) Some Munka Ljungbyans commented with sadness on the social functions shopping has assumed and on isolation in Swedish society:

You used to meet people, to socialize, at church. Now, it's at the shops. This new commercial life has a material message. We listen to salesmen instead of to the minister. It's really sad. Retired people stand outside Brännborn's and wait for the store to open. They meet their friends there sometimes instead of going to homes.

One old man comes here [the Munka grocery] five times a day to buy one thing, just because he is so lonely. This is an "acceptable" way for him to get some contact with folk. It's just too bad that he has to spend money to do it!

As in Foley, shopping is said to be a popular conversation topic at some workplaces.

Sweden's economic downturn in the early 1990s inhibited shopping somewhat. Munka residents said that increasingly, people try to stay with lists of what they needed when shopping. They also reported less frequent turnover of household goods than in the 1980s, and the increasing popularity of flea markets and garage sales. Economic factors aside, more Munka Ljungbyans than Foleyans express dislike of shopping. The following comments are typical:

[Wrinkles nose.] Ugh. We would rather be out in nature. Something is missing, you are empty, if going shopping is what you want to do most.

Shopping has become a popular entertainment. I think it's because people lack hobbies. And they have lots of time on their hands.

Shopping is a big waste of your free time! A more worthwhile activity would be a walk in the woods. Outdoor life is much more wholesome, beneficial.

ORIGINS OF CONSUMERISM

Ethnologist Orvar Löfgren (1990) points out that contemporary culture is often described in terms of the arrival of a new kind of consumerism—such as postmodern consumerism, late consumer capitalism, or advanced consumer culture. He argues against trying to identify any one prime factor behind consumer behavior, "such as status-seeking, social insecurity, cultural compensation, need for social distinction, or market manipulation" and warns against such reductionist explanations. Certainly, both Foleyans and Munka Ljungbyans communicated a variety of functions of consumerism.

Recall Paul Ekins's (1991) definition of consumerism: a cultural orientation that maintains that the "possession and use of an increasing number and variety of goods and services is the principal cultural aspiration and the surest perceived route to personal happiness, social status and national success." I presume that "use" refers exclusively to services, since people have many things that they do not use either because the initial thrill of ownership has died or they no longer like them, they received them as gifts, or—most importantly—they don't have the time to use all they have! Durning (1992) writes of elaborate sports equipment, fancy shoes, and so forth, and concludes, "Leisure wear has replaced leisure as the reward for labor."

Even though they may be spending a little less time shopping, Foleyans assured me that the urge to buy things is still widespread. Informants were asked why they think it is so strong. Responses from Foley and Munka Ljungby illustrate all three dimensions of consumerism addressed by Ekins: personal validation and reward, social affirmation, and national economic health. Many Foleyans began explaining acquisitive urges by referring to advertising, offering statements like "We see these things on TV," "We're exposed to all those ads," and "The carrot's always being dangled in front of us." When asked what makes them susceptible to the carrot, most informants stopped, baffled. Those who could continue speculated that buying things affirms existence, and that consumption confers feelings of being important, powerful, adult, and successful:

A splurge will give them the mental feeling that they're *there*.

People equate having things with success. Not even any particular thing—just "things."

People think, "I must be important now because I have this *thing*."

I like to shop and buy things *because I can*. It makes me feel like I am beyond adolescence, you know?

Others came up with an interesting conundrum: that buying things with money they earn somehow validates what they do to get the money. Also, consumption can be a way to reward oneself for work.

Buying things . . . makes what I'm doing for a living worthwhile.

Buying things validated my work [part-time job] somehow: "Now I can go *spend* it!"

I buy something for myself. It feels good, like I really deserve it. I "earned" it through my work.

Munka Ljungbyans also tie the acquisition of things to affirmation of self and self-reward. They added that buying things is a way of expressing personality.

One buys new things because one lacks a good sense of self. Many people buy new cars even if they don't have the means, to make themselves feel better about themselves.

Buying or getting things is one way of showing yourself that you *are* something.

You're stressed, so you give something to yourself. A reward to keep going.

You consume in order to show. You show your personality through your possessions. You also get a CD, a big TV, a computer, and so forth, in order just to show that you *can*.

Given the overthrow of tradition and the speed of social change, buying things becomes one way to feel that you are successfully keeping up with society and not being left behind, an isolated loser. Social relationships can also precipitate buying, according to Foleyans, who spoke of parents compensating for time away or winning the affection of their children with gifts. Some Foleyans also speculated that people acquired things in attempts to compensate for bad marriages.

You reward yourself and make up for time not spent with kids: "Here's an article of clothes; love me."

Shopping is like a drug; it makes her happy. . . . Of course, she has a bad marriage.

Munka Ljungbyans identified similar ways in which relationships can foster consumption. For example:

You compensate your kids for the time you don't give them with things. You buy stuff for them whether or not you have the money to pay for it!

In addition to affirmation of self and compensation to others, both Foleyans and Munka Ljungbyans describe consumption as compensation to self: compen-

sation for dull jobs, general stress, and lack of family or other close relationships. One Foley couple told of a bachelor in his early forties:

He has to buy something major on a regular basis or he becomes extremely restless.
[Something major?] Like a pontoon boat or an RV. Last year, building a house cut down
on some of his large purchases, but then he was adding a deck, furniture, and so forth.
[Why is he restless?] Because he wants a family, and roots.

To further illustrate this relationship-compensation hypothesis, this couple
referred to the common pattern of widows replacing home furnishings when
their husbands die.

The theme of compensation appears in Munka responses as well. Informants refer to lack of contact with nature, job satisfaction, and social contacts as
prompting consumption. More than one Munka Ljungbyan used the term
tröstköpa (buying to comfort oneself), forged from the older concept of *tröstäta*
(eating for comfort).

People like to shop because they don't have a positive daily environment. It all depends
on job, social life, who your friends are. They are probably lacking contact with nature:
the forest and the shore.

Tröstköpa parallels *tröstäta*. We are very isolated from each other here in Sweden.
Shopping gives us contact with others. It's comforting.

You comfort yourself because you are having problems at work, your teenagers drink or
do drugs, you can't get a day-care place for your youngest child, and so forth.

Especially now, with so much unemployment, there's shopping for comfort and for
distraction from these problems. If you don't have money for more expensive things, you
buy potato chips!

Isolation is a fact of Swedish life. Ethnologist Åke Daun (1994) writes that
36 percent of all Swedish households consists of only one person, with an even
higher proportion of such households (44%) in central Stockholm. Daun says,
however, that this statistic is a function of individual preference and compares
Swedish with American students—the former more often living alone, the latter
having roommates. In the United States in the 1990s, 25 percent of all households consisted of one person. (Besides their social consequences, the implications of one-person households for embodied energy consumption are deep—
another study in itself.)

Buying to Fill a Spiritual Need

Half of the Foley core households speculated that buying things is an
attempt to fill a spiritual need, an inner void:

Buying makes people think they're keeping up with society, filling a void. We think we
can get inner peacefulness by finding material things we can put our hands on.

Consumerism results from the lack of something deeper, such as spirituality. Material possessions become your god. They end up controlling you.

People think, "I got *this* for myself. It makes me feel good. But it doesn't last very long, so I have to keep doing it." There's a horrible sadness down there somewhere.

Munka Ljungbyans also acknowledged that only temporary comfort and satisfaction comes from buying things:

People buy things to compensate for a lack of security, for an essential meaninglessness they feel in their lives.

If I feel that I must have it, I *must*, then something is wrong. There is something else that is missing. People long for *something*.

Munka Ljungbyans referred to feelings of meaninglessness or longing that lead to consumption, but unlike Foleyans, they did not overtly identify the spiritual origin of these feelings. Rather, they characterize consumption as compensation for lives lacking inner content or a lack of imagination.

You compensate with things for feelings you want . . . [like] love, comfort. You compensate for stress. You compensate for a boring life, a life without inner content: "Buy a pink dress or a chocolate cake—you'll feel better."

Shopping is done because people lack imagination: they have money and don't know what else to do with it.

Some Munka Ljungbyans prescribed more contact with nature as the antidote to consumerism. The following comment is typical:

If people would get out in the woods more, get in contact with nature, they would find these urges to get more and more things disappearing.

CONSUMPTION AND THE ECONOMY

In addition to individual and social motives, informants cited economic rationales for consumption. One Foley informant questioned intensive Christmas shopping and gift giving:

All these Christmas things, this is nuts. You ask yourself, "*Why* are we doing this?"

He then provided his own answer, couched in terms of national economic health and social obligations:

Our economy is based on consumption. Someone will lose a job. Also, it's the tradition of "payback time." Who gave to who. Who gets back.

The widespread conviction that consumption is necessary to support jobs, discussed in Chapter 5, appears again in the context of discussion of the origins to buy. If people stop buying, the economy suffers, and jobs will be lost. Yet, this belief was much stronger in Foley than in Munka. The 1990s questionnaire asked, "Should we consume more to foster the economy?" Nearly three quarters (71%) of Foley respondents answered yes, but just one quarter (23%) in Munka agreed. Holding dissonant beliefs—that the environment is more important than economic growth and that the consumption of goods must continue in order to keep the economy healthy and provide jobs—leads to contradictions between consumers' statements and their behavior.

Just as they failed earlier to associate their fuel consumption with environmental consequences, consumers now do not associate the goods they buy with the environmental costs of their production, distribution, and disposal. They conceive of the economy as mystifying and abstract forces, which have consumers at their mercy. Additionally, "industry" is an (often vilified) abstraction, having nothing to do with them. Consumers do not recognize the true implications of choosing environment over economic growth. Supporting the environment or "the ecology" is now socially sanctioned, but such support is abstract and theoretical—largely lip service.

The delusion that we can have it all, what anthropologist Alf Hornborg refers to as the "image of unlimited good," is addressed in Chapter 9. Industrial society is marked by the inability to conceive of alternative ways of defining "growth" or of structuring society—among individual consumers but among theorists and policymakers as well.

RESISTANCE TO VOLUNTARY SIMPLICITY

Why does consumerism persist and spread, if there is awareness that it compensates for but does not, cannot, satisfy nonmaterial needs? Three quarters of respondents in a 1986 American survey stated that they would prefer a simpler life over a higher standard of living and wanted less emphasis on material success (Research and Forecasts, cited by Elgin [1993]). Most Foley and Munka questionnaire respondents, however, felt otherwise. In the 1990s under half—46 percent in Munka and 41 percent in Foley—agreed with the statement, "I would like to live a simpler life, with fewer possessions."

In contrast, over half of respondents said that they want to simplify their schedules. Sixty-nine percent in Foley and 59 percent in Munka responded positively to the statement, "I would like to live a less stressful life, with fewer obligations and activities." (This is further evidence of the conviction that we can have it all: more time *and* more stuff, as well as environmental protection, economic growth, and cheap energy.)

Those choosing to reduce consumption of goods in a material- and image-based society incur negative social reactions. Further, voluntary simplicity may deeply threaten some community members. One couple living outside Foley chose to spend their money for 40 acres of land rather than a house. They live simply in a weatherized yurt and enjoy their wooded surroundings. They had this to say about the reaction their way of life invoked:

[Our way of life is] a threat to the larger community. Our culture says happiness comes from *things* and *power*. People believe that and go after these things. Many exhaust themselves getting a big house. And our saying "No, we don't need this" challenges everything they're doing.

This couple was described by other Foleyans as a "throwback from the sixties" and "way out there" and was generally perceived as "weird" for living in a yurt. Sadly, the tires on their truck have been slashed more than once, and they have found dead animals in their mailbox. Although most Foleyans would be appalled by these events, such acts show that voluntary simplicity can trigger deep feelings and indicate how conformist America can be, despite its touted individualism. The couple are solid local citizens, teachers. I did not hear much about their politics or religion, just about that "tent" and another peculiar dimension of their lifestyle: bicycling to work!

People living in voluntary simplicity are considered distinctive in Munka Ljungby as well. Åke Daun (1994) has described the narrow range of social acceptability in Swedish culture and the importance of fitting in with one's neighbors and coworkers. One Munka couple who chose to live simply were described as "special" (negative, given Swedish conformity) and were considered by some to be eccentric, stingy, or strange. This couple, well aware of others' appraisal, emphasized, "We're not stingy but rather, *rational*, in our expenditures."

Another woman who lived outside Munka was described as a curiosity whom I could not miss the opportunity to meet. She lives in the woods with her two children in a small, energy-efficient house she designed herself. Their only heat source is a ceramic oven, and they use electricity only to heat water. The pantry is chilled by underground air brought up by pipes. She bicycles over five miles to work, borrowing her mother's car for major grocery shops and trips to the recycling center. A vegetarian ("the Earth's resources would suffice if everyone were vegetarian"), she grows much of her own food. That the family recycled its own bodily wastes was seen as peculiar in the extreme, but this family was afforded overall tolerance, and there were no attacks such as those in Foley. But then this family lives in a ordinary house, not a yurt. This informant commented on others' opinions of her:

People think I'm a little strange . . . extreme. No one wants to live in all aspects the way I do. Some say, good about the low use of electricity, some say good about vegetarianism, and so forth. But nobody wants it all.

When asked why she thought others did not adopt "all aspects" of voluntary simplicity, she replied: "It's too much work, too hard to go against the flow, to ignore criticism and judgments, to dare to be different!"

In order to have a "green" lifestyle or live a life of voluntary simplicity, other Munka Ljungbyans told me, you must have a deep inner conviction "from somewhere" or be deeply religious. One informant stated, "There's an enormous group pressure on how one should live. You'd need to have the whole village change." Another said, "Society, the *kommun*, would have to encourage this lifestyle. Right now, it's just always money we focus on. "

In 1981 Duane Elgin estimated that 10 million American adults were experimenting with voluntary simplicity. Durning (1992) calls this number optimistic, declaring voluntary simplicity an unattainable ideal because of the ways in which physical infrastructure, institutional channels, and social sanctions constrain individuals' choices. Juliet Schor (1992) also writes of the constraints of American society's "work-and-spend cycle," from which there is seemingly no escape. Bill McKibben (1989) thoughtfully adds, "A voluntary simplification of life-styles is not beyond our abilities, but it is probably outside our desires. . . . Even if our way of life has destroyed nature and endangered the planet, it is so hard to imagine living in any other fashion." In addition to economic and social constraints and channels, another equally strong force operates. Consumerism distracts us from our fears—both existential fears and those generated by materialist, competitive society.

CONSUMERISM AND FEAR

Why do people find it so difficult to reduce their levels of consumption, even if they are motivated by desires for energy or environmental conservation? The dynamics supporting consumption override these motivations, which are themselves essentially material in their goals. The universal need for social affirmation becomes a powerful force for consumption in industrial society, where material image is all and social engagement mandates consumption of commodities. Both Foleyans and Munka Ljungbyans say that buying things confirms existence. Individuals also learn to allay existential questions through consumption. This deflection was addressed by a Foley informant:

[Through buying things] . . . you try to fulfill a deeper need you might even know is there but choose [instead] to go off into the material aspects of life. . . . We have all this modern technology but so many unanswered questions . . . *big* questions.

Eugene Linden (1979) traces the relationships among consumer society's structure, its members, and the material appetites that it "coaxes and services" in *Affluence and Discontent*. He believes consumerism to be a result of the hegemony of science over spirit in contemporary life. Members of consumer society can potentially enjoy countless material benefits, but this material certainty is accompanied by a metaphysical uncertainty: loss of a sense of place in the greater order of existence. "Outlaw" spiritual energy and unmet spiritual needs create an anxious restlessness. However, consumer society identifies unsatisfied *material* desires as the cause of this unhappiness. In attempts to still spiritual anxiety and driven by the secondary fear of rejection, people purchase things. Linden concludes, "Thus we have the paradox of a society that is fueled by the very dissatisfactions it creates." Through the act of consumption, the individual is integrated into society and is given a sense of self and place. A purchase establishes or maintains identity; it is, as Linden puts it, "the transfer of protection money for the buyer's self-esteem." Of course, this attempt to satisfy deeper needs with material means cannot last. Anxiety looms again, and is again (temporarily) assuaged by consumption.

Many other authors have addressed this consumer society paradox. Some emphasize the delusions into which we have been socialized. During (1992), for example, writes that "hoodwinked by a consumerist culture, we have been fruitlessly attempting to satisfy with material things what are essentially social, psychological, and spiritual needs." Wendell Berry describes the seductiveness of the deceptive consumerist paradigm:

The knowledge that purports to be leading us to transcendence of our limits has been with us a long time. It thrives by offering material means of fulfilling a spiritual, and therefore materially unappeasable, craving: we would all very much like to be immortal, infallible, free of doubt, at rest.

The opiate of the masses is not religion, but the reaffirmation of the self and calming of anxieties through purchases from an ever-expanding catalog of goods and services. Through this catalog the self is "free to divert itself endlessly from itself" and from the question of its place in the universe, as Walker Percy (1983) writes in *Lost in the Cosmos*, his study of the self in a "post-religious," technological society. What Percy calls the immanent self exists in and is centered by the material world, solving the predicament of identity and place either through a "passive consumership" as a member of mass society or by a more "discriminating transaction with the world." In urbane circles, consumerism is merely more sophisticated and refined. The dynamic described by Linden and Percy has been referred to aptly as "self-actualization through good taste" (Miller 1984).

Anthropologist Jules Henry (1963) writes that in industrial society, "[technological drivenness] . . . harnesses human effort to the very machines that nourish the consuming appetites." He also stresses, however, that humans have the capacity to learn to want almost any conceivable material object, and he illustrates this diversity with the golden stools of the Ashanti of West Africa; the feather cloaks and curare of native South Americans; and the totem poles, cedar boxes inlaid with mother-of-pearl, and engraved six-foot copper plates of the Kwakiutl of Northwest North America. Henry reminds us of the lavish consumption among the elite of ancient Greece, Rome, and Egypt as well. In contemporary industrial societies, of course, it is the scale of the energy and resources devoted to satisfy wants that wreaks unprecedented damage on the environment and perpetuates global exploitation of peoples.

Consumption is currently a popular topic in the social sciences (see Miller

1995a, 1995b; Friedman 1994). Many authors relate consumption to the formation and communication of identity and other information through possessions (for example, anthropologists Douglas and Isherwood 1979; McCracken 1988). Consumption may very well serve in self-definition for us muddled postmoderns. Such analyses of the cultural and symbolic aspects of consumerism are intrinsically interesting. However, they are ultimately neofunctional, precluding a more critical look at industrial consumerism and the crucial questions of sustainability and equity. Some social scientists, it should be noted, do broaden the analysis of consumerism with questions of environment, morality, and justice (for example, Gullestad 1995; Otnes 1988; Uusitalo 1983, 1986). And other authors, such as Paul Wachtel (1983) and Robert David Sack (1990), relate consumerism to the breakdown of a sense of community and belonging which followed the industrial revolution. They assess industrial society more critically and see consumerism as our attempts to create places for ourselves out of fragmented social order and kaleidoscopic culture and to obtain some feeling of security through possessions. Philosopher Andrew McLaughlin (1993) challenges consumerist society most boldly, calling it a "psychologically frustrating and ecologically lethal mode of forming personal identity."

Certainly, most members of consumer society struggle to resolve questions of personal identity, social acceptance, and life's meaning. I would argue that both American and Swedish society are driven by fear. The American system engenders economic fears with its individualistic, competitive economy; anxiety about social acceptance it generates and then promises to allay with the products it offers; and existential fears and spiritual hunger which cannot be appeased by material means. Even though Sweden's social welfare state relieves its members of fears of destitution, Swedes are engaged in the same social dynamics of consumer culture and are subject to rigid demands for social conformity. Further, the highly secular nature of Swedish society offers little spiritual solace. (Friends have asked me why Swedes are such a secular people. I believe that it is because many of their cultural values, such as equality and humanitarianism, are spiritual in origin, and this resonates in individuals. Further, the contacts and bonds with nature that Swedes have feed them spiritually.)

Thirty years ago, Jules Henry (1963) discerned that what he called "technological drivenness" was largely based on fear, and that industrial capitalism relies on its (individual and corporate) members' fears of competition and of becoming obsolete. In his essay, "The Ecological Crisis as a Crisis of Character," Wendell Berry (1977a) eloquently describes the dynamics of fear in consumer society:

People whose governing habit is the relinquishment of power, competence, and responsibility, and whose characteristic suffering is the anxiety of futility, make excellent
spenders. They are the ideal consumers. By inducing in them little panics of boredom,
powerlessness, sexual failure, mortality, paranoia, they can be made to buy (or vote for)
virtually anything that is "attractively packaged."

Anthropologist Ernest Becker (1973) posits a direct relation between materialism and fear of death. In *The Denial of Death*, he writes that societies in which death is greatly feared are likely to be highly materialistic. Certainly, buttressing the ego with possessions, things seemingly more real and more durable than our mortal, transitory selves, distracts and buffers against the thought of death—or maybe, we hope, even against death itself. Illustrating what anthropologists call contagious magic, we feel that a transfer of the seemingly immortal properties of our goods to ourselves can occur. I presented Becker's hypothesis to several Foley core households and asked for their reactions. Most agreed with his idea:

People fear death, but don't want to talk about it. We find alternate means to get away from it.

Yes, there's a connection between death and materialism. If you have the belief that this is just a stopping-over place, material things are not so important.

Yes, that is true, but people aren't usually conscious of doing it. I guess that explains why we also get older, decaying people out of sight: too anxiety-provoking.

The self "distracting itself endlessly from itself" reaches the pitch permitted and encouraged by industrialism. We distract ourselves with activity as well as things. "Keeping busy" is a formula for keeping happy and warding off the questions of being that arise during times of quiet. As members of a culture where the material has primacy over the spiritual, we deny death and, as a consequence, distance ourselves from evidence of our biological and mortal nature. We don't do well with the organic or messy dimensions of life. We dislike disorder, smells, and decay—primary reasons given by Foleyans and Munka Ljungbyans for not recycling, let alone composting kitchen (or human!) wastes. An ad slogan for a vacuum cleaner reads, "Life is messy. Clean it up!" America's anal tendencies are symbolized by scented and pastel-colored trash bags on the market. Swedes were stunned when I told them about this product. "That's America," they muttered, shaking their heads.

It makes sense that if we want new, shiny, inoffensive things around us, we want new, shiny people, too. America's cult of youth and desire for youthful-looking bodies and faces is stronger than ever, paradoxically coupled with a quest for longevity. P. O. Hallin commented to me, "You Americans seem to be really *worried* about your cholesterol." I responded by saying that we believe that if we could just find the right mix of behavior and diet, we could live forever (and look fabulous, as well)—attested to by the recent manias for oat bran and fish oil and the current preoccupation with antioxidants and fat-free foods. We reject illness, and certainly do not accept pain. These crimp our blitz of (distracting, economically "productive") activities and our attempts to transcend our mortal nature. One painreliever's advertising jingle avers, "You haven't got time for the pain." Pain interferes with our careers, with our "busy, active lifestyles." In another ad, a woman is asked, "How is your headache?"

She replies, "How do you know I have a headache?" "It *shows*," comes the fearsome answer—the worst possible news in an image-based and competitive world, where you can all too easily become the wounded gazelle in the herd.

Given a materialist orientation toward the world and a system that engenders and depends on economic and social insecurities and that socializes for the ineffectual deflection of nonmaterial needs into material channels, of *course* consumers will continue to focus on the material and the short term. This perspective governs energy, environment, and consumption choices.

Chapter 9

Worldview

It is clear that industrial, money-market economy assumptions shape awareness of consumers in Foley and Munka Ljungby. The Swedes' awareness of the environment and the rest of the world is broader and more holistic, informed by the policies and positions of the welfare state. Yet, both Foleyans and Munka Ljungbyans belong to industrial consumer society and have been effectively socialized into a scientific-materialist worldview and consumerist values. In this chapter, their beliefs about future energy supplies and behavioral versus technological solutions are contrasted. Their stated conviction that they will have to be forced in order to reduce their consumption is documented. How they define quality of life, and gaps between ideal and real behavior, are investigated. Four dimensions of the industrial worldview, held by both individuals and institutions, are considered: emphasis on efficiency and growth, the "image of unlimited good," infatuation with technological solutions, and distance from the realities of production and consumption. The displacement of "conservation" by "efficiency" in energy discourse is considered. Industrialists assume unlimited resources because the money-market economy ignores thermodynamic and environmental constraints. Ingenious technology (especially cyber technology) is promoted as the solution for obstacles or shortages. Consumers perceive no context for their consumption choices, being cut off from the realities of agricultural and industrial production, as well as from the international dynamics and inequities of industrialism.

THE ENERGY FUTURE:
POTENTIAL SHORTAGES AND SOLUTIONS

Shortages

Skepticism about the authenticity of declared oil shortages was expressed by some Foleyans in the 1980s and by even more in the 1990s. They suspect "big business" of engaging in a ploy to maximize profit, and the collusion of government and the media in this deception as well. Some Foleyans added that even if the oil shortage was real, oil companies took advantage of the situation. Such skepticism colors views about the possibility of future shortages as well. Currently, Foleyans feel frustrated by conflicting estimates of fuel reserves. Foley opinion remains divided about the potential for fossil fuel shortages in the future. Foleyans express confusion, asking why there is inactivity regarding alternatives if future fossil fuel shortages are certain.

In the 1980s no one in Munka expressed disbelief in the reality of fuel shortages. In the 1990s a few Munka Ljungbyans did raise this question, but they communicate resignation ("It's business") rather than the angry scorn of the Foleyans. Despite their skepticism about the reality of the 1970s oil crises and confusion about present reserves, Foleyans continue to predict a closer date for a worldwide energy shortage than Munka Ljungbyans do. Additionally, more in Munka think that such a shortage will never exist. That Foleyans continue to believe in potential shortages in the near future contributes to greater energy conservation efforts and investments in improving the heating efficiency of their homes.

New Era: Behavioral Change versus Technological Innovation

In the 1980s most Foley core households responded positively to the question as to whether a new era in fuel acquisition and use was beginning. With fuel prices at formerly unimaginable levels and still climbing, Foleyans stressed energy-conserving behavior over new and more-efficient technology. The Foley minority emphasizing technology over behavior referred vaguely to Yankee ingenuity or miraculous-sounding developments. For example:

There are going to be some products coming down the pike . . . little pellets you drop in water . . . and we're going to have our energy out of *water*!

Some Foleyans evidenced continuing faith in nonspecific technology to solve environmental problems in the 1990s, illustrated by the following statement:

If they destroy it [the ozone layer], they should be able to remake it. . . . Our technology is at a stage that we should be able to undo these problems.

Only one core household in Munka Ljungby in the 1980s spoke of the need for conserving behavior, the majority stressing technological breakthroughs to solve energy supply problems. However, Munka references to technology were more grounded in reality than Foley's were. Specific government research projects for solar, wind, and geothermal alternatives were cited.

In the 1990s Foleyans puzzle over the size of remaining fuel reserves, and a sizable minority expressed confidence that some new supplemental or replacement fuel would become available. More Foleyans have joined the Swedes in faith in technology. Only a very few specified reality-based possibilities, however; vagueness and improbable tactics still characterize responses.

Several Foleyans expressed confidence in America's continuing economic ascendancy, declaring that this will ensure the country's fuel supply. The strong majority of Foleyans, however, envisions a more modest way of living and conserving behavior, reflected by the following statement:

Too many people are relying on technology. Future generations will be living at a lower standard than what we are now, and that's all there is to it. People are going to have to get used to living with less.

SOLVING ENERGY AND ENVIRONMENTAL PROBLEMS

In the 1990s Foley and Munka Ljungby core households were asked who should take the lead in solving energy and environmental problems. Foleyans expressed wistfully the hope that it could be, *should* be, individual citizens. They emphasized the need for consumers to say what they find unacceptable to business and industry as an impetus for changing wasteful and damaging practices.

Stern and Aronson (1984) write that "information alone will generally be insufficient to get energy users to change their stock of energy-using equipment or to use it differently, in ways that will save them money." Foley and Munka informants agree with them. Questionnaire respondents in both locales ranked technology as the best way to get families to conserve energy, followed by information; a combination of technology and information; and last, price (selected as best by only 5% in each community).

The need for forced change resonated in both communities. Residents say they need, even want, to be forced to conserve energy and to engage in pro-environmental actions such as recycling. They emphasize how hard it is for individuals to make choices against the flow of social opinion and to break ingrained habits. The behavioral change and simpler way of life Foleyans envision will come about, they say, only when external forces limit choices or make choices for them:

You know, I was secretly kinda glad when we had the energy "crisis." It forced us to do something we wouldn't otherwise have done, to cut back . . . to cut out the fat. There's too much waste, everybody says that, but nobody does anything.

To really change, most of us are going to have to be "helped" to change—to be *made* to change. . . . You get caught up in the hustle and bustle and don't follow through with your good intentions [about using less and recycling].

Munka Ljungbyans also identify a need for external forces to conserve energy and effect change:

It's not just supplying me with information; I must be forced to [use less energy]. It doesn't help if I do something and my neighbors do nothing. We must all do something in an imposed way. People don't practice what they preach.

People have it too good. They don't feel they are pressed, forced, to decrease. They must be forced. The state should provide [economic] help, though.

Foley informants say that while they would resent imposed constraints on their behavior, they would concede to some external arbiter. They describe energy and environmental problems as being vast and incomprehensible to individuals, who lack an overview. Foleyans debate just who the larger entity should be: government, business, environmental agencies, or educators. Suspicion of government—its lack of accountability and true initiative—characterizes this debate and is reflected in the following quotations:

Not the government. Lobbyists have made it out of whack. Leaders don't make *real* changes because they want to stay in office.

Taxes on energy would *always* go somewhere else. If the money went to research for alternatives, o.k., I'd pay—but it *won't*. We don't have any control on that.

Foleyans identified the private sector as being more efficient than government at, for example, operating recycling services. However, business is also suspect because of the primacy of the profit motive and perceived collusion with government.

Private industry wouldn't be honest with research findings on, say, alternative types of energy. Why should they threaten their profits?

Logging and clear cutting in northern Minnesota won't stop unless people say it's not acceptable. Logging companies have no qualms.

A few Foleyans advocated a disinterested agency, specifying the Environmental Protection Agency or the Minnesota Pollution Control Agency. A few others favored educators; two nominated Ralph Nader.

In responding to the question of who should take the lead in solving energy and environmental problems, Munka Ljungbyans nearly unanimously chose the government over individuals or private organizations. Although they share some of Foley's irritation with government and described declining confidence in Swedish politicians, they say that government can synthesize research findings and input from all sectors of society in order to come up with both the fairest and the most-realistic strategies. Government, they feel, can best address the diffuse, long-range, and international nature of energy and environmental issues as well. And critically, it is government that can mandate desired changes, both for industry and for citizens, while supplying them with information relative to the problem.

It's ultimately everybody's problem, but politics should take the lead. Research is

important and must be organized, and results communicated, on a larger scale. . . .
Information must be provided in combination with laws, so that people know how
serious it [the environmental situation] is.

Swedes are so authority-oriented . . . so law-abiding . . . so *Lutheran*! If the *kommun* says
[so], *then* it's a crisis. Otherwise, people won't respond. So, government must lead.

Cooperation from individual citizens is deemed essential to successful
solution of energy and environmental problems, however. Unlike Foleyans,
Munka Ljungbyans can cite a successful tradition of individual initiative
through folk movements and consumer organizations to bring about change—
recent examples being packaging and garbage reduction laws. Like Foleyans,
however, Munka Ljungbyans lament the politic indecision of politicians:

Who should take the lead? Any party whatsoever! But we're still waiting.

Politicians could decide, and should decide, about energy. But they won't. It isn't
workable politically. No one is ready to make a decision. Politicians listen too much to
the public and sway back and forth, back and forth.

Both communities, then, opt for force instead of discipline, for outer rather than
inner control. It is ironic that in the "individualistic" United States we want
someone else to do it for us, but in "socialist" Sweden more personal initiative is
taken, and people's movements are common.

QUALITY OF LIFE

A 1989 Gallup Poll showed that when given a list of physical health, family
life, betterment of society, and other goals, most respondents ranked "nice
home, car, other belongings" last (cited in Schor 1992). Foley and Munka core
households echo these priorities in their definitions of quality of life, both in the
1980s and the 1990s. They name good health, family and friends, and basic
material security as the essential components of quality of life. Whereas Foleyans say that what they have is sufficient for good quality of life, over half the
Munka core households declare their material standard *already* too high. A
typical Munka comment was: "We are overwhelmed by things now. Consume,
consume, consume: it's sickening." One household succinctly summed up
material quality of life as *"Lagom av allt! "* (a moderate amount of everything).
Six Munka households added that feeling content, not wanting more than can be
easily satisfied, is essential to quality of life.

Material things creep back into more detailed discussions, however.
Although no Foley household says that it desires a higher material standard, a
few include material dimensions in their definitions. For example, one young
couple said that quality of life means:

Living life to the fullest. Having a few nice things. . . . Having something that's better than somebody else's.

Another Foley household said that "toys" are important to high quality of life. Additionally, some Munka Ljungbyans said that pleasant home surroundings contribute to quality of life.

Economist Juliet Schor (1992) describes consumers being trapped in what she calls the work-and-spend cycle: employers rewarding increased productivity with higher income instead of more free time, to which employees become habituated. She points out the irony that Americans, when asked, nevertheless say that they reject consumerist values. In discussions, Foleyans and Munka Ljungbyans say that material things are not essential to quality of life, but many opt for these things when making real-life choices. (Recall that fewer than half of Foley questionnaire respondents said that they would like to live a simpler life with fewer possessions.) Likewise, informants' harrying activity schedules contradict their philosophies. That their behavior belies their philosophy is due to entrapment in the cycle of work and spend, and to attempts to succeed in a system ordered and defined by economic productivity and growth goals.

Foleyans more often identify having more time and less stress as components of quality of life than Munka Ljungbyans do. That having more time would enhance life was cited by 10 Foley households but by only 3 in Munka. (It should be noted that Swedes have more structured free time: all workers are guaranteed a minimum five weeks' paid vacation annually and enjoy more holidays per year as well. There is a permissive ethos about leaving early on weekends, especially in the summer, and the state often pays when parents take time away from their jobs to care for their children.) Six Foley households said that less stress would be desirable. Three Munka households specified less stress, and 3 responded, "Peace and quiet!" Additionally, 2 Munka households emphasized peace of mind and loosening up from "the shoulds" as desirable for high quality of life.

Two Foley households incorporated altruism into their definitions, emphasizing that they wanted to "help society work, help the community" or to "do something with life that will benefit others." Individualism characterizes Foley responses more strongly, however—having choices and doing and getting what one wants:

It's a freedom thing. To do *what* you want, *when* you want.

In the 1990s only one Foley household cited a clean environment, but half the Munka households specified access to nature, as being important to quality of life.

Foleyans are much more likely than Munka Ljungbyans to name faith in God as integral to quality of life. Seven of the 20 core households in Foley did so, but no Munka household included religious faith in its definition. Instead, Munka Ljungbyans emphasize social solidarity. A democratic or free society is said to be essential to quality of life, and Sweden is judged to be providing well for its citizens in that respect.

GAPS BETWEEN IDEAL AND REAL BEHAVIOR

It is a commonplace that people say one thing and do another. A classic problem for anthropologists is the dissonance between ideal and real behavior (what people say they do or think versus what they actually do) in the societies they study. This dissonance was evident in Foley and Munka Ljungby. In the 1980s, for example, many Foleyans railed against the restraints of conserving behavior but proceeded to conserve in order to control fuel bills. And in the 1990s, Hallin found *no* statistically significant correlation between expressed environmental concern and pro-environmental behavior in either Foley or Munka Ljungby. Even though they express certain frustrations with consumer society, Foleyans and Munka Ljungbyans largely accept its values and comply with economic and social mandates to consume and conform. As is apparent from their consumption rationales and explanations of resistance to change, when goals conflict, social and economic considerations win out over energy and environmental conservation.

Even within households, members conserve in some ways but remain indifferent to, or even splurge in, others. In one Munka household, the husband faithfully bicycles to his work in Ängelholm, but his homemaker wife takes their car and drives, fast and far, whenever she feels restless (as she said, *Lappsjuk*, or cabin fever). Another household is distinguished by its hand lawn mower, but, atypically for Munka, has an electric can opener and many other small appliances and gadgets. One Foley household sets the indoor temperature relatively very low and got rid of paper towels and a few small kitchen appliances—but bought a powerful, high-speed motorboat and other "pleasant" recreational items.

One example from Munka shows how two households can have very different interpretations of the same issue: driving versus bicycling to work. Two neighbors, men, both work in Munka's industrial park and return home for lunch. One drives and one bikes to work. One man laughs, amused at the very idea of walking or biking instead of driving: "I come home for lunch and let the dog out, so I *must* take the car." The second man says he bicycles to work because that way he gets exercise and fresh air, saves money, pollutes less, and "can hear the birds. . . . Besides, I come home for lunch, so it would be even *sillier* for me to use the car so much."

INDUSTRIAL WORLDVIEW

Efficiency and Growth

In both the United States and Sweden, a semantic shift has occurred over time. Energy efficiency replaced energy conservation in the media. (In Sweden, *energisparande* became *rationell energianvändning*.) Unlike conservation, efficiency connotes no depriving cutbacks and is in keeping with dominant cultural values. Further, efficiency means that we can maintain existing patterns by lowering their energy demands.

Efficiency is a much more appealing proposition than conservation, to those in the energy field and the public alike, in that it harmonizes with other goals of industrial society—such as improved technology, greater productivity, and scientific solutions. Further, as Lutzenhiser (1992) writes, focusing on increasing efficiency precludes critical examination of industrialism's social structures, consumerism, and corporate and government influence on consumption. The issue of equity is ignored.

Ultimately, cultural analysis cannot support the argument that the contents of habit, practice, lifestyle, utility or servicing are unimportant (i.e. that they simply need to be made more efficient across the board). An attempt to take that turn was made in the 1980s, when energy research broke with its historic concern for conservation, and adopted an interest in efficiency. While securing a more broadly-based legitimacy for the movement, this turn also served to direct attention away from the comparative consumptiveness of various lifestyles and social structures, the issue of equity . . . and the influences of corporations and governments upon public and private sector consumption and conservation.

Likewise, increasing energy efficiency (or recycling) is preferable to reducing consumption of goods for many analysts and consumers. The primary rationale given by consumers for their continued consumerism—despite expressed weariness, disenchantment, or distaste for this behavior—is that consumption provides jobs. Economists and politicians, fixed on economic growth and GDP measures, exhibit similar circular thinking. On the international level as well, growth in its industrial conception is assumed: for example, the Brundtland Report (that from the U.N. World Commission on Environment and Development 1987) prescribes an annual growth rate of 3–4 percent. Challenging this assumption, Dutch economists Jan Tinbergen and Roefie Hueting (1991) advocate halting further growth in the production of "rich countries," as well as developing appropriate technologies, stabilizing global population, and making international income distribution more equitable. John Peet (1992) likewise criticizes the Brundtland Report for avoiding "the real issue, the requirement for rich nations to consume less so that the poor can consume enough, while keeping total global resource and pollution flows at a manageable level."

Some energy researchers as well challenge the constricted perspectives of consumers, economists, politicians—and their own colleagues. One of these, Danish physicist and sustainability analyst Jørgen Nørgård (1995), addresses the need to expand thinking beyond growth and efficiency goals in his insightful paper, "Efficient Technology in an Inefficient Economy." Nørgård urges us to recognize that a fundamental redefinition of the current money-market system is necessary for the achievement of true environmental sustainability. The theme of his paper is that in Europe, "modest gains in technological energy efficiencies are more than offset by an increasing inefficiency of lifestyles and political systems aiming for economic growth." Nørgård gives examples of political resistance toward proposals that in any way constrain the growth economy— such as doubling the longevity of durable goods or the Danish leave of absence program to reduce unemployment and increase leisure time. He underscores the irony of GDP accounting: "When a society is geared towards economic growth, a more expensive solution to a problem will somehow get most attention, for instance by creating more jobs." The most inefficient behavior generates the largest GDP.

Nørgård also exposes what he calls the "myth of the harmless service sector," which assumes that as an economy becomes increasingly based on services over goods, its energy intensity will be reduced. He cites analyses by Danish economist Jesper Jespersen that indicate that public service (child and elder care, education, health) is less than half as energy intensive as manufacturing, but that private service (trade, hotels, and transport) is close to manufacturing in energy intensity. Nørgård further contrasts the inherently limited demand for public services with the boundless demand for private services.

The Image of Unlimited Good

Swedish anthropologist Alf Hornborg (1992) incisively indicts the fragmentary and distorting nature of the industrial society worldview. Hornborg describes how industrial societies, disregarding thermodynamics, assign a high "utility value" (an artificial, culturally based concept) to the products they manufacture—with consequences that are ecologically damaging, economically exploitative, and socially unjust. Hornborg calls this worldview "the image of unlimited good." His phrase is an ironic contrast with "the image of *limited* good," a concept created by anthropologist George Foster (1965) to characterize the outlook of Mesoamerican peasants—in which desired things in life exist in finite quantity, so that gains in one area imply losses in another. Hornborg states that contemporary expectations of unbounded material growth and prosperity arise from assumptions and values propounded by industrial economies, which ignore the more essential dynamics of energy and ecology.

What is the difference between market "utility value" and thermodynamic "real value?" Real value refers to the available energy contained in naturally occurring entities or manufactured products. This usable energy is also referred to as "order." The second law of thermodynamics, the entropy law, states that all processes of energy conversion must entail a net reduction of order in the universe. Constant input of energy from the sun maintains organic systems; otherwise, all order would dissipate and all life on earth would expire. However, the second law applied to "industrial technomass" means that "the earth's limited stocks of mineral exergy are disordered into waste and pollution." ("Exergy" is negative entropy—that is, high order or high use value.)

There is no way of reversing the entropic process. Further, it is accelerated by the industrial market economy's assigning of an artificial high utility to its products. Hornborg (1992) points out that conventional economic ideology obscures entropy by misrepresenting industrial production and consumption as generating value. Members of industrial society fetishize the machine, regarding it as having productive force in itself and not recognizing the "flows of exergy which sustain it." Further, we fetishize money: a growing GNP disguises the fact that production is merely the creation of symbolic value, based on the abstract notion of the utility of industrial products.

The current low prices of raw materials (high in useful energy, or exergy) and high prices of consumer goods (low in exergy) subsidize industrialism. "Merely to manage maintenance, industry must be paid *more* for its products than it spends on raw materials, even though it has achieved a *decrease* in the overall sum of order" (Hornborg 1992). Hornborg identifies industry as an essentially wasteful form of production which can continue only through subsidization by what he calls "an asymmetric world trade in energy." He adds in another article that "Only from a local perspective can it appear 'productive' or 'efficient.' . . . The ideology of 'growth' is a local, industrial perspective which excludes the entropization of non-industrial sectors from its field of vision" (1993).

Further, these inversions of real value maintain industrial imperialism: we are not only deluding ourselves but also exploiting others. Industrialists define world market prices, which disregard more fundamental measures of value. Hornborg (1993) calls the global money-market economy an artificial "house of cards," in which international credit institutions have encouraged Third World countries to take loans with escalating debt payments, "stimulating continued, unequal exchange. . . . What is being exchanged is intact exergy for spent exergy . . . [because] from a thermodynamic point of view, products are deteriorated materials."

"Perhaps, in the long run, the only way to liberate human bodies and souls from the grip of this parasitic, synthetic biomass . . . is to refuse to define nature as 'raw materials' and life as 'labour.' Such a cosmological shift might make us stop rewarding 'production' (i.e. destruction) *for its own sake*" (Hornborg 1993).

Infatuation with Technological Solutions

The industrial image of unlimited good gives rise to collective searches for solutions to energy and environmental problems based on high-tech approaches—just what got us into these problems originally. Smart houses, cars, and smart everything else are promoted with seeming indifference to the resources they would consume or to the Third World, and reflect deep infatuation with cyber-technology. What McKibben (1989) calls the "mindless worship of a miracle future" to rescue us from problems has led to proposals of orbiting solar collectors, satellites of thin film to throw shadows on the earth in order to counteract the greenhouse effect, and lasers to eliminate CFCs from the atmosphere.

McLaughlin (1993) also challenges our fanciful and uncritical attitudes toward technological solutions:

There is a recurrent fantasy that some kind of technological invention will suffice to resolve all our problems. One could sense this reaction sweep through the United States a few years ago when it appeared that the process of "cold" fusion would offer unlimited energy in the not too distant future. Almost no one pondered whether such a development would be good; its virtue was assumed. There was almost no awareness that access to unlimited energy by this society might be catastrophic for the good of humans and certainly would be so for other forms of life. Is giving a drunk an automobile that runs on air a good idea?

According to leading energy analyst John Holdren (1992), another 20–30 years of research is needed to determine the feasibility of cold fusion—and even such a breakthrough may not result in cheaper energy. Whether it does or not, it would not correct the consumerist trajectory we are on. Further, availability of cheap energy would accelerate resource depletion and environmental destruction.

Bill McKibben (1992) questions the assumption that technology will confer limitless advances and advantages:

What is there that we can't do now that we will be able to do when we've developed artificial intelligence and virtual reality and smart houses and all the other shiny promises of the technological future? What convenience or comfort does the average American life lack? If you could pick three conditions on earth to change in the next 50 years, would you want "advances"—picture phones, virtual reality, computer shopping—or would you want more quiet, more community, cleaner air?

The problem is, we want both, as our culture implies is possible, and don't understand why this can't be so.

Recall the Foleyan who predicted making energy from pellets dropped into water. Other Foley statements reflect faith in technological solutions, such as the "fixing" of the hole in the ozone layer. Although Munka Ljungby's faith in technology and science is less fanciful, it is even more pervasive. Munka Ljungbyans nearly unanimously stressed technology over behavioral change to solve energy and environmental problems. As Lundgren (1992) points out, technological solutions are often more costly but generally faster and easier to implement compared to "politically costly" behavioral solutions. Stern, Young, and Druckman (1992) characterize the Montreal Protocol as a "paradigmatic" case of a quick technical fix, something "that can be used for exactly the same purposes without requiring any fundamental change in human economies or societies."

Hornborg (1992) urges us to recognize that "There is no technology for gaining a human livelihood more *efficient* than those which sustained human-kind prior to the Industrial Revolution." He expands on this conviction:

A part of this awakening, also, would be to realize that the global technomass is indis-solubly linked to the combustion of fossil fuels, and to stop dreaming about a means of harvesting solar exergy more efficient than photosynthesis. If modern technologies for generating electricity from renewable sources (sun, water and wind) were not subsidized by the global appropriation of fossil fuels, as Georgescu-Roegen has argued, what do we mean by saying that the under-developed countries cannot afford these technologies? And what makes them so unprofitable even in developed countries? When the destruc-tive nature of our economic system is emphasized, economists will often reply by expressing confidence in better technologies, but when technologists are asked why these have not yet been introduced, they tend to refer to faulty economics. (Hornborg 1993)

Detachment from the Realities of Production and Consumption

Economic theory and institutions have become disconnected from thermo-dynamic and environmental realities, and consumers in turn internalize this distortion. Robert David Sack (quoted in Stern, Young, and Druckman 1992) argues that "environmental degradation is ultimately tied to social forms and mechanisms that have *divorced the consumer from awareness* of the realities of production, hence leading to irresponsible behavior that exacerbates global change." Certainly, this is clear in Foley and Munka Ljungby—detachment from industrial, and lately agricultural, processes. Recall Foley's earlier illusion of invulnerability to energy crises and its only recent recognition of agriculture's heavy oil dependence. Though Munka Ljungbyans' perspectives are broader, they too evidence a fragmented awareness of production.

Detachment from the physical realities of land and production finds a parallel in disconnection from the material realities of our own bodies. That we are fooling ourselves with our perennial quest for a free lunch is apparent in thermodynamics-defying advertisements assuring us that we can have whatever we want, immediately and without effort. Weight-loss pills and patches "melt fat while you sleep," and a cream rubbed into thighs will "reduce and slim and firm" them. In our image-based society, even the illusion of such results is equally acceptable: control-top pantyhose ads read, "Don't do leg lifts when you can buy them" and "Don't skip dessert—Just look as though you did!"

The very nature of the modern industrial world obscures it from the consumer, its complexity and the speed of its constant change making it an unfathomable kaleidoscope. In *Place, Modernity, and the Consumer's World*, geographer Sack (1992) characterizes mass consumption as a means of creating context, creating places for ourselves through products, in a culture that feels fragmentary and impermanent. Sack's analysis is distinguished from other social science functionalism, however, by his insightful critique. Sack writes that whereas the products we consume empower us to create contexts, these contexts are distorted because we place ourselves at their centers. According to Sack (1992), places of consumption "encourage us not to think of ourselves as links in a chain but, rather, as the center of the world." This false positioning blocks us from awareness of larger dynamics of cause-and-effect:

From the perspective of the consumer's world, it is virtually impossible to understand the real effects we have. . . . A shop that sells Colombian coffee does not reveal the social structure that produces the coffee, the economic impact of coffee production on the Colombian economy, or the way coffee growing affects the Colombian government. Instead, Colombian coffee is advertised as though it were picked by fictitious planters, like Juan Valdez, in a coffee-producing paradise.

That we are unaware of both the antecedents and the consequences of our world-transforming consumption choices in this "context without a context" impedes us from choosing responsibly. Sack (1992) writes:

The consumer's world undermines our ability to act morally and responsibly because it obscures the consequences of our actions at the very outset. The consumer's world portrays itself as a context without a context, a front stage without a backstage. . . . The world of consumption denies the existence of a broader reality. Moreover, consumption is . . . a principal means by which we transform the world. . . . It makes it appear as though there is no world supporting consumption and, therefore, no need to understand this world. Mass consumption thus fosters irresponsibility.

Conclusion

Previous chapters have described factors shaping the awareness and choices of Foleyans and Munka Ljungbyans with regard to energy, environment, and consumption. In this concluding chapter, obstacles to change in consumers' everyday lives and outlook, and potential routes to overcoming them, are considered. I believe that we must outgrow consumerism and not just reform industrialism but profoundly restructure our economic life. Otherwise, containment of energy and resource demand will be sporadic and incomplete (as the industrial model spreads throughout the world), and ecological catastrophe merely forestalled.

Both Europe and America initially achieved substantial reductions in residential energy demand after the 1970s oil crises—largely due to retrofits and the displacement of older technology and appliances by new, more-efficient models. Behavioral efforts also contributed to these reductions. In Foley and Munka Ljungby, some energy-conserving practices begun under duress continue even after fuel prices stabilized and anxiety subsided—for example, lower indoor temperatures and cold water laundering (in Foley) and operating full dishwashers and clotheswashers (in both Foley and Munka). However, the decline in residential fuel demand in both the United States and Europe slowed in the mid 1980s and is currently on the rise. Larger homes, increased saturation of appliances, and a gradual rebound in indoor temperatures all contribute to this trend (Schipper, Haas, and Sheinbaum 1996).

The price motivation for conservation which Foleyans and Munka Ljungbyans identified as absolutely essential to their efforts no longer exists. Consumers have become inured to the prices that stunned them in the late 1970s, and these prices have declined substantially in real terms since then. Fuel costs represent an even smaller portion of household budgets than they did earlier. Energy use is no longer infused with the emotion that it once was: fear and anger in Foley and the call to national solidarity in Munka. Of course, regardless of trends in direct energy consumption, demand for embodied energy and resources will continue to rise in order to satisfy consumerism's relentless voracity. Recall that even during the period of high oil prices, new home size continued upward, and consumers acquired more and more appliances—and the current shift in energy demand from production to pleasure.

Environmental rebound has also begun, signaled by reports appearing about declining interest in green consumerism and a return to products such as disposable diapers in the United States. Arguments against the effectiveness of recycling (Tierney 1996) further indicate the pendulum's return. In isolation from other change, and deflecting as it does more-basic questions about the assumptions of industrial consumerism, recycling is merely a stopgap measure. However, those who argue against it are not coming from this perspective but instead stress the abundance of remaining landfill space and resources.

Foleyans and Munka Ljungbyans reflect the consumerist societies to which they belong. Although perspectives have broadened in Foley since the 1980s, the household economic unit continues to dominate awareness; few Foleyans are conscious of the larger environmental, economic, or sociopolitical contexts of their household activities. Munka Ljungbyans have deeper personal bonds with the environment. They embody Sweden's pervasive moralism, more quickly identifying ethical dimensions of energy use and environment and advocating equity in resource distribution. Munka Ljungbyans evidence broader and more holistic perspectives, and greater ecological and international awareness. Yet, they too are engulfed by consumerist institutions and worldview.

Foleyans and Munka Ljungbyans alike dislocate what they personally have and do, the choices they make in daily life, from the larger problems they lament. In Foley especially, informants convey feelings of helplessness and isolation with regard to these problems—unable to experience the feelings of solidarity that Munka Ljungbyans have. Residents of neither community fully relate consumerist demand for products to its consequences for energy, environment, and equity. They censure what they call "excessive" consumption but feel that it can be remedied without any change in personal standards or patterns of living. Though they feel that environmental protection should not be subordinate to economic growth, they also think that such growth is necessary for economic health. And the conviction that we should buy more to foster the economy persists, especially in Foley.

Both Foleyans and Munka Ljungbyans emphasize nonmaterial dimensions when defining quality of life. They also say that they want fewer possessions and fewer obligations and activities, more time for themselves. They indicate environmental concern as well. Even though on one level they mean these statements, their everyday choices belie them. Caught up in the enervating work-and-spend cycle, Foleyans and Munka Ljungbyans lack the psychic energy to act on their convictions. Further, they share the image of unlimited good fostered by industrial consumer culture and believe that they can have it all: more time, more things, cheap energy, unlimited social and physical mobility, unending economic growth, and a clean and protected environment. Many are caught up in social emulation and in personal validation through material possessions and achievements. They persist in attempting to satisfy nonmaterial needs with material things, even when they acknowledge this as misdirected. Fearful of potential social rejection and personal anomie, they are unable to break through and take even the first steps toward simplifying their lives.

In Foley especially, consumers feel politically powerless in the absence of a tradition of consumer movements and strong advocacy groups. Certainly, the grip of vested interests on the government and the survival needs of office-holders make the status quo seem intractable. Additionally, the institutions and economic premises of consumerist society are themselves narrow, separating consumers from awareness of the realities of production (both agricultural and industrial) and its international dynamics. Consumers are socialized into a truncated and fragmented awareness that excludes thermodynamics, international relations, and social injustice. Yet they have begun to question not only the environmental costs but also the personal toll of industrial consumerism. In earlier chapters, Foleyans and Munka Ljungbyans testified to the difficulty of initiating change, even change that they desire, when it goes against internalized cultural values and social sanctions. How might consumers break out of consumerism, so socially pervasive and personally deep-seated?

THE ABERRATION OF INDUSTRIALISM

On the institutional level, breaking out of the industrial consumerist paradigm means acknowledgment of the thermodynamics which underlie all human economies and redirection toward sustainability as overarching goal. A commonly-used definition of sustainable development is that of the World Commission on Environment and Development: "development that meets the needs of the present without compromising the ability of future generations to meet their own needs" (WCED 1987). The only appropriate framework for such deliberation is a global one, not that of the individual nation. The concept of sustainability is generally out of awareness in Foley and Munka Ljungby, although some residents of each town conveyed their feelings that something is profoundly wrong about the consumerist trajectory we are on. Global citizenship? Of all the core households, only one Munka informant brought up a global issue, that of the world's burgeoning population.

Industrialism can be seen both as a type of material production and a particular kind of culture, consumer culture. In retrospect, industrialism will be viewed as an aberrational phase, a detour, in the collective evolution of humanity. It is a destructive system:

- *Energetically*, with heavy fossil fuel subsidization of industry and agriculture accelerating entropy
- *Economically*, built on artificial and arbitrary exchange values of a culturally-created money-market system

- *Politically*, with exploitation of and blatant disregard for nonindustrialized peoples and cultures
- *Psychologically*, providing its members no means of identity formation other than occupation and possessions
- *Spiritually*, its consumerist premises and rewards antithetical to spiritual development

However, industrialism is tenacious. Andrew McLaughlin (1993) writes:

It seems hard to imagine that human societies will shift from industrialism toward some other social formation by choice. Recent events in Eastern Europe show that people, when they can grasp a chance for material abundance, will do so. Industrialism, urbanism, alienation from the earth, division of one's life into work and leisure, the perception of nature as a mere resource, and the resultant consumerist orientation toward life seem to hang together as a social formation that most modern societies strive to realize.

Ecological crises and shortages of energy and other resources could force new environmental awareness and appreciation. Without fundamental changes in old industrialist attitudes toward nature and systemic thermodynamics, however, quick technological fixes will continue to dominate proposals for solutions of energy and environmental problems. And without concern for equity, rich nations will continue to buy their way out of problems. Steady-state economist Herman Daly (1988) declares that a "great ecological spasm" would be needed to convince people that something is wrong with the economics of industrialism, predicated as it is on unending growth. Daly writes that crisis conditions by themselves, however, will not create a responsive public "unless there is a *spiritual basis providing moral resources* for taking purposive action" (quoted in McLaughlin 1993, emphasis added here). The need for such spiritual grounding is addressed later in this chapter.

GOVERNMENTAL INITIATION OF CHANGE

Feeling oppressed by consumerist culture, Foleyans and Munka Ljungbyans say that they want to reduce consumption and live in greater balance with the environment. What will enable them to bring about such profound change in their lives? Government implementation of truly progressive energy and environmental policies is doubtful because, as Foleyans attest, "politicians want to stay in office." The conundrum is that such proposals die or weaken in legislatures, victims of what representatives think their constituents want or of vested-interest lobbies (for example, the emaciation of the broad energy tax proposed by Vice President Gore into a trivial 4.3-cent-per-gallon gasoline tax). Such "political gridlock" (Lovins 1996) effectively stifles attempts at substantive change. American citizens do not have a true voice in their system. Swedes, though more justly represented, express concern about the increased priority their government gives to economic over environmental issues and its waffling on the nuclear power referendum decision.

John Peet (1992) writes that there is a "moral vacuum presently character-izing attitudes" and that by default the marketplace will determine future policies. Our current artificially-low fuel prices, resulting from direct and indirect subsidies and not reflecting environmental and sociopolitical costs, are predicted to rise only very gradually over the next two decades. We can assume that under these conditions government will continue to act from short-term economic interest and leave resultant major energy and environmental problems for future generations to contend with.

Even if one country should take bold environmental action, its effectiveness would be limited. Environmental damage is clearly a global problem, for which sustained international cooperation and commitment are needed. As Stern, Young, and Druckman (1992) write, "Efforts to cope with some large-scale environmental changes such as ozone depletion and global warming seem doomed to fail if some of the major national actors do not cooperate." They cite as precedents for cooperation the 1946 convention for the regulation of whaling and the 1973 restriction on international trade in endangered species. Nonsub-scribers of course sabotage the effectiveness of such efforts—for example, Norway's announcement in 1993 that it would increase its catch beyond the limits sanctioned by the International Whaling Commission. Another example of political obstruction is the United States not signing the biodiversity agree-ment until two years after the Rio conference. Even when accord among nations is achieved, individual opportunists can undermine it. The Montreal Protocol of 1987, which mandates cutting CFC production and consumption in half by the year 2000, has led to the smuggling of tons of outlawed CFCs into American and European black markets (Hanley 1996). Though they are heartening, advances in international cooperation are not substantive enough to truly redirect consumer society—to redefine ends and restructure means, to address the sources rather than the symptoms of the problems we face.

A global frame of reference which goes beyond opportunistic (and danger-ously outmoded) nationalism is now essential. We need as well more than just a broadening of institutions within society (such as those proposed by ecological economists to incorporate "external costs")—we need a whole new system, an alternative to money-market industrialism and its consumerist corollaries. For, as McLaughlin (1993) writes, "Accommodating industrialism, as realistic as this may appear to be in terms of political change, seems to implicitly advocate either continued domination of the Third World by the industrial nations or a totally unrealistic image of an ecologically unlimited biosphere." Hornborg (1993) also urges the radical rejection of money-market thinking:

Unless we are prepared to reorganize society in a much more fundamental way, any green taxes or other breaks on the system substantial enough to have a real impact on consumption would create economic chaos. . . . More likely, the green taxes would never reach the magnitude at which such effects would follow, in which case they would remain symbolic and pointless. . . . Our only hope is to replace [the logic of money] with a new systemic intentionality.

Herman Daly and theologian John Cobb (1989) offer just such an intentionality in *For the Common Good: Redirecting the Economy toward Community, the Environment, and a Sustainable Future*. They critique misplaced concreteness in economics and other academic disciplines and discuss the implications of a thermodynamic orientation for truly progressive change. Further, they present specific policies they have formulated for such areas as free trade, population, agriculture, industry, and taxation.

ENVIRONMENTAL ETHICS

Change will have to come from the people, rather than from the political institutions which currently exist. Recent social science research documents growth in popular concern for the environment. On the basis of their survey results, Kempton, Boster, and Hartley (1995) conclude that pro-environmental values have become central to American culture. Dunlap and Van Liere (1978) perceive that the earlier "dominant social paradigm," in which humans are seen as separate from and above nature, is changing into a "new environmental paradigm" in which humans are seen as just one element of complex nature.

Environmental ethics contribute essentially to the effort to alter consumerist value systems. Originating in both religious and secular philosophies, burgeoning publications about these ethical systems reflect the appeal of the new environmental paradigm. The land ethic of Aldo Leopold has received renewed appreciation and is joined by the work of "geologian" Thomas Berry, Charlene Spretnak's ecofeminism, Brian Swimme's cosmogenesis, and James Lovelock's Gaia. J. Baird Callicott's (1994) cross-cultural survey of cultural and religious environmental ethics, *Earth's Insights*, and Edward Goldsmith's *The Way: An Ecological World-view*, raise awareness of potentially unifying environmental values that transcend place and time. Goldsmith (1983) presents expressions of the concept of "the Way" of the cosmos, a single order of unity prevailing in the biosphere, from religions and philosophies, both contemporary and historical. A change in environmental ethics is necessary to prevent global environmental disaster. Clearly, this change must be more than a veneer of newly adopted postures over a persistent consumerist base. Where will these new ethics come from? What is the origin of deep feelings for the environment?

Altruism and Love of Nature

How feasible and enduring is conservation of energy and natural resources out of motives of altruism? Though the Swedish social welfare state may be grounded by an ethos of solidarity, the daily lives of Foleyans and Munka Ljungbyans are more similar than not. Greater differences exist between the policies of the two countries than between the behaviors of their citizens. Altruism and solidarity are strongly valued in Sweden, but these feelings are eroded by economic downturn. Additionally, Sweden has witnessed attenuation of this ethos in younger generations and in an increasingly heterogeneous population. Further, socialization for these values is inherently limited, because it springs from a political and materialist base. Altruism and solidarity are, of course, largely overwhelmed in America's aggressive and individual competition. Lars Lundgren (1992) warns emphatically against any expectation that altruism will contribute to the solution of environmental problems.

As several authors stress, nature has become for many another consumer product. Outdoor vistas and experiences are snatched up by nature lovers, who, though smug about their ability to appreciate and to commune with nature, also lust after top-quality, high-price gear—status symbols among outdoorsy peers. "Love of nature" is ultimately a weak motive, vulnerable to co-optation by environmental consumerism—and also to what Alain Touraine (1989) calls "green fundamentalism": baby-with-the-bathwater rejection of rationality and science in the course of rejecting "the god of Progress." Tactics such as Earth First!'s tree-spiking shows callousness toward other humans. What can generate altruistic motivation deeper than socialization for solidarity or feelings of love of nature?

Deep Ecology

One source of environmental ethics is deep ecology, a perspective developed by Norwegian philosopher Arne Naess. Deep ecologists (Naess 1973, Devall and Sessions 1985, Fox 1990) challenge the industrial view of humans as separate from and dominant over nature, maintaining that humans are just one part of the organic whole. Deep ecology is welcome in that it radically challenges the industrial money-market view of nature as an aggregation of resources and the illusion of humanity's independence and separateness from nature. It also offers a mode of creating identity that is an alternative to the consumerist formula of identity through possessions. Its adherents say that individuals embracing the tenets of deep ecology will come to discover their "ecological selves," expanding the boundaries of identification beyond the ego as far as possible. Ideally, this entails identification with the entire ecosystem, so that you believe that if you hurt any part of the ecosystem, you are hurting yourself and all your fellow inhabitants as well. Warwick Fox (1990) writes that such ecological self-realization must precede environmental ethics and laws— that you have to know who you are before you can decide how to act.

Awe Inspired by Nature

Agnostics and even atheists feel awe or respect for nature, a spirituality in nature. Participants in the Kempton, Boster, and Hartley study (as did Foleyans, and to a lesser extent, Munka Ljungbyans) invoked beliefs about human responsibilities as caretakers of divine creation as the basis for their pro-environmental values. It is logical that respondents who said that they belong to an organized religion were likely to agree with the survey statement, "Because God created the natural world, it is wrong to abuse it." But a surprising finding is that 69 percent of those who are not members of any organized religion agreed with this statement—and of those who do not believe that a spiritual force in the universe even exists, 46 percent agreed!

On the basis of Genesis 1:28, the Judeo-Christian tradition has been accused of disdaining the environment and fostering anthropocentric environmental destruction, because the translation of humanity's "dominion [over . . . every living thing]" connotes imperialism to the industrial reader. Evidence can be gathered to blame this religious tradition for damaging the environment and for ravaging indigenous peoples and cultures. However, such spoilage is linked more closely with industrialism than with theology—both industrialism's dissociation from nature and the destructive nature and scale of industrial processes. The scientific-materialist, industrial worldview removes us from both from God and nature, resulting in the loss of the sense of our place in the cosmos and engendering great fearfulness. Rudolf Bahro (1989), one of the founders of Germany's Green Party, writes, "Einstein thought the ultimate task of science was to establish a trust in the order of the cosmos so that man would lose his destructive fear." Theodore Roszak (1995) also sounds this theme of trust as essence: "The problem is that in the Western industrial societies we seek to achieve it [security] through domination rather than trust. And if I understand the real meaning of deep ecology and other environmental philosophies, they are summoning us back to a sense of trust as the secret of society."

But what are we to trust *in*? Increasingly, a purely scientific approach to the problems we face is seen as ineffectual—and the past damages of this approach recognized. Trusting in "the Way," a "single order of unity prevailing in the biosphere" (Goldsmith 1993), seems a little impersonal, rather a philosophical stretch—and, like deep ecology and other environmental philosophies, hard to translate into action. The biosphere holds no inherent morals or ethics. Also, ethics based on environmental care are not enough, because ultimately they remain secular philosophies. Deep ecology replaces anthropocentrism with biocentrism but largely retains a materialist (in the sense of *matter*) foundation. In order to transform industrial consumerism, Robert Ornstein and Paul Ehrlich (1989b) declare, we must "make available to students the conclusion of all the world's great religions of the unity of humanity . . . and [offer a] *new synthesis* between modern *scientific* understanding of the world and elements of *religious* traditions that provide moral guidance not offered by science" (emphasis added).

Daly and Cobb (1989) concur, writing that "the real possibility for change depends on an awakening of the religious depths in a world whose secularity has gone quite stale" and that

The changes that are now needed in society are at a level that stirs religious passions. The debate will be a religious one whether that is made explicit or not. The whole under-standing of reality and the orientation to it are at stake. . . . Idolatry in the guise of misplaced concreteness and [academic] disciplinolatry have brought us to the present crisis. Overcoming these is a religious task.

Daly and Cobb urge the embrace of theocentrism, or God-centeredness. Such a "theocentric undergirding of the biospheric perspective" incorporates both ecological thought and justice issues. Theocentrism further functions as a check against idolatry, defined by these authors as "treating as ultimate or whole that which is not ultimate or whole"—such as one's self, nation, or even environment. It "makes ethical life more authentic and heightens sensitivity to aspects of reality that are otherwise neglected . . . gives real importance to what happens in the world, especially to the despised."

SPIRITUAL RESTORATION

Even radical changes in social and economic paradigms are ultimately insufficient for crisis resolution, for these orientations are materialist at base. A spiritual impetus is necessary to achieve truly enduring change that is unaffected by transient political currents and alliances, social trends, or economic circumstances. America, though profligate, is more likely a source of this impetus than highly secular Sweden. Foleyans acknowledge the importance of spiritual values. Even if some of this is only lip service or ideal culture, such overt naming is a beginning. Spiritually grounded individuals search for identity and satisfactions outside the material framework (including material philosophies). Regarding the environment as a divine creation reflecting divine attributes, they feel both deep reverence and personal responsibility toward it, rather than using experiences in nature as an antidote to the stresses of workaday "reality." They love and care for all environments, the mundane as well as the pristine and picturesque. Further, they express solidarity with all people, born of the recognition that all share an essentially spiritual nature.

In recognizing this oneness, true humility is reclaimed—and core stuff, not merely intellectual or ethical reform. Such humility enables life in harmony with what Wendell Berry (1987) calls the Great Economy or the Kingdom of God. The Great Economy is beyond any money-market economy, and beyond any economy based on energy as well. The all-inclusive Great Economy is "both greater and more intricate than we can know," containing as it does everything visible and invisible. Like Hornborg, Berry stresses that human economies cannot make real value, but can only add artificial, culturally constructed value to the real entities that they alter. He writes, "When humans presume to originate value, they make value that is first abstract and then false, tyrannical, and destructive." Industrial economy is based on "invasion and pillage" of the Great Economy, where real value originates.

Berry declares that we can call it whatever we wish, but that we cannot describe the Great Economy except through reference to religious tradition, and cites parallel Christian, Buddhist, and Tao allusions to the concept. Berry addresses the error industrialists make in seeing themselves as limitless, and the dangerous consequences of such self-aggrandizement:

The great events of our era may all have to do with the democratization of aristocratic vices. We have now completed the democratization of ostentation and hedonism, and we are well advanced in the democratization of hubris. A lot of people are now acting on the assumption that they are gods. Industrial acts of power that seem ordinary to us would have astonished Zeus. The Pentagon and the Kremlin have far outmoded Milton's war in Heaven. Dabblers in atoms, genes, toxic chemicals, social, psychological, and anatomical engineering all have promoted themselves far above their intelligence. One must hope for the democratization of a fear appropriate to the danger, and of a courage appropriate to the fear. (Weinreb interview in Merchant 1991)

Stern, Young, and Druckman (1992) write that "beliefs, attitudes, and values related to *material possessions* and the *relation of humanity and nature* are often seen as lying at the root of environmental degradation" (emphasis added). To these two key relationships with possessions and nature can be added a third, that of humanity to the *rest* of humanity. Failure to recognize our fundamental equality and interconnectedness fosters a narrow nationalism, leading to the degradation of others' environments to sustain our own industrial processes and lifestyles. Additionally, it makes us indifferent to prevailing inequities. Only a spiritual orientation can bring about the three profound changes in relation (to material possessions, to nature, to all of humanity) that are necessary for the truly lasting resolution of crises of energy and resources, environment, and social justice. I use the Bahá'í Faith, the most recent world religion, to illustrate the nature of these relationships because it directly addresses them—but the unity of all religions means that all people truly living the universal truths of their faith would recognize and work to embody them.

Spiritual Orientation to Material Possessions

Until we stop defining ourselves and our worth with possessions, and stop trying to fill spiritual needs with material means, we will not rid ourselves of destructive levels of consumption. Only through reaffirming our essentially spiritual nature can we discern our true longings and the means to their enduring satisfaction, and only through such spiritual grounding can we act in harmony with nature and in unity with others. Otherwise, as environmentalist Robert White (1989) writes, we are violating our spiritual purpose—our reason for being—and thwarting our spiritual growth:

Reshaping the world to gratify humanity's misconceived wants is clearly a violation of our spiritual purpose. It is, in fact, the view of society as primarily a vehicle for organized economic activity to exploit Nature for the provision of material goods that prevents us from realizing any real satisfaction in their consumption. . . . Spiritual growth can only occur when we begin to relate to all people and our earth home in a spirit of unity and cooperation. Given the total interconnectedness of humanity and Nature, it would be impossible for humans to attain spiritual perfection at the expense of Nature.

Spiritual Orientation to Nature

Deep ecologists allude to the spiritual dimensions of the organic whole that is nature and state that in going beyond a "narrow materialist and scientific understanding of reality, the spiritual and material aspects of reality fuse together" (Devall and Sessions 1985). Arne Naess developed two "ultimate norms" or intuitions that transcend deep ecology's deductive reasoning processes: self-realization and biocentric equality. Although the deep ecology goal of what Robert White (1989) calls a "deeper reconciliation between humanity and Nature" can be applauded, efforts toward self-realization remain ego-centered and ego-bounded—rather like the false contexts of consumption Sack describes. Is the ecosystem the cosmos? Deep ecologists do not address this question directly. They speak of the ecological self, but not of the cosmological self. When some biocentrists insist that humans are no more distinguished a species than sandworms, they seem to convey more hostility toward other humans than love for other species. This posture feels like inverted egoism, a parallel to the sin of excessive scrupulosity in the Catholic Church. Further, then what? What are the behavioral implications of such a stance? Environmentalism can become a kind of religion, with the environment or nature as God. Communion with nature gives the illusion of the conferring of immortality, much as material goods seem to transfer timelessness to their possessors. However, an environment-god is harmed easily, and can even be destroyed, for the environment is, after all, vulnerable *material*. Bill McKibben (1989) writes of the end of nature, our sense of nature as eternal and separate now gone. He declares that we are living now in a "postnatural world," the result of pervasive human intervention.

The awe that the environment inspires in its religionists is understandable. They are sensing the spiritual reality underlying our material surroundings. For those who believe in a Creator, nature is a repository of divine mysteries, reflecting divine attributes. Nature then becomes an indirect experience of the sacred, a way of beginning to apprehend God. We honor creation, recognize its sacredness, and humble ourselves in relation to it when we recognize that "the ecological interdependence of life on earth can be understood as the physical representation of a unifying spiritual reality" (White 1989). This realization gives us the immutable respect and humility necessary for ecological harmony. Such humility was addressed directly by the founder of the Bahá'í Faith:

Every man of discernment, while walking upon the earth, feeleth indeed abashed, inasmuch as he is fully aware that the thing which is the source of his prosperity, his wealth, his might, his exaltation, his advancement and power is, as ordained by God, the very earth which is trodden beneath the feet of all men. (Bahá'u'lláh 1891, rev. ed. 1979)

Spiritual Orientation to All of Humanity

Those concerned with environmental issues are not always concerned with social justice. Deep ecology, for example, focuses nearly exclusively on the dynamics of personal enlightenment. Our spiritual and ecological awareness depends on acknowledging our absolute and profound dependence on the earth, and further, realizing our commonality with all humankind in this. Without such awareness, we will continue to attempt to resolve problems through adversarial political strategies and fickle political alliances. Only spirituality enables us to go beyond efforts at political solidarity to inner conviction of the essential unity of humanity. Such certitude yields enduring and respectful concern for and cooperation with all people. Because of its tenets on the oneness of humanity and of all religions, as well as its statements on ecological sustainability and the models it offers, the Bahá'í International Community was the only religious nongovernmental organization invited to participate in the 1992 U.N. Conference on Environment and Development. Its plenary statement, "Sustainable Development and the Human Spirit," identifies the solution to the overwhelming problems of today to be the recognition of humankind's spiritual essence and oneness:

The problems facing humanity cannot be fully addressed without a magnitude of cooperation and coordination at all levels that far surpasses anything in humanity's collective experience. . . . A true resolution of the dangerous state of affairs in the world can only be realized when the spiritual dimension of human nature is taken into account and the human heart is transformed. . . . [For the] spiritual dimension of human nature can be understood, in practical terms, as the source of qualities that transcend narrow self-interest. . . .
The fundamental spiritual truth of our age is the oneness of humanity. Universal acceptance of this principle—with its implications for social and economic justice, universal participation in non-adversarial decision making, peace and collective security, equality of the sexes, and universal education—will make possible the reorganization and administration of the world as one country, the home of humankind. Over one hundred years ago, Bahá'u'lláh challenged the rulers and peoples of the earth to make their vision world-embracing: "It is not for him to pride himself who loveth his own country, but rather for him who loveth the whole world." This challenge has yet to be answered.

Robert White (1989) declares that "conventional remedies such as resource management amount to little more than 'fine tuning' a continuous process of environmental degradation." Into this category of tinkering I would also put attempts to reduce residential fuel consumption through improved technical efficiencies or conservation campaigns, and certainly the emphasis on "green" or informed selection of the products we buy. Although these remain worthwhile goals, we must aim for more. We must transform culture profoundly and lastingly by restoring its spiritual basis—by moving beyond anthropocentrism, ecocentrism, and biocentrism to theocentrism.

Appendixes

APPENDIX 1: SAMPLE SIZES

Questionnaire Sample Sizes

	Foley	Munka Ljungby
1980s	243	106
1990s	140	148

The 1980s Foley questionnaire sample is larger than the Munka sample because over 500 questionnaires were mailed out to all single-family dwellings in Foley, but I hand-delivered 110 questionnaires in Munka. In the 1990s questionnaires were mailed to a randomly selected sample of 250 single-family dwellings in each community.

Heating Fuel Consumption Sample Sizes

	Foley	Munka Ljungby
1980s	91	41
1990s	106	36

Heating fuel samples are comprised of those households in the questionnaire samples authorizing release of their utility records and reporting consumption totals of heating fuel not furnished by utilities. In both Foley and Munka Ljungby, these non-utility heating fuels were wood and fuel oil, and in 1980s Foley, LP gas as well. In order for households to be included in the heating fuel samples, energy consumed for heating had to be distinguishable from energy consumed for purposes of household operations (see discussion in Appendix 3).

Household Fuel Consumption Sample Sizes

	Foley	Munka Ljungby
1980s	91	63
1990s	106	36

The Munka 1980 household fuel sample (n=63) is larger than its heating sample (n=41) because household electricity data were readily available from the utility company, but heating fuel data for wood and oil were dependent on self-report in the questionnaires. That Munka Ljungby's 1993 heating and household operations samples are substantially smaller than Foley's reflects the rise of all-electric housing in Munka, for which heating fuel consumption could not be distinguished from fuel consumption for all other household purposes.

Core Sample Sizes

	Foley	Munka Ljungby
1980s	22	21
1990s	20	20

Randomized samples of core households were recruited from the pools of completed questionnaires. Samples were matched for proportionate representation of all life-cycle stages. In the 1980s the average core household size was 4 persons in Foley and 3.4 in Munka Ljungby. In the 1990s the average sizes were nearly identical: 3.5 in Foley and 3.4 in Munka Ljungby.

APPENDIX 2: CALCULATION OF FUEL CONSUMPTION

Actual fuel consumption was compared for a subset of questionnaire-answering households for which complete fuel consumption data were available. A permission form allowing access to electricity and natural gas billing records accompanied each questionnaire sent out, and roughly 100 households in each community signed these forms. Records were obtained for Foley households from Northern States Power Company; Ängelholm's power company (*energiverk*) provided electricity records for Munka households. In both communities, oil and wood consumption data came from self-report on questionnaires.

Fuel measurement periods for this study, determined by utility billing cycle, were as follows:

Foley: March 20, 1980 through March 19, 1981 (called "1980")
          December 16, 1992 through December 15, 1993 (called "1993")
Munka: August 15, 1979 through August 14, 1980 (called "1980")
          January 1 through December 31, 1993 (called "1993")

Fuel consumption totals had to be converted to an energy "common denominator" in order to make meaningful comparisons among households. The joule, the International System unit of energy, served the purpose for this study. A joule is equal to the work done when a current of one ampere is passed through a resistance of one ohm for one second. One Btu equals 1,055 joules. Because the energy represented by one Btu is about the same as that of a wooden kitchen match, totals of joule-equivalents of fuel consumed by households are understandably large. They are expressed commonly as MJ (megajoules, millions of joules) or GJ (gigajoules, billions of joules).

For each household, the totals of all of the various fuels consumed during the measurement period were converted to their joule equivalents. The following equivalents were used in calculations for this study:

Joule Equivalents of Diverse Fuels

Fuel unit	Joule equivalent	Expressed in MJ
1 kWh electricity	3,600,715	3.6
1 ccf natural gas	105,500,000	105.5
1 gallon fuel oil	147,700,000	147.7
1 gallon LP gas	97,060,000	97.1
1 cord wood	20,256,000,000	20,256.0

APPENDIX 3: DISTINGUISHING HEATING FUEL FROM HOUSEHOLD OPERATIONS FUEL

Heating fuel is defined for this study as the fuel used for space heating of homes, and household operations fuel as that fuel used for all household operations other than space heating, such as heating water, cooking, laundry, and lighting. Differing sample sizes in Foley and Munka Ljungby reflect differences in availability of data and the feasibility of distinguishing heating from household operations energy.

In Foley, heating fuel could be distinguished readily from household operations fuel consumption when the heating fuel is oil or wood, because these fuels are not used for household purposes. For those Foley households using natural gas for both heating and household operations, summertime fuel use, when heating systems are shut down, was assumed to represent year-round energy demand for household operations. The summertime monthly average was multiplied by 12 to yield estimated year-round natural gas demand for household operations. This operations total was subtracted from the combined fuels total; the balance was ascribed to heating fuel.

Because meter readings occur just three or four times per year in Munka Ljungby, the summer-use technique for separating heating fuel from household operations fuel was not possible. Only those Munka homes where *different* fuels were used for heating and for household operations could thus be included in the heating and household operations fuel samples. This excluded Munka's all-electric homes and homes with combination furnaces (electricity and oil and/or wood), for which household electricity is impossible to isolate.

APPENDIX 4: ESTIMATING FUEL USED TO HEAT WATER

Homes that heated with oil or wood also used that fuel to heat water, a task I put in the category of household operations. It was impossible to determine which portion of oil or wood went to space heating and which went to heat water. Therefore, estimates of energy used to heat water were based on Swedish national averages: a household of 3.2 members uses 25 GJ of oil for hot water. To adjust for various household sizes, I multiplied the square root of the (N of household members over 3.2) by 25 GJ. (Swedish statistics; formula from Schipper 1994). I used the same number of GJ for wood as for oil. This is a rough estimate, but wood is complex to calculate, given that energy intensity varies by type. In 1993, only three Munka households used wood for heat and hot water, and only three used a combination of wood and oil for these purposes.

APPENDIX 5: USING DEGREE-DAYS TO ADJUST FOR DIFFERENCES IN CLIMATE

In order to compare heating fuel consumption in Foley and Munka meaningfully, adjustment for differences in climate is necessary. This is possible through comparison of the "degree-days" in each locale during its measurement period. A degree-day is the number of degrees below a selected baseline temperature the average temperature in a 24-hour period falls. In the United States the baseline is 65° F. In Sweden it is 17° C, or 62.6° F. If the daily average temperature is above the baseline, there are zero degree-days entered for that particular day.

Degree-day statistics were obtained for each community's measurement period. Foley's daily records came from the U.S. National Weather Service. Statistics for Munka for 1980 came from the Swedish Meteorological and Hydrological Institute. For 1993 they were provided by Ängelholm's *Energiverk*. Swedish degree-days were converted from Celsius to Fahrenheit by multiplying them by 1.8. To equalize Swedish and American baseline temperatures, 2.4° F were added for every heating day recorded in the Munka area. Totals appear in the accompanying table.

Degree-Days Fahrenheit during Measurement Years

	Foley	Munka Ljungby
1980s	8,074	7,630
1990s	9,205	7,109

Foley had only 400 more degree-days than Munka during 1980, but 2,100 more degree-days than Munka in 1993. During the 1980 measurement period, Foley had 8,074 degree-days, below the area's 10-year historical average of 8,868 degree-days. In turn, Munka had 7,630 degree-days, close to its 10-year average of 7,890. Munka's degree-days were 95% of Foley's 1980 total, but only 77% of Foley's in 1993. Then, Munka had 7,109 degree-days, close to its "normal" year of 7,292 degree-days. Foley had 9,205 degree-days, above its "normal" year.

Foley and Munka heating fuel consumption averages were adjusted for climatic differences by dividing them by the number of Fahrenheit degree-days (DDF) that occurred during the measurement period. For example, Foley had 9,205 DDF during the 1993 period. Foley's 1993 heating fuel consumption average of 100,957 MJ, divided by 9,205 DDF, is 10.967, which I rounded up to 11.

Bibliography

American Petroleum Institute. 1995. *Annual Supply and Demand Review.*

Appadurai, Arjun, ed. 1986. *The Social Life of Things: Commodities in a Cultural Perspective.* Cambridge, UK: Cambridge University Press.

ÄRAB (Ängelholms Renhållnings AB). Ängelholm Refuse Collection Company. 1994. Newsletter. Ängelholm, Sweden.

Bahá'í International Community. 1992. Sustainable Development and the Human Spirit. New York: Bahá'í International Community, Office of the Environment.

Bahá'u'lláh (Mírzá Husayn-Alí i Núrí). 1891. *Epistle to the Son of the Wolf.* Wilmette, Illinois: Bahá'í Publishing Trust. Rev. ed. 1979.

Bahro, Rudolf. 1989. Theology Not Ecology. *New Perspectives Quarterly* 6, 1.

Becker, Ernest. 1973. *The Denial of Death.* New York: The Free Press.

Berry, Wendell. 1977a. The Ecological Crisis As a Crisis of Character. In *The Unsettling of America: Culture and Agriculture.* New York: Avon Books.

———. 1977b. The Use of Energy. In *The Unsettling of America.*

———. 1987. Two Economies. In *Home Economics: Fourteen Essays by Wendell Berry.* San Francisco: North Point Press.

Berry, Winiek. 1978. Saving Energy with Portable Appliances. In *New Demands—New Directions.* In *Proceedings: The Twenty-Ninth National Home Appliances Conference.* Denver, Col.

Bormann, F. Herbert, and Stephen R. Kellert, eds. 1991. *Ecology, Economics, Ethics: The Broken Circle.* New Haven: Yale University Press.

Bourdieu, Pierre. 1984. *Distinction: A Social Critique of the Judgement of Taste.* Cambridge, Mass.: Harvard University Press.

Bullard, Clark W. III, and Robert A. Herendeen. 1975. The Energy Cost of Goods and Services. *Energy Policy* 3, 4.

Bushrui, Suheil, Iraj Ayman, and Ervin Laszlo, eds. 1993. *Transition to a Global Society.* Oxford, UK: Oneworld Publications.

Callicott, J. Baird. 1994. *Earth's Insights: A Survey of Ecological Ethics from the Mediterranean Basin to the Outback.* Berkeley: University of California Press.

Campbell, Colin. 1987. *The Romantic Ethic and the Spirit of Modern Consumerism.* Oxford, UK: Blackwell.

Carlsen, Hanne Norup, J. T. Ross Jackson, and Niels I. Meyer, eds. 1993. *When No Means Yes*. London: Adamantine Press Ltd.

Castensson, Reinhold, and P. O. Hallin. 1981. *Energiflödesanalys: Energikällor, Omvandlare och Användare i Munka-Ljungby* (Energy flow analysis: energy sources, transformers, and users in Munka Ljungby). Stockholm: Swedish Council for Building Research.

Costanza, Robert, ed. 1991. *Ecological Economics: The Science and Management of Sustainability*. New York: Columbia University Press.

Cross, Gary. 1993. *Time and Money: The Making of Consumer Culture*. London: Routledge.

Csikszentmihalyi, Mihaly, and Eugene Rochberg-Halton. 1981. *The Meaning of Things: Domestic Symbols and the Self*. Cambridge, UK: Cambridge University Press.

Dagens Nyheter(DN). Newspaper with national distribution. Stockholm, Sweden.

Daly, Herman E., ed. 1973. *Economics, Ecology, Ethics*. San Francisco: Freeman.

———. 1988. The Steady-State Economy: Postmodern Alternative to Growthmania. In David Ray Griffin, ed. *Spirituality and Society: Postmodern Visions*. Albany: State University of New York Press.

———. 1991. *Steady-State Economics*. Washington, D.C. : Island Press.

Daly, Herman E., and John B. Cobb, Jr. 1989. *For the Common Good: Redirecting the Economy toward Community, the Environment, and a Sustainable Future*. Boston: Beacon.

Daun, Åke. 1994. *Svensk Mentalitet* (Swedish Mentality). Stockholm: Rabén Prisma. (English edition: 1996. *Swedish Mentality*. Jan Teeland, trans. University Park, Penn.: Penn State University Press).

Devall, Bill, and George Sessions. 1985. *Deep Ecology: Living As If Nature Mattered*. Salt Lake City, Utah: Gibbs Smith.

Douglas, Mary, and Baron Isherwood. 1979. *The World of Goods*. New York: W. W. Norton.

Dunlap, Riley E., and Kent D. Van Liere. 1978. The "New Environmental Paradigm": A Proposed Measuring Instrument and Preliminary Results. *Journal of Environmental Education* 9, 4.

Durning, Alan Thein. 1992. *How Much Is Enough?* New York: Norton.

Ehn, Billy, and Orvar Löfgren. 1982. *Kulturanalys: Ett etnologiskt perspectiv* (Culture analysis: An ethnological perspective). Lund: Liber Förlag.

Ekins, Paul. 1991. The Sustainable Consumer Society: A Contradiction in Terms? *International Environmental Affairs*. Fall.

Elgin, Duane. 1993. *Voluntary Simplicity*. Revised Edition. New York: Morrow.

Energy Information Administration (U.S. Department of Energy). 1992a. *State Energy Data Report 1992*. Washington, D.C. : U.S. Government Printing Office.

———. 1992b. *Housing Characteristics 1990*. Washington, D.C.: U.S. Government Printing Office.

———. 1995. *Annual Energy Review 1994*. Washington, D.C.: U.S. Government Printing Office. July.

———. 1996. International Energy Annual. Washington, D.C.: U.S. Government Printing Office. December.

———. 1997. *Monthly Energy Review*. Washington, D.C.: U.S. Government Printing Office. January.

Erickson, Rita J. 1985. *Energy Use in Cultural Context: An Ethnographic Comparison of Households in Minnesota and Sweden*. Ann Arbor, Mich.: University Microfilms International.

———. 1987. Household Energy Use in Sweden and Minnesota: Individual Behavior in Cultural Context. In Willett Kempton and Max Neiman, eds. *Energy Efficiency: Perspectives on Individual Behavior*. Washington, D.C.: American Council for an Energy-Efficient Economy.

Farhar, Barbara C. 1993. *Trends in Public Perceptions and Preferences on Energy and Environmental Policy*. (NREL/TP–461–4857) Golden, Colorado: National Renewable Energy Laboratory.

Foster, George M. 1965. Peasant Society and the Image of Limited Good. *American Anthropologist* 67.

Fox, Warwick. 1990. *Toward a Transpersonal Ecology: Developing New Foundations for Environmentalism*. Boston: Shambhala.

Friedman, Jonathan, ed. 1994. *Consumption and Identity*. Chur, Switzerland: Harwood Academic Publishers.

Frykman, Jonas, and Orvar Löfgren. 1987 [1979]. *Culture Builders: A Historical Anthropology of Middle-Class Life*. Rutgers: University Press.

Gaunt, Louise, and Ann-Margret Berggren. 1983. *Brukarvanor och Energiförbrukning* (Occupant habits and energy use). Gävle: The Swedish Institute for Building Research.

Gladhart, Peter, Bonnie Maas Morrison, and James Zuiches, eds. 1987. *Energy and Families: An Analysis of Lifestyles and Energy Consumption*. East Lansing, Michigan: Michigan State University Press.

Georgescu-Roegen, Nicholas. 1971. *The Entropy Law and the Economic Process*. Cambridge, Mass.: Harvard University Press.

———, ed. 1976. *Energy and Economic Myths*. New York: Pergamon.

Goldemberg, José, Thomas B. Johansson, Amulya K. N. Reddy, and Robert H. Williams, eds. 1987. *Energy for a Sustainable World*. Washington, D.C.: World Resources Institute.

Goldsmith, Edward. 1993. *The Way: An Ecological World-view*. Boston: Shambhala.

Goodland, Robert, Herman Daly, Salaj El Serafy, and Bernd von Droste. 1991. *Environmentally Sustainable Economic Development: Building on Brundtland*. Paris: UNESCO.

Gullestad, Marianne. 1989. Small Facts and Large Issues: The Anthropology of Contemporary Scandinavian Society. *Annual Review of Anthropology* 18.

———. 1992. *The Art of Social Relations: Essays on Culture, Social Action and Everyday Life in Modern Norway*. Oslo: Scandinavian University Press.

———. 1995. The Morality of Consumption. *Ethnologia Scandinavica* 25.

Hackett, Bruce, and Loren Lutzenhiser. 1986. Energy Billing Cultural Variation and Residential Energy Consumption. In *Proceedings: 1986 Summer Study on Energy Efficiency in Buildings*. Washington, D.C.: American Council for an Energy-Efficient Economy.

———. 1990. Social Stratification and Appliance Saturation. In *Proceedings: 1990 Summer Study on Energy Efficiency in Buildings*. Washington, D.C.: American Council for an Energy-Efficient Economy.

———. 1991. Social Structures and Economic Conduct: Interpreting Variations in Household Energy Consumption. *Sociological Forum* 6, 3.

Hallin, P. O. 1993. Miljökris and Gröna Handlingsstilar (The environmental crisis and green behavior). *Nordisk Samhällsgeografisk Tidskrift* 17, September.

————. 1994. Livsstilar och miljö: Hushålls Miljöhandlingar i Sverige och U.S.A. (Lifestyles and environment: Environmental behavior in Swedish and American households). *Rapporter och Notiser* 131. Lund: Department of Social and Economic Geography.

————. 1995a. Environmental Concern and Environmental Behavior in Foley, a Small Town in Minnesota. *Environment and Behavior* 27, 4.

————. 1995b. Environmental Concern and Environmental Behavior in Foley and Munka Ljungby. Lund: Department of Social and Economic Geography.

Hambraeus, Gunnar, and Staffan Stillesjö. 1977. Perspectives on Energy in Sweden. *Annual Review of Energy* 2.

Hanley, Charles J. 1996. Hot, New Crime: Smuggling Coolant for Air Conditioners. *St. Paul Pioneer Press*. March 26.

Hannon, Bruce. 1975. Energy Conservation and the Consumer. *Science* 189.

————. 1980. Energy Use and Moral Restraint. In Herman E. Daly, ed. *Economics, Ecology, Ethics.* New York: Freeman.

Hardin, Garrett. 1968. The Tragedy of the Commons. *Science* 162.

Harryson, Christer. 1981. Brukarbetingade Variationer i Energiåtgång hos Småhus (User-determined variations in energy consumption in single-family dwellings). Gothenburg: Chalmers Tekniska Högskola.

Henry, Jules. 1963. *Culture against Man.* New York: Random House.

Holdren, John. 1992. Prologue: The Transition to Costlier Energy. In Schipper and Meyers et al. *Energy Efficiency and Human Activity.* Cambridge, UK: Cambridge University Press.

Hollander, Jack M., ed. 1992. *The Energy-Environment Connection.* Washington, D.C.: Island Press.

Holm, Fredrik, and Bo Thunberg. 1993. *Nya Handla Miljövänligt* (Environmentally friendly shopping). Katrineholm: Naturskyddsförening Förlag AB.

Hornborg, Alf. 1992. Machine Fetishism, Value, and the Image of Unlimited Good: Towards a Thermodynamics of Imperialism. *Man* 27, 1.

————. 1993. Distinctions That Mystify: Technology versus Economy and Other Fragmentations. *Knowledge and Policy* 6, 2.

Illich, Ivan. 1977. *Toward a History of Needs.* New York: Pantheon.

Jamison, Andrew, Ron Eyerman, and Jacqueline Cramer (with Jeppe Laessoe). 1990. *The Making of the New Environmental Consciousness.* Edinburgh: University Press.

Johansson, Thomas B., Henry Kelly, Amulya K. N. Reddy, and Robert H. Williams, eds. 1993. *Renewable Energy: Sources for Fuels and Electricity.* Washington, D.C.: Island Press.

Kaijser, Arne. 1992. Redirecting Power: Swedish Nuclear Policies in Historical Perspective. *Annual Review of Energy and the Environment* 17.

Kempton, Willett, and Max Neiman, eds. 1987. *Energy Efficiency: Perspectives on Individual Behavior.* Washington, D.C.: American Council for an Energy-Efficient Economy.

Kempton, Willett, James S. Boster, and Jennifer A. Hartley. 1995. *Environmental Values in American Culture.* Cambridge, Mass.: MIT Press.

Kjeang, Are. 1989. *God Energirådgivning på 90-talet* (Good energy advising for the 1990s). Gothenburg: Föreningen Sveriges Energirådgivare (Association of Swedish energy advisors).

Lindén, Anna-Lisa. 1994. *Människa och miljö* (Man and environment). Stockholm, Sweden: Carlssons.

Linden, Eugene. 1979. *Affluence and Discontent: The Anatomy of Consumer Societies*. New York: Viking.

Linder, Staffan. 1970. *The Harried Leisure Class*. New York: Columbia University Press.

Löfgren, Orvar. 1982. Professor, Department of Ethnology, University of Lund, Sweden. Conversation with the author. Lund.

————. 1990. Consuming Interests. *Culture and History* 7.

————. 1992. Varför är det så lätt att älska naturen? Om glappnet mellan ideal och vardag (Why is it so easy to love nature? On the gap between ideal and everyday). In Lars J. Lundgren, ed. *Livsstil och miljö: På väg mot ett miljövänligt beteende?* (Lifestyle and environment: On the way to environmentally friendly behavior?). Hässelby Castle Conference Report. March 18–19. Lund, Sweden: BTJ Tryck.

————. 1994. Conversation with the author. July. Lund.

Lovins, Amory. 1977. *Soft Energy Paths: Towards a Durable Peace*. New York: Harper.

————. 1996. Plenary at the 1996 ACEEE Summer Study on Energy Efficiency in Buildings. August 25-31. Asilomar Conference Center, Pacific Grove, Calif.

Lundgren, Lars J. 1992. Den miljövänlige konsumenten (The environmentally friendly consumer). In Lars J. Lundgren, ed. *Livsstil och miljö: På väg mot ett miljövänligt beteende?* (Lifestyle and environment: On the way to environmentally friendly behavior?). Hässelby Castle Conference Report. March 18–19. Lund: BTJ Tryck.

Lunt, Peter K., and Sonia M. Livingstone. 1992. *Mass Consumption and Personal Identity*. Philadelphia: Open University Press.

Lutzenhiser, Loren. 1992. A Cultural Model of Household Energy Consumption. *Energy* 17, 1.

————. 1993. Social and Behavioral Aspects of Energy Use. *Annual Review of Energy and the Environment*, 18.

McCracken, Grant. 1988. *Culture and Consumption*. Bloomington: Indiana University Press.

McKibben, Bill. 1989. *The End of Nature*. New York: Anchor Books, Doubleday.

————. 1992. *The Age of Missing Information*. New York: Random House.

McLaughlin, Andrew. 1993. *Regarding Nature: Industrialism and Deep Ecology*. Albany: State University of New York Press.

Marknadsföring AB. 1980. *Enkät våren 1981 om bränsleförbrukning i småhus* (Spring 1980 questionnaire on fuel use in single family dwellings). Stockholm, Sweden: Marknadsföring AB (Marketing Inc.).

MEA (Minnesota Energy Agency). 1978. *Energy Policy and Conservation Report*.

Meier, Alan, Leo Rainer, and Steve Greenberg. 1992. Miscellaneous Electrical Energy Use in Homes. *Energy* 17, 5.

Melosi, Martin V. 1985. *Coping with Abundance: Energy and Environment in Industrial America*. Philadelphia: Temple University Press.

Miller, Dennis. 1995a. Consumption and Commodities. *Annual Review of Anthropology* 24.

————, ed. 1995b. *Acknowledging Consumption*. London: Routledge.

Miller, Frank C. 1984. Professor, Department of Anthropology. University of Minnesota, Twin Cities. Conversation with the author. Minneapolis.

Minnesota Monthly. 1995. "Minnesota Firsts." March.

Moran, Emilio, ed. 1990. *The Ecosystem Approach in Anthropology*. Ann Arbor: University of Michigan Press.

Morrison, Bonnie Maas, and Willett Kempton, eds. 1984. *Families and Energy: Coping with Uncertainty*. East Lansing: College of Human Ecology, Michigan State University.

Myrdal, Gunnar. 1944. *An American Dilemma: The Negro Problem and Modern Democracy*. New York: Harper.

Naess, Arne. 1973. The Shallow and the Deep, Long-Range Ecology Movements. *Inquiry* 16.

Nordvästra Skånes Tidningar (NST), a regional newspaper for northwest Skåne.

Nørgård, Jørgen. 1993. Limits to Growth in Europe. In Hanne Norup Carlsen, J. T. Ross Jackson, and Niels I. Meyer, eds. *When No Means Yes*. London: Adamantine Press.

——. 1995. Efficient Technology in an Inefficient Economy. In A. Persson, ed. *Proceedings: 1995 Summer Study on Sustainability and the Reinvention of Government*. Stockholm, Sweden: European Council for an Energy-Efficient Economy.

Nørgård, Jørgen, and Bente Christensen. 1992–93. Towards Sustainable Energy Welfare. In *Perspectives in Energy* 2.

Nørgård, Jørgen, and Jan Viegand. 1994. *Low Electricity Europe—Sustainable Options*. Brussels, Belgium: European Environmental Bureau.

NSP (Northern States Power Company). 1981. *Home Use Study*. Minneapolis, Minn.: NSP, Market Research Section.

——. 1993. Understanding Your Energy Bill. Minneapolis, Minn.: NSP.

NST. See *Nordvästra Skånes Tidningar*.

NUTEK (*Närings- och teknikutvecklingsverket*) (Swedish National Board for Industrial and Technical Development). Stockholm.

Organization for Economic Cooperation and Development. 1994. *OECD Economic Surveys 1993–1994: Sweden*. Paris.

——. 1995. Final Report of the OECD Workshop on Sustainable Consumption and Production: Clarifying the Concepts. Rosendal, Norway, July 2–4.

Official Statistics of Sweden (SCB, *Statistiska Centralbyrån*). Örebro, Sweden.

Olsson, Sven E. 1993. *Social Policy and Welfare State in Sweden*. Lund: Arkiv.

Ornstein, Robert, and Paul Ehrlich. 1989a. *New World, New Mind*. New York: Doubleday.

——. 1989b. New World, New Mind. *New Perspectives Quarterly* 6, 1.

Otnes, Per, ed. 1988. *The Sociology of Consumption*. Atlantic Highlands, New Jersey: Humanities Press International.

Peet, John. 1992. *Energy and the Ecological Economics of Sustainability*. Washington, D.C.: Island Press.

Percy, Walker. 1983. *Lost in the Cosmos: The Last Self-Help Book*. New York: Washington Square Press.

Porro, Jeffrey D., and Christine Mueller. 1993. *The Plastic Waste Primer*. New York: Lyons and Burford.

Rathje, William, and Cullen Murphy. 1992. *Rubbish! The Archaeology of Garbage*. New York: Harper.

Roszak, Theodore. 1995. A Few Beautifully Made Things. *Common Boundary* 13, 2.

Ruth, Arne. 1984. The Second New Nation: The Mythology of Modern Sweden. *Daedalus* 113, 2.

Sachs, Wolfgang. 1989. The Virtue of Enoughness. *New Perspectives Quarterly* 6, 1.

Sack, Robert David. 1990. The Realm of Meaning: The Inadequacy of Human Nature Theory and the View of Mass Consumption. In B. L. Turner et al., eds., *The Earth as Transformed by Human Action*. New York: Cambridge University Press.

————. 1992. *Place, Modernity, and the Consumer's World*. Baltimore: The Johns Hopkins University Press.

SCB. See Swedish Central Bureau of Statistics.

Schipper, Lee. 1994. Senior staff scientist, Energy and Environment Division, Lawrence Berkeley Laboratory, Berkeley, California. Conversation with the author. July.

————. 1996a. People in the Greenhouse: Indicators of Carbon Emissions from Households and Travel. In *Proceedings: 1996 Summer Study on Energy Efficiency in Buildings*. Washington, D.C.: American Council for an Energy-Efficient Economy.

————. 1996b. Conversation with the author. August 28.

Schipper, Lee, and Allan J. Lichtenberg. 1976. Efficient Energy Use and Well-Being: The Swedish Example. *Science* 194.

Schipper, Lee, and Stephen Meyers, with Richard Howarth and Ruth Steiner. 1992. *Energy Efficiency and Human Activity*. Cambridge, UK: Cambridge University Press.

Schipper, Lee, and Claudia Sheinbaum. 1994. OECD Household Energy Use Efficiency after the Oil-Price Crash: End of an Era? In *Proceedings: 1994 Summer Study on Energy Efficiency in Buildings*. Washington, D.C.: American Council for an Energy-Efficient Economy.

Schipper, Lee, Reinhard Haas, and Claudia Sheinbaum. 1996. Recent Trends in Residential Energy Use in IEA Countries and Their Impact on CO Emissions. *Journal of Mitigation and Adaptation to Global Changes* 1, 2.

Schor, Juliet B. 1992. *The Overworked American: The Unexpected Decline of Leisure*. New York: Basic Books.

Scitovsky, Tibor. 1976. *The Joyless Economy: An Inquiry into Human Satisfaction and Consumer Dissatisfaction*. Oxford, UK: Oxford University Press.

Sobel, Michael E. 1981. *Lifestyle and Social Structure*. New York: Academic Press.

Socolow, Robert A. 1978. Twin Rivers Program in Energy Conservation in Housing. In Robert A. Socolow, ed. *Saving Energy in the Home: Princeton's Experiments at Twin Rivers*. Cambridge, Mass.: Ballinger.

Stern, Paul C., and Elliot Aronson, eds. 1984. *Energy Use: The Human Dimension*. Report of the Committee on Behavioral and Social Aspects of Energy Consumption and Production, National Research Council. New York: Freeman.

Stern, Paul C., Oran R. Young, and Daniel Druckman, eds. 1992. *Global Environmental Change: Understanding the Human Dimensions*. Washington, D.C.: National Academy Press.

Swedish Central Bureau of Statistics (SCB, *Statistiska Centralbyrån*). 1994. *Statistical Yearbook of Sweden 1994*. Örebro, Sweden: Statistics Sweden.

Swedish Department of Culture. 1994. *Om Flyktingar* (About immigrants). Stockholm.

Swedish Institute. 1994. Energy and Energy Policy in Sweden. Stockholm.

————. 1993. General Facts on Sweden. Stockholm.

————. 1992. Environment Protection. Stockholm.

Sydsvenska Dagbladet. 1982. Regional newspaper for southern Sweden.

Tierney, John. 1996. What a Waste. *New York Times Magazine*. June 30.

Tinbergen, Jan, and Roefie Hueting. 1991. GNP and Market Prices: Wrong Signals for Sustainable Economic Success That Mask Environmental Destruction. In Robert Goodland et al., eds. *Environmentally Sustainable Economic Development: Building on Brundtland*. Paris: UNESCO.

Touraine, Alain. 1989. Neo-Modern Ecology. In *New Perspectives Quarterly* 6, 1.

Tucker, Mary Evelyn, and John A. Grim, eds. 1994. *Worldviews and Ecology: Religion, Philosophy, and the Environment.* Maryknoll, New York: Orbis Books.

Turner, B. L., William C. Clark, Robert W. Kates, John F. Richards, Jessica T. Mathews, and William B. Meyer, eds. 1990. *The Earth as Transformed by Human Action: Global and Regional Changes in the Biosphere over the Past 300 Years.* Cambridge, UK: Cambridge University Press.

United Nations. 1994. *World Economic and Social Survey 1994.* New York: United Nations.

U.S. Department of Commerce, Bureau of the Census. 1994. *Statistical Abstract of the U.S., 1994.* Washington, D.C.: U.S. Government Printing Office. September.

———. 1996. *Statistical Abstract of the U.S., 1996.* Washington, D.C.: U.S. Government Printing Office. October.

U.S. Department of Energy. 1993. *Residential Energy Consumption Survey.* Washington, D.C. : U.S. Government Printing Office.

———. 1995. *State Energy Data Report* 1993. Washington, D.C.: U.S. Government Printing Office. July.

U.S. Government. *Economic Report of the President 1993.* Submitted to the Congress, February 1994. Washington, D.C. : U.S. Government Printing Office.

Uusitalo, Liisa, ed. 1983. *Consumer Behaviour and Environmental Quality.* Hants, UK: Gower Publishing Company.

———. 1986. *Environmental Impacts of Consumption Patterns.* New York: St. Martin's Press.

Veblen, Thorstein. 1899. *The Theory of the Leisure Class.* New York: Macmillan.

———. 1914. *The Instinct of Workmanship and the State of the Industrial Arts.* New York: Macmillan.

Wachtel, Paul L. 1983. *The Poverty of Affluence: A Psychological Portrait of the American Way of Life.* New York: Free Press.

Weinreb, Mindy. 1991. A Question a Day: A Written Conversation with Wendell Berry. In Paul Merchant, ed. *Wendell Berry.* Lewiston, Idaho: Confluence Press.

Wennerström, Sten. 1976. Review of Sven Olof Olsson's *German Coal and Swedish Fuel, 1939–1945. Economy and History* 19, 1.

White, Robert A. 1989. *Spiritual Foundations for an Ecologically Sustainable Society.* Ottawa: Association for Bahá'í Studies.

Wilhite, Harold, and Richard Ling. 1992. The Person Behind the Meter: An Ethnographic Analysis of Residential Energy Consumption in Oslo, Norway. In *Proceedings: 1992 Summer Study on Energy Efficiency in Buildings.* Washington, D.C.: American Council for an Energy-Efficient Economy.

Wilhite, Harold, Hidetoshi Nakagami, Takashi Masuda, Yukiko Yamaga, and Hiroshi Haneda. 1996. A Cross-Cultural Analysis of Household Energy-Use Behaviour in Japan and Norway. *Energy Policy* 24, 9.

Winteringham, F. Peter W. 1992. *Energy Use and the Environment.* Chelsea, Mich.: Lewis Publishers.

Wolvén, L.-E. 1991. Lifestyles and Energy Consumption in Sweden. *Energy* 16, 6.

WCED (World Commission on Environment and Development). 1987. *Our Common Future.* Oxford, UK: Oxford University Press.

Index

About the Author

RITA J. ERICKSON is a post-doctoral associate of the Department of Anthropology at the University of Minnesota, Twin Cities. She also holds degrees in cultural anthropology from Smith College and Columbia University. She is the author of articles on energy use and environmental awareness. Although the Mall of America is in her backyard, she has never been there.

ISBN 0-275-95766-7

90000>

EAN

9 780275 957667

HARDCOVER BAR CODE